WHAT MAKES
YOU TICK?

ALSO BY DOUGLAS E. SCHOEN

Enoch Powell and the Powellites

Pat: A Biography of Daniel Patrick Moynihan

*On the Campaign Trail: The Long Road of
Presidential Politics, 1860–2004*

The Power of the Vote

*Declaring Independence: The Beginning of the End
of the Two-Party System*

WHAT MAKES YOU TICK?

How Successful People Do It—and What You Can Learn from Them

MICHAEL J. BERLAND
AND DOUGLAS E. SCHOEN

HARPER
BUSINESS

An Imprint of HarperCollins*Publishers*
www.harpercollins.com

FIRST EDITION

Designed by Nicola Ferguson

Library of Congress Cataloging-in-Publication Data is available upon request.

ISBN: 978-0-06-087815-3

09 10 11 12 13   OV/RRD   10 9 8 7 6 5 4 3 2 1

TO MY FAMILY:
MARCELA THE "VISIONARY,"
MATTHEW THE "INDEPENDENCE SEEKER,"
AND ISABELLA THE "DO-GOODER."

I love you guys and the success in life that we have created together.

FOR MY MOTHER, CAROL SCHOEN—

who set the example, which put me on my own path for success.

CONTENTS

• • •

Natural-Born Leaders

Do-Gooders

Independence Seekers

Independents Who Follow Their Dreams

INTRODUCTION

• • •

Books about success typically have one thing in common: They almost always promise that there are simple steps you can take that will all but guarantee you'll get to your destination. They are all basically selling the same idea, that achieving success is about following a prescription.

Our book is different. We believe that success is achieved not by changing your personality, but by enhancing the skills you already have. This book gives you a way to use your own skills, your own attributes, and your own personality as a path to chart your own course. The stories in this book—culled from interviews with forty-five highly successful people—are models of success you can learn from. The book is about how highly successful people actually *think* about success; you learn from their experience and knowledge, not from instructions on how to behave or what path to follow.

After all, success means different things to different people. Sometimes it's so intangible that even brilliant and successful minds have trouble articulating what it means. As best-selling author Bob Woodward told us, "I can't put a definition on success because it's more internal than external. Do you like what you do? Do you enjoy doing it?" Success is not about the score. It's about much more.

People often confuse success with winning. Those two goals have some common traits, but they're not identical. Success moves us into the realm of the thinking man; it's more of an emotional quotient than a number at the bottom of a balance sheet. It's about what we want for our inner selves. It's easy to define winning; the definition of success, on the other hand, inspires an endless discussion.

As professional political and corporate strategists, we're experts in *how* to win. For more than twenty years, we've been in the business of winning hard-fought battles on the campaign trail and in the boardroom. We're hired because we produce results. And our results *can* be defined in terms of winning—whether it's an election or the public's hearts and minds on a serious or controversial issue.

Today, the prospect of "winning" has gone well beyond America's voting booths and corporate boardrooms and become a catchword within our entire culture. It's as if the ghost of Vince Lombardi, the famed Green Bay Packers football coach, has jumped out of his grave and tried to remind all of America—from those in the corner offices to the lowest-level managers to the most struggling blue-collar workers—that they've lost sight of their bottom-line goals. (What Lombardi actually said, remember, was, "Winning isn't everything; it's the only thing.")

"A winning personality," "winning on all fronts," "winning in everything you do." Even Jack Welch published a book called *Winning* in 2005, a primer for strivers who wanted to learn secrets from the man *Fortune* magazine called "the Manager of the Century." Probably the most viral of all clichés in the last twenty years has been "a win-win situation," which refers to a transaction where all parties benefit. So is it any wonder that *BusinessWeek* reminded us in a cover story on competition in 2006 that "Yes, Winning Is Still the Only Thing"?

It's not hard to buy into Vince Lombardi's philosophy. We all like to win. We all like the money, the attention, the recognition, and the rewards that accompany victory. And do you know anyone who likes to lose?

After interviewing forty-five leaders in their respective fields for this book, however, we discovered something very different: Winning is only a one-dimensional reward. Vince Lombardi's mantra really relates only to the smaller matters of life, like football. And for all but a few of us in this world, football is not life itself. Even world-class champions like Tiger Woods and Roger Federer—both already among the greatest athletes of all time—aren't motivated purely by the final outcome of the game. Federer recently said, "I can beat the main rival. But I think that what people like Tiger and I are more interested in is not who we're playing. . . . It's wanting to get the best out of yourself." Woods sees his own golf game as a constant exercise in self-improvement, not something to be defined simply by crushing the tournament field.

Of course, Woods and Federer wouldn't be who they are without winning at the highest level. But in any competitive situation, winning is functional. Winning is no longer an obsessive goal—if indeed it ever really was. It's just one stat on the scorecard of a life well lived. Winning isn't the only thing; it's simply what you do along the way.

So what else is there? Success.

WE CAN QUANTIFY THE SUCCESSFUL PERSONALITY

Over the course of a year, we interviewed captains of industry in business, politics, sports, and entertainment. The insights we gained in our interviews represent an unprecedented exploration of what success really means to a wide range of goal-oriented individuals. We found that these people went beyond the usual media sound bites, becoming introspective about the fact that their lives were shaped around much deeper concerns than simply winning. Success proved to be a much more complex and subtle topic than many of them may have expected.

And when it came time to assess individual experiences—when we delved into the specific personality traits of these high achievers—we hit upon a very important lesson: For all of these people, finding success wasn't a matter of altering their basic profiles, or personalities, or emotions, or ambitions, the qualities that made these people what they are. It was a matter of figuring out what they truly valued, who they were—*what made them tick*—and then using that knowledge to lead them, consciously or not, in the right direction.

In that spirit, we devised this book to help you, the reader, discover what makes *you* tick, so that you can use that knowledge to help you get where you want to go.

None of the people you'll read about trapped themselves by trying to change who they really were. They understood their own makeup—genetic, psychological, emotional—and this was the one thing they all had in common.

In talking with these people, we discovered that success has many different definitions. Upon closer examination, however, we also discerned that these diverse personalities settled into four distinct archetypes. While each success story was unique, there were several consistent character traits that allowed us to separate them into discrete groups. Not everyone interviewed approached his or her challenges in the same way, of course. But in our efforts to describe their personalities and quantify their skills, strengths, and weaknesses, the contours of these four archetypes emerged again and again.

These successful people fell into the following four categories:

- Natural-Born Leaders
- Independence Seekers
- Visionaries
- Do-Gooders

Each of these success archetypes exhibits unique strengths and potential. None of them was limited to a specific field or certain kinds of people. These types exist at the most fundamental level of human behavior; the personality tics and traits that define them seem to be present from childhood throughout adulthood and retirement. The interviewees themselves recognized these things as unchangeable and chose to work with them rather than against them.

Within each archetype, we also isolated three different aspects of personality—inner personality traits, motivational traits (internal and external), and external traits—that play an important role in under-standing which archetype someone is.

1. **INNER PERSONALITY TRAITS**: Core characteristics
   Which traits dominated their makeup? Which traits defined their character?

2. **MOTIVATIONAL TRAITS**: The goals individuals set for themselves and the ways they want to reach them
   What role does achievement play in their life? How do they get there? How important is it that they do?

3. **EXTERNAL TRAITS**: How they leverage relationships with others and larger organizations to achieve those goals
   How do they interact with the people in the organization? What is their role? How do they delegate?

As we studied the people in this book, we quickly realized that un-derstanding success involves understanding the interaction of these three aspects of personality. Looking at a single aspect in isolation can give you a false reading; all three parts must be looked at simultane-ously to understand the true archetype.

Let's explore the archetypes.

NATURAL-BORN LEADERS

These are people who find their fulfillment in managing complex chal-lenges on a national and global scale. They are confident in themselves and their abilities. They were born to the task. They take success as a given: They expect to succeed, and they know they will. They revel in the process of taking on challenges and moving up the ladder. And more than the members of any of our other groups, they are eager to climb as high as they can and be recognized faster and younger than anyone else. The telltale characteristics of the leader:

Inner Personality Traits

1. **SELF-CONFIDENCE:** They have a sense, from early on, that they can succeed at anything they want to do.
2. **BIG-PICTURE THINKING:** They have a macro perspective on how things come together; they don't get stuck on details.
3. **TAKE-CHARGE PERSONALITY:** They take control of any task or position given them.
4. **INSPIRATIONAL/MOTIVATIONAL SPIRIT:** A big part of their leadership involves inspiring others, especially within an organization.
5. **HELPFUL APPROACH:** They help the people around them succeed; they see the success of those around them as a reflection of their own success.

Motivational Traits

1. **THEY ALWAYS HAVE TO BE THE BEST IN ANYTHING THEY DO**—school, sports, business.
2. **THEY STRIVE FOR ORIGINAL ACHIEVEMENT,** aiming to be the first, to do things faster/younger than anyone else.
3. **THEY ENJOY COMPLEX ORGANIZATIONS;** they like working in large hierarchies, with multiple opportunities to succeed and move up.

External Traits with Organization

1. **THEY'RE COMFORTABLE DELEGATING;** they expect others to do a good job without having to micromanage them.
2. **THEY PUT THE COMPANY FIRST;** their personal interests come second.

INDEPENDENCE SEEKERS

These people want to live life on their own terms—to do what they want when they want. They set hard-to-achieve goals and change them frequently. They are inspired and challenged by a specific project rather than a position. After doing one thing for a while, they grow restless to move on and take on something new. They consider themselves "on their own," intellectually and financially. To them, money is important for the freedom it brings, not for the yachts it buys. Once they achieve a level of financial independence, money becomes a secondary issue in their lives. In many cases, it's never the prime motivator.

Independence seekers may work in a corporation, but such structured environments often feel like traps to them, and they leave. If they create their own company and it becomes too big or unwieldy, independence seekers sense a trap—and, as likely as not, leave to reinvent themselves.

Independence seekers have the following characteristics:

Inner Personality Traits

1. **GOAL-ORIENTED/CAN-DO OUTLOOK**: They'll always think about new and better ways to get tasks done; their satisfaction comes from reaching the goal.
2. **SELF-CONFIDENCE**: They'll do whatever they need to do to be successful; failure is not an option.
3. **ENTREPRENEURIAL/RISK-TAKING ATTITUDE**: When they see opportunities, they're willing to take chances to realize them.
4. **RESTLESS SPIRIT**: They periodically reinvent themselves and set new goals.
5. **SELF-DEPRECATING PERSONALITY**: They don't take themselves too seriously.

Motivational Traits

1. **PREFERENCE FOR REACHING GOALS OVER ACHIEVING PERFECTION**: They don't have to be the best, just good enough to fulfill their definition of success.
2. **NEED TO BE THE STAR**: They require recognition that they made things happen and that without them they wouldn't have worked.

External Traits with Organization

1. **DESIRE FOR HIGH-PROFILE RECOGNITION**: They thrive on personal validation, although being CEO is rarely their goal unless they started the company.
2. **INTEREST IN PERSONAL RATHER THAN ORGANIZATIONAL SUCCESS**: Their personal goals come before those of the organization.
3. **PRIDE IN ASSOCIATION**: They wear their affiliation with their organization as proof of their abilities.

For some independence seekers, independence itself becomes the goal. As marketing guru Sergio Zyman says, "For one thing, success meant having screw-you money. I wanted—and was able—to get to the point where I could say to an employer, 'Screw you. I have enough money now, and I don't need you anymore.'"

For others, independence is an attribute that helps them stay focused on their core dreams and not get sidetracked along the way. This group we call "independents who follow their dreams." They have the same characteristics as the independence seekers, but they are motivated by a single career goal or dream rather than by the quest for independence itself.

VISIONARIES

Put succinctly, visionaries see what others do not. What's most note-worthy about the group of visionaries we've assembled is not simply that they rose to the top of their fields, but that they all did it while single-handedly revolutionizing their respective industries.

Visionaries are single-minded and relentless and have the most inventive personalities. These are the people who change our world, who see beyond the accepted models. They look not at what we are doing, but at what we could be doing. Visionaries tend to frame their views in terms of a philosophy. They see something—a product, a service, a process—and try to improve it. If it ain't broke, they try to fix it anyway. They create new paradigms in our lives, and their ideas become touchstones for everyone who follows them.

For visionaries, setbacks are temporary, not a reason to quit. Failures are just part of the process; they learn and move on. Their driver is passion—the passion to realize their vision. Their common traits:

Inner Personality Traits

1. **RISK-TAKING APPROACH**: They don't accept the status quo and aren't afraid to gamble on changing it.
2. **DESIRE FOR CHANGE**: They tend to ask "Why not?" rather than "Why?"
3. **CAN-DO SPIRIT**: They find ways to make things happen.
4. **BIG-PICTURE THINKING**: They tend to look at issues creatively, from many angles.
5. **FOCUS**: They believe they're on a mission to make something better.

Motivational Traits

1. **RELENTLESS DRIVE**: Their ideas keep them going in pursuit of their vision, no matter how many setbacks they experience.
2. **INNER SATISFACTION**: They're less concerned with public recognition than with personal fulfillment.

External Traits with Organization

1. **PREFERENCE TO DO THINGS THEMSELVES**: They're not good at delegating but think they are and wonder why people don't get it or see what they see.
2. **PREFERENCE FOR TRUE BELIEVERS**: Everyone must drink the Kool-Aid to work with them.
3. **DEPENDENCE ON GOOD MANAGERS**, although only the best know this about themselves or manage to act on that knowledge.

DO-GOODERS

These are people whose greatest satisfaction comes from working toward the greater good and helping other people. They're very focused on other people and derive their greatest pleasure from improving the lives of others. Their management style is based on personal contact and connection. They tend to see their goals and the goals of their organization as intertwined with the progress of the people around them. Do-gooders have these things in common:

Inner Personality Traits

1. **STRONG MORAL COMPASS**: They do what they think is right.
2. **COMFORT WITH CRITICISM**: They view it as vital to growth and better results.
3. **IDEALISM/OPTIMISM**: They believe in the potential of humanity.
4. **TENACITY**: They never give up on something they know is right.
5. **SERIOUSNESS**: They are deeply interested and involved in their work.

Motivational Traits

1. **WILLINGNESS TO SACRIFICE**: They prioritize the greater good and social change over self-interest.
2. **DRIVE TO BE THE BEST**: Why compromise quality or effort when the stakes are so high?

External Traits with Organization

1. **PURSUIT OF GREATER GOOD OVER ORGANIZATION**: They take a genuine interest in helping others succeed.
2. **PREFERENCE FOR LIKE-MINDED PEOPLE**: They gravitate toward those with shared goals.
3. **IDENTIFICATION WITH THEIR ORGANIZATION/ CAUSE**: They define themselves in terms of the organization or cause they work for.

So how are we to choose which definition of success is right for us? Do we follow the CEO, the entrepreneur, the artist, the athlete? How do you know which one you are? Which of the people in this book offer the best lessons for you?

Many books take a one-size-fits-all approach in the advice they give; others offer a long menu of characteristics and expect the reader to choose them randomly. They compile a laundry list of attributes—*perseverance, single-mindedness, trust*—or a series of disassociated lessons the authors have learned from life: *Understand your past so that you can create your future. Don't let others define you. Reinvent yourself.*

Our insight is different.

In our work on the political campaign trail, we always implore candidates to be true to who they really are. Why? Because pretending to be someone or something else never works. Even if a false persona gains a candidate a temporary advantage, in the long term it will always be a liability—and it certainly won't lead to a legacy in which the candidate is likely to take pride.

The same holds true for each of us, in both our professional and our personal lives. Being successful, we've learned, isn't about trying to be what you wish you were—or what someone else thinks you should be. Trying to live someone else's definition of success is fruitless, and it will eventually come back to haunt you. The key to real success and fulfillment is to accept what you are and what you really care about. Don't look at others' successes simply to admire or envy them: Look at them in order to become more aware of who *you* are. Which person do you identify with and feel best represents you?

When we explored the personalities of the high-achieving people you'll read about in the following pages, we discovered that they looked at their lives and careers through a much different lens from what you might expect. They are almost all their own toughest critics, more willing and comfortable submitting to serious self-analysis than we could have hoped.

We talked with a wide range of people from varying backgrounds: men and women; young and old; people from different ethnic backgrounds; people from different professional worlds—sports, entertainment, government, multinational corporations, and small-scale entrepreneurial operations. We ran the gamut of high-level achievers who make the world turn faster—and allow most of us to live more fulfilling lives.

Their single common thread was that they felt the true measure of success was not how much money they made, or how well they lived, or where they lived, and especially not whether they won or lost specific battles along the way. Rather, it had more to do with self-motivation and reaching personal goals. And they all defined their goals in specific, personal ways.

For the truly great achievers, it's all about today and tomorrow, not yesterday. It's about life goals, not goalposts. It's about *how* they live their lives and how they want to live, not about past victories or future contests. It's about the serendipity of the journey, the strange and un-expected detours.

Bud Selig, for example, wanted to be a history professor. His father wanted him to join the family car dealership. He ended up becoming the commissioner of Major League Baseball, a job plenty of people would covet. We'd call him a natural-born leader; otherwise he'd be still looking over the hood ornaments of cars.

Or take NBC News anchor Brian Williams. Williams was a ter-rible student, but he knew he wanted to be a network news anchor. He couldn't fathom the idea of being chained to a desk. That's one reason he's also a quintessential independence seeker.

Craig Newmark, the man who brought us craigslist, had planned to become a paleontologist. Somewhere along the way, he decided he wanted to do something "cool" that also had a social conscience. That made him one of our classic do-gooders.

As you'll discover in the following pages, many of these successful people share fascinating character traits. Jason Binn, the publisher, ex-hibited a bulldoglike personality and will to succeed from the day he finagled his way into a job interview at an ad agency. Don Hewitt was floundering at CBS, thinking he was all but finished as a news pro-ducer, when he "stole" the best ideas from Edward R. Murrow's news program and created *60 Minutes*. When asked why he was successful, he unabashedly admitted he was lucky.

Binn and Hewitt are at different ends of a generational divide, but they share the traits that characterize all independence seekers: Both are confident; both march to their own rhythms; and both were entrepreneurial enough to forge their own way—one within a large organization and the other by creating his own company.

Arturo Moreno, owner of the Anaheim Angels, told us that much of his success came about because he was never afraid of being told "no." He imparted this advice to those around him.

A number of people said they were simply in the right place at the right time. Many of our respondents, Don Hewitt among them, used the word *lucky* when describing the arc of their lives or careers. While they may have indeed been fortunate in different ways, we should take this as a sign that they're thankful for their success— that they understand the value of humility. Most people understand that chance favors the prepared. Hard work, risk taking, refusing to quit, and the will to get to the next waypoint no matter how formidable the obstacles appeared helped to define these people. These are just a few of the traits that define many of their achievements.

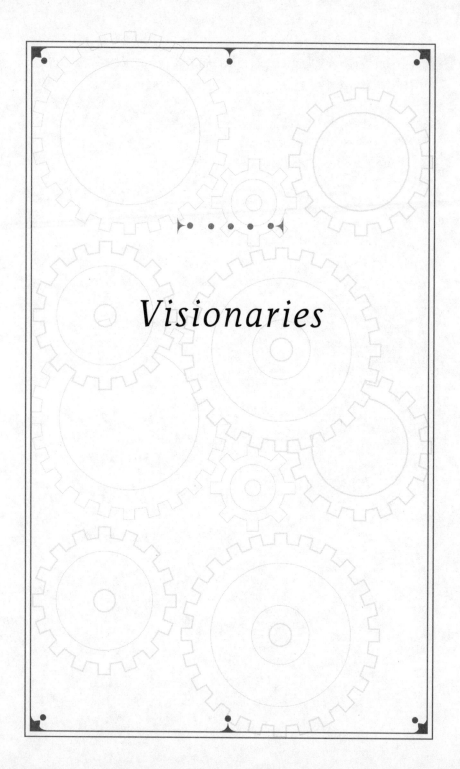

Visionaries

CHAPTER 1

• • •

Mark Burnett

EXECUTIVE PRODUCER, *SURVIVOR*

A pioneer in reality television, Mark Burnett is best known for creating the Emmy Award–winning reality show *Survivor*. In doing so, he revolutionized the "unscripted" drama series and introduced millions of people worldwide to an entirely new television genre.

Burnett is a former member of the British Army Parachute Regiment, with active service medals in both the Northern Ireland and Argentina conflicts. He began his television career by creating the trailblazing adventure series *Eco-Challenge*. He served as executive producer on nine Eco-Challenge events and programs, earning a Sports Emmy Award for Outstanding Program Achievement for *Eco-Challenge: Morocco*.

Since *Survivor*, Burnett has also produced the popular reality shows *The Apprentice*, *The Contender*, and *Rock Star: INXS* for network television, and he partnered with Steven Spielberg to produce a filmmaking competition series called *On the Lot*. In 2004, Burnett was featured in *Time* magazine's "*Time* 100 List" of the most influential people in the world and has been cited several times by *Entertainment Weekly* as one of the "Top 101 Most Powerful People in Entertainment."

Mark Burnett is the quintessential visionary. When most producers were focused on discovering the next hit sitcom or drama, Burnett was building a reality television empire—and changing the American appetite for small-screen entertainment. Every task he sets his mind to has to be bigger and better than the last. And one key to Burnett's immense success is his incredible work ethic: No job or task is beneath him if it means accomplishing his goals.

"TO ME, SUCCESS PROVIDES THE GLORIOUS PRIVILEGE OF BECOMING INDEPENDENT."

I grew up in London. As a kid I was enamored of *Rambo*. My idea of adventure was being in the military, with bandoliers and bullets hanging over my chest. Becoming a Special Forces soldier was all I ever wanted to do at that time, so at the age of eighteen I joined the British Army Parachute Regiment.

I served in Ireland and in the Falklands. It was way scarier than I imagined. And in retrospect, as an older man, the fact that bureaucrats are sending young kids to do things that they probably wouldn't do themselves is kind of annoying.

After the Falklands War, which was the first trench warfare in many decades, I didn't see another war on the horizon. I also didn't particularly want to go back to firing blank ammunition in training, and the idea of spending many more years waiting for another war began to wear thin.

Instead, I decided to seek out the American dream—but in order to make that happen, I needed money. I had heard there was work available in Central America for experienced foreign soldiers. I had a contact who was recruiting from California. Fresh off a stint in the British paratroopers, I felt that soldiering in Central America was the best use of my skill set at the time and the best way for me to save some money and give myself a start in America once I was done.

What I hadn't counted on was how horrified my parents would be. I had just finally left the parachute regiment, and already I was planning to carry weapons again. They didn't even know the truth; they thought I was going to do some bodyguard-type work in Los Angeles.

At the airport, as I was leaving, my mother looked into my eyes and said, "Don't you think you've put us through enough?" She made me promise before boarding the plane: "No carrying guns." As an only child, I had major guilt. But there was no way to avoid the issue, so, reluctantly, I promised her. I got on that plane to California with a one-way ticket, $600, and no idea what I would do when I got there.

I had no advanced formal education. No family wealth to fall back on. No business connections. No marketable skills. For the first time in many years, I felt a nervous, sick feeling in my stomach.

When I got to L.A., I called the only person I knew there—an English guy named Nick I'd known since I was ten. He had a chauffeur-type job, and almost immediately he managed to hook me up with a nanny job in Beverly Hills.

I didn't really think about the humor in that—a commando one day, a nanny the next. I just knew I needed a job, and that nanny job solved the problem. That's one thing about my personality: I live in the now, and I'm always looking for solutions to problems. I'm focused on prioritizing, and my priority at that moment was finding somewhere to live, food, and money. Driving someone's kids to school and vacuuming the living room carpet certainly wasn't glamorous, but it was a start. I've since noticed that people who truly want to make it don't consider any task beneath them; they just do whatever it takes. The first job I ever performed in America was unloading a dishwasher—and it was the first one I'd ever seen. At home, *my mother* was our dishwasher!

I learned a lot in that nanny job. I learned about American culture and the American way of life. I also learned that despite their lavish lifestyle, their education, and their big bank account, the people I worked for weren't that much different from me. My logic and intelligence was absolutely on a par with theirs. I also learned that Americans in general are very open-minded people who are willing to give you a break. Americans lack cynicism.

Americans are results-based; they're open to giving people a chance.

If you were at a party and half the guests were Americans and half British, and somebody said, "Oh, my God, there's a seventeen-foot purple giraffe in the front yard," the Brits wouldn't bother to get off their asses; their cynical nature requires them not to believe any outrageous claim for fear of looking stupid. Most Americans, on the other hand, would rush to look out the window—but they'd also quickly realize it was a joke, and they'd laugh heartily at themselves.

The moral of that story is that on the day a purple giraffe finally appears out in the yard, only the Americans will see it! They will not miss any opportunity. I'm an American citizen now. I always look out the window for the purple giraffe.

What I took away from the nanny experience, and from spending time around such wealthy people for the first time in my life, was simple: "Work for yourself. Start a small, low-capital business and become independent." So I started selling T-shirts on Venice Beach and eventually expanded into having five outlets.

By 1991, I'd finally achieved some level of success in America. Less than a decade after arriving, I had a home, a car, and a growing business. I no longer woke up dreading that I was on the verge of ruin. Life felt good. But then came one of the worst setbacks ever: I discovered that my mother was dying of cancer. Probably as a search for meaning, I started going to Tony Robbins's seminars to analyze and reevaluate my life plans. "Stop working for a living and start designing a life," he said. "You need to write down what you really want." What I really wanted was adventure—which goes right back to why I joined the parachute regiment in the first place. And I also wanted to be wealthy.

The universe works in mysterious ways, and it was around this time that an article in the *Los Angeles Times* caught my eye. It was about a French adventure competition called the Raid Gauloises. The Raid was held in a different exotic country every year. That year, the location was Costa Rica.

The races were grueling. They lasted up to two weeks and covered several hundred miles. The goal was for each team to race three hundred miles nonstop, over mountains, down rivers, and through jungles so snake-infested that the teams carried their own supply of antivenin.

They also carried all their own food, water, and gear. They were so driven to reach the finish line that the winner slept just one hour per night. It reminded me so much of my parachute regiment days—only without the weapons—that it seemed the perfect competition to indulge the adventurous, hardship-loving side of me.

But could it also be a way to make money?

The concept of expedition racing wasn't new to me. I had read articles about similar races being held through the glaciers and fjords of New Zealand's Southern Alps. The French race grew out of that concept. But reading the *Times* that morning, I suddenly became consumed with an idea: I should launch an expedition-length race of my own in the United States.

Around this time, *Outside* magazine was also doing quite well. Clearly, Americans were becoming more interested in the outdoors. I did some research and found that sales of tents and sleeping bags and backpacks had skyrocketed. And I read a study that said the 1990s would be about three dominant themes: the ecology, extreme sports, and self-actualization through challenge. In my mind, no other format combined all three like expedition racing.

I purchased the rights to the French race and decided my race would be called the Eco-Challenge. I had it all mapped out in my head. I envisioned a rigorous Eco-Challenge expedition race, with a stunning television show beamed into homes shortly thereafter. That goal became the driving force in my life.

Part of my strategy for launching Eco-Challenge was to take part in the French Raid Gauloises. Participating in that race, I figured, would give me a better understanding of what future Eco-Challenge contestants would be going through, and it would help me become a better race producer.

I ended up racing three times in the Raid Gauloises, in Oman, Madagascar, and Borneo. It was much harder, actually, than anything I had done in the army. It was brutal, but I did very well in my second outing: My team became the first American team ever to complete the Raid Gauloises.

To defray my costs of competing, I secured sponsors—and those sponsors needed TV exposure. So for this second race in Madagascar, I managed to convince KCAL Channel 9 in Los Angeles to send a reporter to produce a one-hour special on the race, and specifically on our team. I also convinced the Raid organizers to provide me with free copies of all the footage their ten camera crews shot of the race, and in return I'd get the race publicized on American television. The other side of this deal was that I convinced KCAL to produce a one-hour show with all the footage.

It was a win-win for everyone: The Raid was happy to have gotten exposure in America, and KCAL was happy to end up with a one-hour special that would have cost more than $1 million to produce if they'd shot it themselves. I had achieved my major goal of satisfying my sponsors, but the best part of the entire deal was that KCAL would get to air this show only once; then the show became my property to distribute. I went on to sell it to ESPN, and the show got fairly good ratings. This is where I really began to learn how to be bold and creative in putting together a national television deal.

I first heard the idea that would become *Survivor* in 1995, while I was at Fox television in Los Angeles pitching *Eco-Challenge*. The Fox executive hearing the *Eco* pitch told me about this game show concept where a bunch of people were starving on a desert island. They competed for luxuries such as food and pillows. Meanwhile, a host living on a luxury yacht offshore eliminated them from the contest one by one.

The brains behind the show's concept was a brilliant producer from England named Charlie Parsons. But the Fox exec believed that it would take someone with previous experience producing large-scale adventure-reality TV in a remote setting to pull it off. She believed *Eco-Challenge* qualified me.

I made it my goal to meet Charlie and show him *Eco-Challenge*. We hit it off immediately, and I ended up buying the North American rights to the show in 1998. I had a gut feeling that I could make this great concept even greater. In the months following our meeting, I thought about the island game show often, but in my mind I saw it less as a game show and more as a drama. When I traveled for business, I would look about the plane at my fellow passengers and imagine us crash-landing on an island. Where would I fit into our new society? Who would lead? Who would follow? Who would find the ordeal too hard and quit?

I wanted my *Survivor* to be bigger, more dramatic, and more epic than any nonfiction television ever seen.

The important thing to know is that one thing that was really beneficial to me was my naïveté. I had no clue back then about the television industry. If I had known what I know now, I might never have attempted it. Looking back, I realize it should have been impossible.

Even when I closed the deal with CBS, I wasn't certain that I could actually pull it off. I had a belief that somehow it would work out, but I wasn't certain. I think the important thing to remember is this: Those who need certainty don't do anything, because nothing is ever certain. Somehow, my dogmatic, persevering nature, coupled with the naïveté of just believing it would all work out, *made it* work out.

The challenges and adventures of *Eco-Challenge* had taught me to rely on my gut, but it was *Survivor* that made me put that skill to use every day. I had a gut feeling all along that *Survivor* was going to be a big hit. I felt this so strongly that when I pitched the show to Leslie Moonves at CBS, I began by handing him a mock issue of *Newsweek* with *Survivor* on the cover. I wanted him to know I truly believed *Survivor* would be that huge. And when the show became a hit, both *Time* and *Newsweek* actually did end up putting *Survivor* on their covers!

One of my favorite poems is by the Scottish poet Robert Burns. It's called "Epistle to a Young Friend." Here's a verse that has always driven me:

To catch dame Fortune's golden smile,
Assiduous wait upon her;
And gather gear [wealth] by ev'ry wile
That's justified by honour;
Not for to hide it in a hedge,
Nor for a train attendant;
But for the glorious privilege
Of being independent.

It's from the 1700s, but it is equally relevant today. Think of what it says: If you want to become wealthy, you really have to work at it—*assiduously*. But the motive shouldn't be to hoard it. The motive should be independence.

To me, success provides the glorious privilege of becoming independent.

CHAPTER 2

• • •

Tamara Mellon

FOUNDER AND PRESIDENT, JIMMY CHOO

Designer-shoe mogul Tamara Mellon was born with a bent for both fashion and business. Her mother, Ann Yeardye, was a former Chanel model; her father, Tom Yeardye, was a successful entrepreneur and co-founder of the Vidal Sassoon hair care company.

Mellon began her career with a short stint in public relations and retail sales before transitioning to the editorial side of the fashion business. In 1990, she became accessories editor at British *Vogue*.

While she was at *Vogue*, Mellon's entrepreneurial instinct and eye for fashion led her to perceive a gap in the luxury shoe market: She believed the offerings of the time lacked both style and variety. Mellon saw the potential for developing her own ready-to-wear brand, in collaboration with a talented—yet relatively unknown—Malaysian shoemaker named Jimmy Choo.

Mellon launched the business in 1996 and soon became her own company's muse, generating a glamorous global image for the little-known brand. And it wasn't long before Hollywood took notice. Beyoncé sang about them, *Sex and the City* women drooled over them, and A-list actresses considered them good-luck charms on Oscar night. In eight short years, Mellon turned a £150,000 loan from her father into a £100 million global phenomenon.

Tamara Mellon had a successful career at a fashion magazine, but her instincts and vision proved that she was destined for greater heights. She saw a market for luxury women's shoes and took a first-class cobbler and turned him into a worldwide brand name. Like others with a strong sense of what they want, Mellon is her company's muse; she designs shoes that she wants to wear, and millions of women worldwide follow suit.

"I DEFINE SUCCESS AS FOLLOWING YOUR PASSION. I'VE ALWAYS BEEN PASSIONATE ABOUT FASHION. I JUST DIDN'T KNOW IT WAS GOING TO END UP BEING SHOES."

I was always terrible in school. I was probably voted the least likely to succeed. I just knew I wanted to be in fashion, but I didn't know exactly how. I had no real strategy. I started off working the floor in a clothing shop. Back then I thought, "Oh God, what am I doing this for?" But all the things I've done can be traced back to working in a shop, because it was there that I learned how to run a store.

Then I went and worked for a public relations company. I learned how to do PR and promote a brand. Then I worked for a fashion magazine, and that trains your eye to pick the right products and predict trends. All of that, all the previous jobs I've had, have led me to where I am today, because they gave me the tools to do what I'm doing.

I define success as following your passion. I've always been passionate about fashion. I just didn't know it was going to end up being shoes.

I don't have a stereotypical head for business; I didn't go to business school, and I didn't get an MBA. A lot of what I do is based on intuition. Intuition is probably the number one tool you can have in your toolbox.

Eventually I started working at British *Vogue*, and at that time there weren't really any great shoes around. There was Manolo Blahnik and that was about it. But there was a guy in the East End of London named Jimmy Choo who was a cobbler making handmade shoes for private clients. I used to get him to make things for fashion shoots for me. Over a five-year period I kept giving him credit in *Vogue*, so his name started to be recognized. And I thought this was a great platform to start a business.

So we had a name—but there was no business there. It was my idea to find factories in Italy to produce the shoes in volume, open stores, find wholesalers, do PR.

What I didn't expect was that I also ended up designing the shoes. It turns out that there's a big difference between making a pair of shoes and designing a full collection. Jimmy's talent really is in making them, not designing. So I ended up doing the collection as well.

I think the key to the success of Jimmy Choo is that I totally relate to my customer. I know exactly who she is, what she wants to wear, how she wants to wear it—because at the end of the day, *I am* the customer. Relating to a customer's needs is very important.

Very early on, I opened a store in London. Then I opened one in New York, because I knew America was one of the most powerful countries in the world and that was where we needed to move to. Usually, it takes British brands twenty years to make that move. We did it within a year.

The hardest thing was getting factories to work with us, because they aren't interested in small volumes. They want to work with big brands that can give them orders for ten thousand pairs of pumps in black. When I was doing it, you had a lot of color, a lot of accessories on the shoes, and in the beginning we were ordering small quantities. So it was a real fight to get good-quality factories to work with us. I had to convince them that this would be a long-term project that eventually would pay off.

My father was a huge influence on my life and career. Up until the day he died I spoke to him every day, and we always talked about business, so I learned a lot from him. Two things I learned were not to let lawyers negotiate your deals and not to let accountants run your business. He taught me that it's very important in the beginning to keep your overhead down—to make sure you've got more money coming in than going out.

You need a lot of determination and focus to succeed in a start-up business. You also need to be able to take risks. It was obviously a huge risk to start a company from scratch. I've probably always been a risk taker. I don't think you achieve true success without taking risks.

Ten years ago, I had a goal. Then, when I got there, I thought, "Oh, it's not enough. I want to do more." Then I thought, "Okay, if I can achieve this, I'll retire by the time I'm forty." And now I've got there and I'm thinking, "I'm not ready to do that; I want to do more." So you set your mind on something, and you get there, and you want to keep going. I'm the kind of person who always needs a challenge in my life.

Some people say, "Oh, you're disempowering women by putting them in heels." And it's absolutely not true. It's just the opposite. Wearing heels makes you taller; it empowers you. I feel much more empowered when I have more height. Men can be very patronizing in business, and that's frustrating. It shouldn't be a man's world. They may wear the trousers, but they don't wear the heels.

CHAPTER 3

• • •

Steve Forbes

PRESIDENT AND CHIEF EXECUTIVE OFFICER, FORBES
EDITOR IN CHIEF, *FORBES* MAGAZINE

Steve Forbes assumed his current position as president and chief executive officer of Forbes and editor in chief of *Forbes* magazine in 1990.

The company's flagship publication, *Forbes*, is the nation's leading business magazine, with a circulation of more than nine hundred thousand. Together, *Forbes* and *Forbes Global* reach a worldwide audience of nearly five million readers.

In 1997, Forbes entered the new-media arena with the launch of Forbes.com. The site, which attracts more than seven million unique visitors a month, has become the leading destination site for business decision makers and investors.

Forbes campaigned vigorously for the Republican nomination for the presidency in 1996 and 2000. Key components of his platform included a flat tax, medical savings accounts, and a new Social Security system for working Americans, ideas he continues to promote passionately today.

Steve Forbes built on one of the best-known brands in business when he
recognized the Internet as a new-media opportunity long before most of
his competitors. More important, he understood the medium when others
were still wondering how to make it work for them. And his foresight paid
off. Today, Forbes.com is one of the most successful business content sites
on the Internet.

"THE KEY TO ACHIEVING SUCCESS IN BUSINESS IS PASSION. DON'T APPROACH THE BUSINESS WITH A FORMULA OR JUST EXPECTING TO MAKE A QUICK BUCK. YOU MUST HAVE A DESIRE, A VISION, AND THEN GO AT IT HAMMER AND TONGS."

We grew up with stories about our grandfather, who started *Forbes*, which had great success in the 1920s. In the late twenties, William Randolph Hearst offered my grandfather the equivalent of tens of millions of dollars to buy the business. My grandfather refused. Then came the Great Depression, and the company nearly went broke. We heard about how our grandfather couldn't even cash his own paychecks because there wasn't enough money in the bank. So we learned early on that success and setbacks are part and parcel of the real world—that life doesn't go in a straight line. Business requires constant attention; if you don't have a passion for it, you ultimately won't succeed, or you'll lead a miserable life.

When I was growing up, the magazine, the whole business, was a dominant presence in our household. My father taught my siblings and me at an early age how our bread was buttered. Business doesn't just happen; you have to go out and make it happen. He would take us to business functions, and we were expected to be more than mere ornaments. We were expected to know who was there, and why, and to contribute to the process. We learned that business was something that needed constant attention and nurturing.

My father also made us learn to play the bagpipes. We'd have these miserable lessons on Sunday afternoons. Whatever genes we have, they are not music genes. But we played our bagpipes at business functions anyway.

When we were entertaining business executives on our yacht, *The Highlander*, we were expected to give tours and things like that. Business wasn't just preached; it was practiced. We were involved. Period.

My father was also involved in New Jersey politics when we were growing up, so we were taken to political events as well. He was in the state senate and ran for governor; as he put it, he was nosed out by a landslide. I followed that campaign closely, on a day-to-day basis. When he lost, I took it personally.

I never intended to go into politics myself, but in the early 1990s I became head of an organization called Empower America, which was founded by Jack Kemp, Bill Bennett, and Jeane Kirkpatrick. It was a reform organization, Reaganesque in its approach. We all assumed that Jack Kemp was going to run for president in 1996. He'd been in the Housing Department in the Bush administration, and he'd run for president in 1988; he'd been a very pro-growth political figure and candidate. By early 1995, though, Kemp decided not to run, which surprised all of us. I looked around at the field of candidates who were running and felt none of them had the Kemp-Reagan approach.

Finally, I took a page from my grandfather, who had started out as a journalist, a reporter for the Hearst papers writing a syndicated column. Then he decided that instead of merely writing about doers and shakers, he'd become an entrepreneur and start his own business. So instead of complaining about politicians and their lack of the right kinds of principles and programs, I thought, "Why not run myself?" And in 1995 I took the plunge, making the flat tax the center of my platform. I tried twice for the Republican nomination but did not succeed.

The amazing thing, however, is that the flat tax, while yet to be enacted in the United States, is now in place in some ten countries, mostly in Central and Eastern Europe.

The lesson you learn from losing is to step back, figure out why it happened; then figure out how you can do better the next time. You don't quit the field: You figure out how to win or how to change the field.

I'm not involved in running for office now. Instead I have elected to be an agitator, an instigator, someone who's constantly stirring the pot. That means pushing causes such as tax reform, pressuring candidates, trying to make things happen.

In my family's line of work, you expect setbacks. We had a technology magazine that was successful for a while but eventually had to be pulled into the regular magazine in 2001. These things happen. But you have to keep probing and pushing, or you'll fail. It's like riding a bicycle: If you don't keep moving, you'll fall over.

One of *Forbes*'s biggest obstacles was overcoming skepticism, especially from outsiders, in the early part of this decade, when the core business was collapsing. No one foresaw that the business magazine category was going to take a huge hit, especially after 9/11. But you don't control circumstances; you're not a master of the universe. So you have to adjust. If you believe in the mission, you have to figure out how to make it happen when things don't go as planned.

When we started our Web site ten years ago, most publishers thought electronic media simply meant taking what they printed and throwing it on a screen, and voilà, you're in high-tech land. It's like what happened a hundred years ago, when Thomas Edison invented movies. Some people thought that making feature films was merely a matter of filming stage plays. They quickly learned that the two were very different media and had better be treated separately. Even today many publishers treat the Web as, in essence, an adjunct to their printed publications. They still don't get it.

From the start, we treated our Web site as a separate medium, with separate staff and separate offices. We poured lots of money into developing the site, even though it was losing money, especially after the high-tech bubble burst in 2000–2001. At that time a lot of publications, including *BusinessWeek* and *Fortune*, put their Web sites into deep freeze. We continued to expand ours, even though our core business was taking a huge hit.

The platforms may change, but the constituency does not. We recognized that our focus was the business community, and entrepreneurial capitalists in particular. I think that focus, along with our firm belief in entrepreneurial capitalism and its principles, distinguished us from our competitors and has enabled us to achieve success at a time when others are floundering. We had focus and direction.

It was a very risky venture. We didn't know if the site was going to work. We had to tighten our belts, make painful adjustments, while pouring huge resources into something that had no guarantee of succeeding. Each day we asked: "Is this the right thing to do? Are we jeopardizing everything by going against the grain?" It sounds glamorous to say we bet the company, but in a sense it's true: If our dot-com hadn't worked, we would have been in trouble.

It's important not to do anything this complex alone. Without my brother Tim, we would have been in much more difficult circumstances. He is brilliant when it comes to operations. He recognized the importance of the dot-com as much as, or even more than, I did. When you're a lone ranger, it's tough to succeed.

The key to achieving success in business is passion. Don't approach the business with a formula or just expecting to make a quick buck. You must have a desire, a vision, and then go at it hammer and tongs. Life never runs in a straight line. Without that desire and drive, you will flounder.

One of the better commencement speeches I've ever heard or read was given by Steve Jobs a little more than a year ago. One of the things he told the graduating class was that he had pursued his passion for calligraphy when he was a student. Most people would think, "Well, that was a nice indulgence, but a waste of time." He pointed out that his study of calligraphy ultimately enabled him to approach designs with Apple and iPod that were, to use the cliché, outside the box.

You can draw on your passion and your interests in ways that you never expected. If you want to be an actor, that doesn't mean you have to wait tables the rest of your life when you're not acting. Your skills may lead you to success in other areas.

I think you have to recognize that even with vision and passion, most of what you do is work. Hard work. Training for an athletic event—say, a baseball game—takes a lot of practice and hard work. There's nothing glamorous about it. The *result* may be glamorous, but getting there takes a lot of detail work.

You must also recognize that there's more than one way to achieve a goal and that even if you don't succeed in achieving a particular goal, you may achieve other things that lead to success. Again, look at Steve Jobs. He got thrown out of Apple twenty years ago and had setbacks in other areas. Some of the things he tried flopped. But then he created Pixar and the iPod.

I think the greatest inspiration for me and my siblings was our father. When he suffered a setback, he licked his wounds, put the problem behind him, and moved on. You can't stay focused on what didn't happen. Don't let the past poison you; move on. As my father put it, your trip on this earth is not a dress rehearsal; you'd better make the most of it.

CHAPTER 4

• • •

Arturo "Arte" Moreno

OWNER, LOS ANGELES ANGELS OF ANAHEIM

In 2003, billionaire Arte Moreno made history by becoming the first Hispanic to own a major sports team in the United States, buying the Anaheim Angels baseball franchise from the Walt Disney Company.

Named one of *Time* magazine's "25 Most Influential Hispanics in America" in 2005, Moreno, a fourth-generation Mexican American, made his money in billboard advertising and in the process revolutionized the industry.

After an army tour of duty in Vietnam, he returned to his home state of Arizona and enrolled at the University of Arizona. He graduated in 1973 with a degree in marketing and went to work at a small outdoor advertising company. Several years later he joined a rival company, Outdoor Systems, where he rose to become the company's president and chief executive officer. Under his leadership, the company's total profits grew from $500,000 to $90 million in less than ten years. In 1996, Moreno took Outdoor Systems public. The company's stock soared, and two years later Moreno sold it to Infinity Broadcasting for $8 billion.

Shortly after assuming control of the Angels in 2003, Moreno cut ticket, souvenir, and concession prices at the stadium and demonstrated a willingness to spend whatever was necessary to sign premium players, endearing him to the team's fans.

In 2005, despite a bitter backlash, Moreno made the gutsy decision to change the team name from the Anaheim Angels to the Los Angeles Angels of Anaheim—a key component of his overall strategy to increase revenue by expanding the team's marketability beyond Anaheim.

Arte Moreno has a remarkable ability never to lose sight of one of the most important principles of business: Have a good product and make more than you spend. By keeping it simple and remaining unshakably confident in his values, Moreno has been able to stay focused on building and growing successful organizations.

"MOST PEOPLE GO THROUGH LIFE AFRAID TO TRY TO ACCOMPLISH SOMETHING BECAUSE THEY'RE AFRAID SOMEONE WILL TELL THEM 'NO' OR THEY'RE GOING TO FAIL. . . . I'M NOT TOO AFRAID OF BEING TOLD 'NO.'"

When I was younger, my mom was home all the time. When we came home from school, she was always there. I have four brothers and six sisters, so it was a busy household. My mother was always taking care of the kids, whether it was getting us ready for school or helping with our homework. She was a very bright lady. My mom was really the manager of the house, while my dad was working.

My brothers and I shared a room. We spent a lot of time together playing sports, talking, wishing, and dreaming. We did not have a television when I was very young, so we would sit around on my mom's bed and listen to the radio. I think I was eight or nine before we got our first TV—back when there were only a couple of stations!

I probably started establishing my goals when I was in the army.

Out of high school I went to college, but I didn't do very well. I ended up getting drafted and spent two years in the army. One of those years I was deployed in Vietnam, and I spent a lot of time thinking about where I was going to go to school when I returned. I knew I could use the GI Bill to pay for it.

My dad was a high school dropout, so his goal was to make sure we all finished high school. I remember in high school wondering how I was going to get to college. I was certainly no Einstein. Even today, I consider graduating from college perhaps my greatest personal success.

One of my goals in college was to work for a corporation, to become a "corporate guy." Part of my motivation was status: You work for a good corporation and with luck you get paid well and receive all the benefits.

I attended the University of Arizona, and I received a good education. I was an accounting major before switching to marketing. But I have to admit, I was also looking to enjoy the other aspects of college life as well. *Where are we going tonight?* It was Thursday night this and Friday night that. Today, I have a son who's getting ready to go to college. I tell him, "Your social experience in college is going to stay with you just as long as your educational experience. The socialization you get going to school is just as valuable as what you learn in the books."

I went to work for Gannett, the newspaper chain. Al Neuharth, the chairman and CEO, was a very, very positive influence in the company. I loved the way he operated the business. Listening to Neuharth make a presentation was motivating. It was very powerful to see how he had planned and structured the company's future.

I got a management position in the company; I made good money and even had some stock options. I was very happy. I loved having an office on Madison Avenue and Fifty-fourth Street. As I moved up the ladder, though, there were fewer and fewer management positions available. I had to decide whether I was going to stay with Gannett or leave and go on my own. I would say that decision was probably the largest professional risk I ever faced.

I remember talking to a young lady at a cocktail party around that time. She told me—to my face—that by giving up my job at Gannett,

I had committed career suicide. I just smiled and said, "Your call." Ironically, I ended up buying a company that her husband was working for.

I learned early on that if you just look at business simply and logically, you can become successful. It's addition and subtraction: If your expenses are greater than your revenues, you lose money. If you can add and subtract, you're very dangerous. Also, you don't need a real high intellectual level to push forward and compete—to say, "Here's the goal, and we're getting there."

There is one principle I've adhered to for a long time, and it's something that's helped me achieve what I have throughout my career: I'm not too afraid of being told "no." Once, back east, I hired a black person who was going to junior college. He had a labor job in a shop, and I went back and talked to him. He was a very nice-looking, well-groomed young guy. I said, "We're going to move some people around here, and we're going to give some people an opportunity to go from the shop to the office. We're going to put you in a training program."

After some time passed, I asked this guy's supervisor how he was doing. He said, "Terrible. We send him into areas and he just clams up."

I called him in my office and asked him, "Are you black?"

"Yeah," he said.

I said, "People have been telling you 'no' your whole life, haven't they?"

He said, "Yeah."

I said, "Now all of a sudden it's hurting your feelings?"

Most people go through life afraid to try to accomplish something because they're afraid someone will tell them "no" or they're going to fail. A teenager in high school doesn't walk across the dance floor to ask a young lady to dance, because if she says "no," that walk back to his friends looks like a football field. So he doesn't even try. The same thing happens in business all the time.

It takes a combination of things to be successful. The number one thing is discipline. Obviously, you have to maintain focus. You have to set a goal, and then you have to be focused and disciplined. I tell people to put their goals on paper, because if you keep them in your head, they're like little Ping-Pong balls bouncing around. You can't keep them all in focus.

When I bought the Angels, I drew up a seven-year plan. We bought this company from Disney, and I spent a lot of time studying how they'd been running the business. I ended up getting hold of a training tape from Disney. The Disney people know that some people save their whole lives to go to Disneyland. They did a very good job training their employees to understand they were in a service business.

Service has probably been the number one key to my success—or, I should say, our business's success. It's the *level* of service that matters most to me. If you tell someone you're going to be there at ten o'clock, you're there at ten o'clock. If I can't be there at ten o'clock, I need to let you know and apologize for not being there.

I evaluate things from the perspective of a family and what satisfies them. Many times I've used input from my wife, Carole, and the kids when making certain business decisions. When someone brings their family to a baseball game at Angel Stadium, they're welcomed when they enter. They walk in and it's clean. They're guided to their seats. We try to make the experience as affordable as possible.

If you're in the entertainment business, you need to entertain. Friday nights we always have fireworks. If we lose a game, it's tough for me to sit there because I'm mad that we lost the game. But then here come the fireworks, and everyone is still in the stadium cheering for the fireworks.

I love winning! I always laugh at these football players dancing around the end zone. I prefer the attitude of someone like Warren Buffett—the easy smile, the nice midwestern confidence. I like the idea that the richest guy in the world can still walk out of a building carrying his own briefcase, smiling, saying, "Have a good day."

CHAPTER 5

• • •

Barry Sternlicht

CHAIRMAN AND CHIEF EXECUTIVE OFFICER, STARWOOD CAPITAL GROUP

In addition to running the Starwood Capital Group, a private investment firm he formed in 1991, Barry Sternlicht is the founder and chairman emeritus of Starwood Hotels & Resorts Worldwide Inc., a company he founded in 1995.

Today, Starwood Hotels is one of the leading hotel and leisure companies in the world, with more than 850 properties in eighty countries. Starwood is a fully integrated owner, operator, and franchiser of hotels and resorts, with seven internationally renowned brands, including St. Regis, the Luxury Collection, W Hotels, Sheraton, Westin, Le Méridien, and Four Points.

Sternlicht has been hailed as a dynamic innovator. In addition to creating and launching W Hotels, he is credited with the creation of Westin's Heavenly Bed and Bath, Westin Workout, and the world's first frequent traveler program with "no blackouts."

In his current role as head of Starwood Capital Group, Sternlicht has structured more than three hundred separate investment transactions with a cost basis of more than $30 billion. The firm manages

more than $12 billion of assets on behalf of its high-net-worth and in-
stitutional partners.

*Barry Sternlicht's career has taken some twists and turns, but a review of
his accomplishments reveals a gift for seeing opportunities his colleagues
and competitors did not. He made his mark early as a smart and gutsy
real estate deal maker but discovered his true passion in the hotel industry, where he proved to be a dynamic innovator. Sternlicht saw a gap in
the luxury hotel market and envisioned a group of stylish urban "boutique" hotels to fill that gap. His creation of the W Hotels chain combined
his real estate savvy with his talent for design, operation, and customer
service and allowed him to successfully bring together all the pieces of his
vision. It wasn't about money, it was about building his personal legacy
from scratch: His vision was realized in the form of a dynamic enterprise.
Sternlicht continues to march to the beat of his own drum, turning down
leadership opportunities at other companies in order to further his new
passion, philanthropy. To each new endeavor he brings the same creativity,
commitment, and innovation that fueled his previous successes.*

"PERSEVERANCE IS GENIUS IN DISGUISE. IF I CAN PERSEVERE, I CAN SUCCEED."

I grew up in an upper-middle-class background, working summers at
two jobs and trying to earn enough money to pay for small things like
a shirt, a fish tank, or a basketball. My idea of success in those days was
earning enough money not just to survive financially, but to have the
simple comforts: the ability to buy a shirt, take a date to a nice dinner,
and buy that fish tank I wanted. And as I extrapolated that philosophy forward, I dreamed of someday having a house with a pool and a
tennis court. It's amazing to reflect back on my notions of success and
see how they have evolved.

I decided at an early age that being passive just wasn't a part of my
character; I would never be happy merely letting things happen to me.

After my liberal arts education, I turned down the pressures of law school and went in search of a job. Although I was hopeful and idealistic about all that I could do, I couldn't find a good fit for myself. In the next two years, I held three jobs. I wanted to see what was out there. Life was far too interesting—the world far too complex—to sit in a job that didn't spark me. So I took what I could from each experience, immersed myself in each new world, and moved on to the next. Finally, after my third job, I left my position as a stock trader and filled out an application to business school.

After business school, I went on the job search. I knew I wanted to work in private equity; I wanted to do deals, and I wanted to be with people. Those things all sparked me. Well, in the end I had two job offers that had me conflicted: a prestigious Goldman Sachs offer and another from a company called JMB. I took JMB.

JMB was based in Chicago; at that time, it was the largest private owner of real estate in the nation. They recruited me hard, and I remember thinking, "Well, if they're taking that much of an interest in me, I should go there." So I went. As with any complicated decision, I had a number of reasons. They had money to invest and wanted to do deals. (You have to have somebody who actually wants to spend the money they have to invest.) JMB also seemed like a flat, entrepreneurial environment where I could pursue good ideas and have the opportunity to be taught, guided, and mentored. I was convinced that JMB was a flat enough organization that if I came up with a good idea, I could pursue it. I'd never even thought of living in Chicago; I was an East Coast kid. It seemed challenging enough to step away from the comfort of the East Coast life I'd come to love. But everyone from Chicago seemed to love the city, so I figured, What the hell. I signed the letter and put it in the mail. Now it was time to work. My net worth then was negative $8,000. I had motivation to work, and work I did, for six years.

I got what I wanted, and so did they. I was a wunderkind at JMB; I was one of the top ten largest equity participants in the company and the fastest-rising star in their history. I was making money, making deals, and making friends. I was making a life for myself. They were high times, and life was good. But it was also the late 1980s in the real estate world. When the bottom fell out in 1991, I was too expensive; JMB needed to cut costs, and I was let go.

I was shocked. Everything I had was lost: the dream job, the huge deals, the great salary, all of it. Of all the great tragedies in the world, this wasn't the greatest. But when that conversation came, it didn't feel that way.

But it didn't take me long to realize where I stood: I had a couple hundred grand in the bank, an education of a lifetime, and I was thirty-one years old. Sure, I needed to get a job. But this time I took my time. Some of the people I worked for tried to help me find a job. They put a high "ask" on what I was worth and sent me to market, but many employers balked. Then I got a job offer from Marvin Davis. Despite how tempting the job was, I wasn't sure he would actually commit capital. Then Richard Rainwater offered to hire me for no salary. I couldn't afford that. After these struggles and still no job, my wife had had enough: She sent me to the unemployment line. I'll never forget standing in that line.

In the end, I realized I really wasn't meant to work for someone. After turning down these offers and standing in that line, I decided to go off on my own. I figured that all the things that made me successful at JMB could make me successful on my own. I was creative and had stamina and desire. I saw that my greatest strengths were my passion, memory, and perseverance. And it was around then, after the challenges of crashing down from the highs of the years before, that I realized just how important that last trait is. Perseverance is genius in disguise. If only I could persevere, I could succeed.

But it was still a time of global recession. My career was just starting, and my family life was just starting. My first child was growing in my wife's stomach. I thought, "If I'm ever going to do this, I'm going to do it now." Though I came from a real estate firm, I had focused more on corporate deals. I had never actually led a pure real estate deal. But I've always been amazed by what one can learn on the go. A friend offered me the chance to invest money for a high-net-worth family he was advising, and I started my first fund: $21 million, $10 million each from two families and $1 million from my former boss at JMB, Neil Bluhm. I felt tremendous pressure to perform. This was my one chance to make it. I put everything that I had, $150,000, into the fund and borrowed another $1 million from the investors to cover the overhead and start-up costs. And then I began working.

First I needed to come up with a name. One of the original family investors suggested the name Starwood Capital Group, after a community in Aspen. I liked it. It had a ring and it wasn't pretentious, like other names out there. When I started Starwood Hotels and Resorts a few years later, I kept ownership and leased the name to them.

We started SCG with three guys and began buying apartments. I recruited a partner from business school who was in charge of asset management. I was in charge of acquisitions and strategy. We worked like mad. Eighteen months later, we decided to sell all of our assets. We had done it. We may have lost more bids than we won, but we executed our strategy and we succeeded. The families had increased their investments to $51 million—and they made $150 million! Our ten-year business plan was complete in less than two years. After that wonderful two-year period, my partner wanted to move to Texas. I used the opportunity to move back to the East Coast so my kids could grow up near their grandparents. Every single employee but one came with me to Connecticut.

For Starwood Capital's first two years, we focused on buying apartments. Now that I was on my own, I wondered, "What do we do next?" We started buying land and then started buying hotels. We quickly realized you could buy hotels much cheaper than they cost to build—just as we did apartments. Hotels were completely out of favor; nobody was looking at them as investments, because institutions considered them an operating business, not real estate, and lenders were terrified of the asset class. I thought hotels were great. Not only did the numbers work out for me, but it allowed me to exercise both the left—the creative—and the right—the financial—side of my brain, all in one industry. I love business, and I love architecture and design. Where else could I so closely marry my two passions?

As I entered the hotel business, I had an idea of what I wanted to do in the industry. I wanted to create a hip, branded hotel chain. I even had the name for it: W Hotels. There were no branded boutique hotels at that time, and I was told that it was a crazy idea. But the idea just seemed to make so much sense to me. You could bring together everything people love about a boutique hotel with the operational and brand benefits of a chain. How could it not work? So we started buying a lot of independent hotels. We bought the Marque in Atlanta, the Midland in Chicago, and the Westwood Marquis in Los Angeles. I was going to renovate them, tear down the signs, and put our new brand name up. And with that, we'd have a new national, distinct brand for our young company.

That was my initial goal. The rest of what we built was based on a series of opportunities. People loved the idea, and we ran with it. We went on a buying spree, buying and then merging Westin Hotels and ITT/Sheraton into our Starwood Lodging Trust. We went public. The company grew from an enterprise value of less than $200 million to $20 billion in less than three years. The stock rose from $6 to $60. We were bigger than Marriott. I was doing this while I watched over the affairs of Starwood Capital Group in the evenings. I soon recognized that we'd built a true global player. I realized I had a shot at changing the industry. And that charge required change.

When I looked at my management team, I recognized that I had some work to do. It struck me that the challenge was quite similar to building a football team. I had some good athletes, but once we stepped up to play in the "NFL," we needed to continue to improve our team. We needed superstars in every position if we were going to win the Super Bowl. The next several years were about finding, recruiting, and retaining an excellent team filled with "best in class" executives.

The transition was noisy. I was thirty-eight years old, and I'd never run a Fortune 300 company before. Over the years, I built very strong relationships with most of the talented executives. I had more difficult relationships with others, because I think they knew that, like the coach of a championship contending team, I was often looking for somebody who could be better than them at the job. We were there to rally a group of extraordinary people behind the mission of revolutionizing an industry. Like a football team, we weren't there to make any one team member feel good. We were there for something far greater than any one person. And my job, like that of the coach, was to build the best team I could and be ruthless in benchmarking our performance—not just against other hotel industry companies, but against companies outside our small world. It took brutal honesty and a never-ending passion for innovation and change. This is how the world evolves toward greatness. And with that philosophy, I set out to turn our commodity brands into category killers, with distinct personalities that were instantly recognizable through differentiated design and attitude.

W was a huge success. On the strength of our Heavenly Bed and Bath, Westin zoomed past Marriott and Hyatt as the best of the upper-upscale hotels. We revolutionized and innovated at the product level. We built very strong brands. The industry was in full recovery. But ten years later, I quit my job as chairman and CEO of the public company and returned to my private firm, Starwood Capital Group. In the end, among the dozens of reasons I walked out the door, one stands out in particular. I really thought we had organized our company incorrectly. There were certain fundamental problems, and I didn't want to be the one to reorganize the corporate structure. I loved building things, not restructuring things. I knew I would be criticized in the press if I stayed on to make the changes I knew we needed to make. All the hotel companies are organized the same way at the corporate level, and I thought that was part of the problem. I thought we needed to do some pretty radical things, and in the end I decided I didn't want to be the guy to do them. I wanted to go back to the private world and get out of the harsh light of being CEO of a public company.

When I take on a job, I want to give it everything I've got. And if I can't get it done, I want to feel like I left nothing behind. That's exactly how I felt at Starwood Hotels. I did everything I could do. I worked so hard, and I gave up so much. I felt responsible for every employee and every shareholder. It consumed me. When I look back, I feel so good about what has come of it all. But I also look back and think that

I should have done more for myself. I still own the stock today. Now I'm watching it do its own thing and enjoying being able to work on the next phase of my life.

Today, I look back on my original conception of success with a smile. It's amazing how much one changes over the course of one's life. I now think my personal philosophy of success is much more about legacy. What do I want to get done in the next ten years and beyond? What do I want to leave behind, both in business and in society? For me, it's about the game, how it's played—being smart, working with smart people, creating excellence, and building a company with a good soul.

Some of the guys in my office say, "Why are you working on designing this hotel? Why are you doing that?" It's easy for me because I like it. That's what I like to do. Following your passion leads to success, as it did with W. And here's a little hint: I think it actually *will* be financially rewarding. Following one's passion, whatever it is, is one of the greatest recipes of success, at least as I used to define it as a child. In my case, I have a passion for design. As I used to say at Starwood Hotels, "Design matters." And it's too often overlooked by MBAs with spreadsheets. In part, it's my passion for design that led Starwood to where it is today.

I'll tell you what I miss: I miss the people of Starwood Hotels. I loved the field. I loved the energy. And I really loved the people. There's no better feeling than to fight for something great as a team. The analogy keeps returning to mind because it is so apt: It's like a football team going through sweat and tears, all to feel the taste of victory together. At the end of those muddy battles, people become close. As they say, iron is forged by fire. And I miss my teammates.

I miss the innocence of starting from the bottom and struggling your way up. In my teens, I worked in mailrooms and in kitchens and I sold knives door-to-door. I kind of miss that. I feel I'm kind of a role model for the American dream. There is something special about working your way up from that first job cutting onions in a restaurant. It makes the ride and the destination all the more satisfying.

I also miss the soft side. When I left the company, I said, "My proudest achievement was that I built the company with a good soul."

When you employ a hundred thousand people, you can't reward everybody with cash alone. Instead, you have to motivate everybody with the fact that they work for a "good" company—a company that cares and does the right thing. That really was fun for me, and I was very passionate about it. I loved having a thousand associates participate in the Juvenile Diabetes Walk, all walking for something meaningful. I don't have the opportunity right now to influence that many people to do that much good that easily, and I miss it.

I do have a different way of helping at a broader level through my personal philanthropy. When my young kids are out of the house, in five years or so, it will be a lot easier for me to spend the time I'd like to on philanthropy. To achieve that goal, we've set up a family foundation. I've realized just how big a difference I can make, especially by supporting juvenile diabetes research, a cause I've supported for years. One of the great satisfactions in making money is the ability to give it away and see all the amazing things that can stem from it. It makes you feel good all over when you give, and even better when you see the impact it has.

I think everybody feels the same way. They want to be remembered for doing good things. They want to leave this world having had a positive impact on it. I feel that running a great business is one way I've already been able to contribute to this world. I ensured that a hundred thousand people had a good job, had job mobility, could meet their personal ambitions, and could be proud of the fact that they worked for a good, socially conscious company. That meant that half a million people, counting their spouses and kids, were better off. I think I made a difference for them. And at a broader level, I helped to revolutionize the hospitality industry in my own little way. In a universe in which every element is constantly marching toward progress, I helped my world evolve to a better place. I hope that those one hundred thousand teammates can recognize and remember that we built something great together.

As I shift through the next phases of my life, I would love to mentor a whole bunch of people. I enjoy coaching. I would like to have fewer "acquaintances" and more strong, close relationships. I want to make a difference in their lives and allow them to do the same for me. I have gotten the ambitious urge out of my system; I'm more focused now on this side of my life. I'm forty-six years old—I'm not quite ready to retire. But now I can focus on other things—things that are more important to me than having enough money to buy a house with a pool and a tennis court.

CHAPTER 6

• • •

William Lauder

CHIEF EXECUTIVE OFFICER,
ESTÉE LAUDER COMPANIES

As a grandson of Mrs. Estée Lauder, the iconic cosmetics pioneer and the company's founder, William Lauder is a member of the new generation of Lauder offspring at the helm of the family business. The Estée Lauder Companies is one of the world's leading manufacturers and marketers of quality skin care, makeup, fragrance, and hair care products, with annual sales of more than $7 billion.

Lauder is a twenty-two-year veteran of the Estée Lauder Companies, occupying numerous positions before becoming chief executive officer in 2008. Prior to that he had been president and chief operating officer since July 2004, and chief operating officer since 2003, overseeing all the company's global operations, including manufacturing, research and development, and human resources.

Previously, Lauder was president of Clinique Worldwide and group president of the Estée Lauder Companies. In this role, he led the worldwide businesses of Clinique and Origins and the company's rapidly growing retail division. From 1998 to 2001, Lauder was president of Clinique Laboratories, and before that he served as vice president/

general manager and later as president of Origins Natural Resources Inc., where he led the introduction and development of the new life-style brand.

Lauder joined the Estée Lauder Companies in 1986 as regional marketing director of Clinique U.S.A. in the New York metropolitan area. Before joining the Estée Lauder Companies, he completed Macy's executive training program in New York City and became associate merchandising manager of the New York Division/Dallas store.

Growing up in a family of tradition, William Lauder has always had to distinguish himself. Lauder's talent is finding innovative yet simple ways to address the most complex issues facing an organization. In a summer job working at the Treasury Department, Lauder came up with a simple idea that by itself changed the cash flow of tax collection in the United States; in his family business, he created a cosmetics brand for his company by focusing primarily on user lifestyle rather than product performance. Lauder's genius is doing seemingly small things that make a big difference.

"I'VE HAD TO PROVE THAT I'M SUCCESSFUL NOT BECAUSE I'M A MEMBER OF THE LUCKY SPERM CLUB, BUT ON MY OWN TERMS."

I grew up in an overachieving household. The challenge for me was to find a way both to continue the tradition and to make my own way. I give my parents a great deal of credit for creating an environment for my brother and me. They said, "You can do virtually anything you want to do, so long as you try your best to be good at it." I think back to that principle often: *Try your best.* It doesn't mean you can be the best, but that you must *try* your best to be the best. If you try your best and you do as well as you could, then you know you've done well. If you achieve something in the process, that's great.

The most influential mentor in my life, in so many areas, is my father. He is a man of enormous accomplishment, warmth, and vision. I feel very confident that he's influenced me in many different ways.

I was always competitive. I was the only one in my family who really was into sports. I wasn't so competitive as to become obsessive, but I liked the idea of winning. Competing was always a favorite part of what I do. It still is.

I wasn't the top student in my class—but the top students in my high school class were all extraordinarily smart. One is at the successor company to Bell Labs. Another is a medical researcher in San Francisco. I don't know how many of them achieved a lot in business, but they've all achieved wonderful objectives academically.

When I was in college, I did pretty well in business school and in some of my law classes, and some law professors encouraged me to become a lawyer. I asked them to introduce me to a happy lawyer. That ended that conversation quickly.

In college I also started learning that I could be, for want of a better word, an opinion leader. In other words, I could rally around an idea and communicate clearly. I spent a summer working for the secretary of the Treasury, Donald Regan. I was given a good deal of latitude to pick a project and work on it and bring people together to help on it. And all I had to figure out was how to motivate people to identify the opportunity.

I had an idea that seemed to make sense and that could actually save the government some money. It was a very simple idea: A ridiculously high number of all revenues from individual taxpayers to the government—about 65 or 70 percent—come in around tax time in the middle of April. Sorting and processing the mail took forever. There were no electronic payments back in 1981; there were billions and billions of dollars sitting there in paper checks, all of them in sealed envelopes, and from the outside it was impossible to tell which ones contained checks and which ones were filing for refunds.

At the time, 70 percent of all envelopes contained returns that actually required refunds; only 30 percent of the returns actually contained a check. I thought, "What can we do to the outside of the envelopes to help the government sort out the checks from the refunds?" Well, you could add a check box marked, "Check enclosed," but no one would check that box—people don't want you to cash their checks fast. But if you added a box that said, "Check here for refund," everyone would check it because everyone wants their refund processed right away. That's just consumer behavior. And that would give you all you need to sort them easily and accurately. Those that require refunds we can open slowly; we put can them in the same warehouse with the Ark of the Covenant from *Raiders of the Lost Ark*. Those without checked boxes? Those we'll open right away.

Did the government implement this immediately? That's an oxymoron. I think it took about eighteen months or two years to get it going. But they did it.

After I graduated, my father said, "You've got to go do something different. You can't just come work for me right out of college. You've got to gain confidence in yourself—to realize that you're successful because of you, not because of me or anybody else." So I went to work for Macy's and spent a number of years there. More than once my father said, "When are you going to come?" I said, "I'm just not ready yet."

Just because I was born on third base doesn't mean I hit a home run. But at the same time, I've had some lucky opportunities fall my way—times when I was thinking in one direction, and then someone said something that sparked a new idea that pushed me in a different direction. We created brands we might not otherwise have created if someone hadn't first sparked that new idea.

A great example is when we created Origins. I'd been working on a project that was very similar in spirit, but not exactly the same. Then, one day, a trend analyst was speaking to our group of senior managers, and a number of the trends she talked about sparked an idea in my head. When I went back and took a look at what we'd been working on, I saw it through a whole different filter.

One way to understand how this idea came to fruition is to look at another phenomenon that was taking shape at the same time—the revolution in rugged terrain vehicles. In the 1980s, Jeep had the market all to itself; the Ford Explorer wasn't out yet, and the SUV revolution hadn't begun. But Jeep had recognized that using the imagery of being outdoors was enough to make people want to drive a Jeep, even if the biggest bump they went over was the speed bump at Burger King.

That struck me when we were working on the Origins idea. One principle that consultant espoused was: "Give them the feeling that they'll be doing good by participating in what your brand is about." It was the idea of having a brand stand for something other than product performance. It was about creating a much more subtle, emotional connection than the traditional, more scientific approach to branding.

I went back to the people I was working with and said, "How are we going to get them to make the connection? And what is it we want them to be getting?" And when we hit upon that connection, we had the key to Origins, which ended up being one of our best brands. We like to *build* brands, if you will, not just buy brands; that's one of our traditions.

I'm an inherently outgoing, engaging person. I believe in my job as a CEO, as a leader; it's as much a political job as anything, because it's all about leadership. I do very little on my own; most of what I do comes about through communication with others. I'm probably a better editor than I am a creator. I take great ideas, try to mix and blend them into a new idea that works, and then figure out how to communicate the new idea clearly. Clarity of communication is so important, whether you're a leader, a manager, or a company that's trying to build a brand.

To me, there's no one definition of success. One man's scorecard is the other one's irrelevancy. There are people who measure their success purely by the amount of money they have earned; there are people who measure their success purely by their level of happiness regardless of what they made; and there are people who are somewhere in between.

When you work in a family business that was created by previous generations of your family, you work twice as hard for half the credit. No matter what you do to be successful at it yourself, some people will just never give you credit for it. Instead, they'll dismiss you: "Well, it was created by others. You didn't come up from adversity." About eight or nine years ago, a management guru spoke to our senior management group. At the end, I introduced myself and asked a question—a fairly innocuous question. After he answered, he mentioned the old saying about how the first generation creates, the second generation builds, and the third generation destroys. It was just a gratuitous shot at me because of my name: Since I was third in line, he was implying that my contribution would be suspect. I swore then that I was going to prove that asshole wrong. I've done my level best to do that.

I've been very fortunate. But then again, the legacy created by my grandmother and my father is a tough act to follow. I've had to prove myself my whole life. I've had to prove that I'm successful not because I'm a member of the lucky sperm club, but on my own terms.

CHAPTER 7

• • •

Geraldine Laybourne

FOUNDER,
OXYGEN MEDIA

G eraldine Laybourne founded Oxygen Media and has served as
its chair and chief executive officer until 2007. Oxygen was
launched in 2000 to fill a void in the television landscape—creating
a network targeted to younger women. Oxygen is the country's only
female-owned and -operated cable network, airing more original series
and specials than any other women's network.

A pioneer in creating innovative, high-quality television programming for children, before founding Oxygen Laybourne had already
revolutionized the children's television landscape in the 1980s and
1990s as the driving force behind the kids' networks Nickelodeon
and Nick at Nite. She spent sixteen years at Nickelodeon, taking over
management of the network in 1984. Under her leadership, Nickelodeon became the top-rated twenty-four-hour cable programming
service.

From 1996 to 1998, Laybourne was president of Disney/ABC Cable
Networks, where she was responsible for overseeing cable programming for the Walt Disney Company and its ABC subsidiary and devel-

oping future television programming for cable and other platforms. In 1996, *Time* magazine named her one of its "25 Most Influential People in America."

Even as a child, Gerry Laybourne refused simply to accept things as they were. At Nickelodeon, her questioning approach led her to reinvent children's programming. A conventional approach would have been faster and cheaper, but she wanted to change children's lives. Laybourne applied the same relentless questioning and revolutionary thinking to women's television. Throwing out all the old accepted myths about female viewing habits, she created an entirely new approach, empowering her audience rather than condescending to it. This was Laybourne's vision for quality—and equality— programming for women.

"MY PHILOSOPHY IS, IF IT AIN'T BROKE, FIX IT ANYWAY. IF YOU'RE NOT THINKING YOU'RE BROKEN, YOU'RE WRONG."

I was raised in New Jersey, the daughter of a stockbroker and an ex–radio actress, a writer/producer who was also a community actress. I was born between two sisters. One was perfect and beautiful, and the other was brilliant and charismatic. My dad said, "You're going to be my business daughter."

I gained a lot of confidence because of my father's efforts to make me his business daughter. When I was eight or nine years old, he would take me to meetings and ask me for my opinion, and I gave it freely and often. But I had a long way to go from being the business daughter to actually being a businesswoman—and as a typical second child, I was born to rebel against conventions or expectations. So before I went into business, first I had to rebel against my father and become a teacher.

I was passionate about being a teacher, and then I was passionate about the nonprofit world I was in, which involved taking on big publishers and creators of materials for kids to make sure that kids were learning from them. Now, when I look around me and see the truly successful people in business, I know it's because they've been passionate about something and dogged about it.

My best mentor was really my worst boss. He had this earnest desire to do really inspirational programming for Nickelodeon, so he did shows like *Against the Odds*, which were biographies of heroic people. They were little tragedies, but all our advertising still followed one principle: "Nickelodeon is fun, fun, fun! Come and watch it—you're going to love it!" And the shows would have a male narrator, because in my boss's view kids listened only to men—which was staggeringly shocking to me. His ambition for Nickelodeon was so low that he did a five-year plan and all it showed was $5 million in profitability. In his vision, the network would even out there and stay there. His motto was, "Be good, on time, and on budget, and stay out of trouble." That drove me crazy, because the reason I was at Nickelodeon was that I saw an opportunity to do something great for kids—to change the landscape.

That boss was like a perfect management school for me. He didn't believe in collaborative thinking, he didn't believe in repairing problems, he didn't believe in creating a team, he didn't believe in aspiring for greatness. It was like I was taking notes in a little notebook the entire time. For three years I thought, "If I get a chance, I'm going to do this the opposite way."

Before Nickelodeon, I had spent ten years with my own kids, and teaching, and in nonprofit organizations working with kids. I saw how flexible and creative their brains were. And then, when I looked at TV and saw its limited animation, its chaotic sound, I thought, "Wow. We're not tapping into one iota of kids' imaginations." I had a lot of theories. A big one was how to include kids in the process. We never put anything on Nickelodeon that wasn't tested or screened at least by my own kids. We didn't have much money, so we would go into schools. It wasn't scientific, but the notion was that it was better to talk to a couple of kids than none at all. So part of our strategy was listening to kids. Part of it was to say, "Hey, let's be on their side. Let's be

Nickelodeon and kids against unfair authority in the world." That was a cause. "Let's make kids feel good about being kids. And let's tap into a completely different creative group. Let's find those creators who have original characters." That's what you saw with *Rugrats* and *The Ren and Stimpy Show* and *Doug*.

My philosophy is, If it ain't broke, fix it anyway. If you're not thinking you're broken, you're wrong.

We set out to explode myths about kids. One was: Program only to boys; girls will watch anything. So we did *Clarissa Explains It All* and turned that on its ear. It wasn't all a bed of roses. We made mistakes along the way. One show we developed, *Turkey TV*, was so bad that when I showed it to my son (who was eleven years old at the time), he burst into tears and told me, "Mom, you'll never work in television again." But we learned from our failures, stuck to our mission, and turned Nickelodeon into the success it is today.

With Oxygen, we took a similar approach. We set out to explode myths about women. One myth was that women aren't funny. And, you know, we're *hilarious*. We just don't tell jokes well. Instead, we find humor in everything. Another myth is that women only like to see size two blondes on TV. That's really not true. We actually like to see women who reflect who we are. So we've done some very bold things—including *Mo'Nique's Fat Chance*, the first ever beauty pageant for large beautiful women.

We want Oxygen to be a place where women don't have to shrink to fit in any way—not their personality, not their size. It's very much the same way we looked at Nickelodeon. How can we show our audience that we like them just the way they are, that we're not trying to make them feel insignificant or dejected?

We're also passionate about exploding the myth that women don't like to help one another. When I came into the TV business, things were tough for women. No one listened to us. We would say something and ten minutes later a guy would say the same thing and everyone would think it was a good idea. But Bernice Coe, an early mentor of mine, really set the stage for the cable industry. Her message was, "You know what? We all get lifted up if we lift each other up." Now we have twenty women who've been presidents of cable networks in the last decade. She touched most of those women at least by one degree of separation. So that was a pretty powerful pull.

Obviously, I'm passionate about women and very proud of what's happened for women in the last thirty years. It's a very different workplace and a very different world for women. The young women we program Oxygen for today are very independent. They don't have the kind of chip on the shoulder that my generation had. They're very confident, very funny, very technologically savvy.

One of the things I'm most proud of is how many graduates we've had from what I think of as my management school. At Nickelodeon, we had a program called Presidents in Training. I offered to train everyone on my executive team to be a president, as long as they promised to check their departmental needs at the door and come to the table thinking about the wider industry. Don't think just about ad sales. Don't think just about programming. Think about the enterprise. It was an informal training program, but everyone sat at the table as an equal thinker. And almost all of them went on to become presidents of something. Bringing on the next generation—I hope that's my legacy.

CHAPTER 8

• • •

Ted Leonsis

VICE CHAIRMAN EMERITUS, AOL LLC

Named one of the "25 Most Powerful People in Sports" by *Sporting News* and "Businessman of the Year" by the *Washington Business Journal*, Ted Leonsis is an Internet and new-media pioneer, a sports team owner, and an innovator in the world of philanthropy.

During Leonsis's fourteen-year career with AOL, he served as vice chairman as well as president of several business units including the AOL Services Company; AOL Studios; AOL Web Services; AOL Core Service; and the AOL Audience Business. During his tenure the company enjoyed its greatest periods of growth and financial success. Leonsis stepped down from day-to-day management at AOL in December 2006.

Before joining AOL, Leonsis founded Redgate Communications Corp., considered the first new-media marketing company. In addition, he participated in the launches of the Apple Macintosh, the IBM PC, and Wang office automation, and founded four computing magazines.

Leonsis is also the founder, chairman, and majority owner of Lincoln Holdings LLC, a sports and entertainment company that holds ownership rights in several Washington, DC, entities including 100 percent of the NHL's Washington Capitals and the WNBA's Washington Mystics. Lincoln Holdings also owns approximately 44 percent of Washington Sports and Entertainment Limited Partnership, which owns the NBA's Washington Wizards, DC's Verizon Center, and the Baltimore-Washington Ticketmaster franchise.

Ted Leonsis has applied his unique outlook and vision to every facet of his life. Whether he was starting a computer magazine at age twenty-five (which he sold for his first fortune), vice chairman of AOL, majority owner of the Washington Capitals, or mayor of a small city in Florida, Leonsis has brought an authentic passion, energy, and commitment to his every endeavor.

"MY DEFINITION OF SUCCESS IS HAVING GREAT RELATIONSHIPS WITH LOTS OF PEOPLE IN LOTS OF DIFFERENT PARTS OF MY LIFE. . . . THE PEOPLE WHO ARE MOST CONNECTED WITH MULTIPLE COMMUNITIES OF INTEREST ARE THE HAPPIEST, MOST SUCCESSFUL PEOPLE IN THE WORLD."

I'm an only child. My dad was a Greek immigrant. He was a waiter; my mother was a secretary. They married late in life. In their best year, they made $27,000. They always told me, "We can't do much for you except make sure you're prepared intellectually and academically and that you have high aspirations." So when I was growing up, they didn't let me watch television. I was very studious: I skipped the eighth grade and went into college when I was sixteen and a half, and I graduated when I was twenty. I was first in my class at Georgetown.

My mentor at Georgetown was a seventy-three-year-old Jesuit named Father Joseph Durkin. At ninety-nine he was still going, beginning work on a book called *God and the Internet*. I used to take him to hockey games; even though he could hardly see, he would sit there picking my brain and asking me questions. He died two years ago at the age of one hundred.

Father Durkin's whole mantra was to find a balance between heart, head, and soul and to know that after you're gone, you'll be measured by how you affected and treated people. You won't say, "Remember So-and-so? He had the second biggest house in his neighborhood." You'll say, "He did so much for this community." He became my mentor my junior year, motivated me, gave me confidence.

I stayed in contact with Father Durkin for the rest of his life. I was actually the last person to see him in the hospital. It's kind of spooky: When we all gathered for his one hundredth birthday party, he fell ill; when we arrived for the party, they said, "Party's canceled. He's in the hospital." That was on a Sunday. The following Saturday was a beautiful day. I said to my wife, "I'm just going to go down to the hospital and see Father Durkin." I went in to see him and he was heavily medicated, on oxygen. I talked to him, I held his hand a bit, and probably spent about seventy or eighty minutes with him. After I left him, I stopped off to do some errands. When I got home about three hours later, my wife was on the telephone. She hung up and said, "Father Durkin passed away about fifteen minutes ago." I don't know what motivated me on that Saturday to get up and go see him, but I was so grateful that I did.

After college I came back to my hometown, moved back in with my parents, and got my first job at Wang Laboratories, a computer company. I worked my way up the executive ladder quickly. Then, when I was twenty-five, I had an entrepreneurial idea and I started a company. We were the first enterprise to focus on software, not hardware. We created a database, and we published newsletters and magazines to a growing audience. Then I took a risk, quit my job, and raised $1 million in venture capital. A year later, I sold that company for $60 million.

So in a very compressed period of time, I achieved what I was supposed to achieve.

I never thought I had a choice. You're either going to work hard, be focused, and be educated or be like your dad, a waiter who worked for tips. We never owned a house; we always rented. My dad never owned a new car. When I hit it, I bought my parents a house and new cars and went on a vacation.

At that young age, I was almost ready to declare victory. I was twenty-six years old and worth tens of millions of dollars and had a big house and all the cars I wanted. And then I got on a plane that lost its flaps and its landing gear. We were coming in for a crash landing. I think everyone in their life has a moment of reckoning: "Oh God, I could die. Does my life have meaning? Did I do the right things the right way?" I really, really prayed. "If I live," I told myself, "I promise I'll live the second part of my life without regrets and I'll do good work."

A lot of the things that seemed important to me, the marks of success—money, admiration, homes, and cars—they weren't what I was thinking about. When you're about to die, you don't miss your second car. Since then I've become a student of happiness, because once you get your second lease on life, every day is a good day. Your mark is on the body of work you're creating, so that when you ultimately do pass, you can look back on the second part of your life and say, "I lived a meaningful life."

After that near miss on the plane, I sat down and made a list of one hundred and one things I wanted to do. By now that list has become cute and funny, but it gave my life some discipline, and it still does. It gave me a scorecard for a more self-actualized, successful life.

Today, I'm involved in research projects on what makes for successful living, how people find happiness and a self-actualized life—how to ensure longevity, great relationships with your family, people you live with and work with, your employees. From what I've learned so far, I boil it down to four things. First, being able to connect your work life, home life, family life, church life, and sports life—having a connective tissue among those communities. That is a hallmark of successful living.

Second, living a life that's positive and filled with gratitude. I believe that people who attack problems as opportunities, who have a can-do spirit and attitude and say "thank you," live a more fulfilled life. The other day, I was with my family walking on the beach where we live, and I literally stopped and said to my wife, "Look at this. Just look at how crisp the water looks and the way the sun is hitting it. You couldn't spec this out any more beautifully." For that little moment, I wasn't thinking about work or anything. I was in that moment, and I was grateful that I was able to share it with my wife. I've come to believe that people who can have that inner stillness and calmness and gratitude are incredibly productive—because they can recharge themselves.

Third, giving back. People who give back, who volunteer and activate goodness in other ways, also tend to have longer lives, better sex lives, more success at the office, great relationships with their families.

Finally, being motivated in your career.

My definition of success is having great relationships with lots of people in lots of different parts of my life. The people who are most connected with multiple communities of interest are the happiest, most successful people in the world. Or, as I often joke, the more people you have on your buddy list, the happier you'll be.

CHAPTER 9

• • •

Jake Burton

OWNER AND CHAIRMAN, BURTON SNOWBOARDS

For thirty years, trailblazing entrepreneur Jake Burton has been the driving force behind the modern snowboarding movement, almost single-handedly legitimizing the sport and revolutionizing the industry.

When Burton was a teenager, "snurfing"—or snow surfing—was just a small-time hobby. By the time he enrolled at the University of Colorado, he had aspirations of making their National Collegiate Athletic Association ski team. Then, just as classes were starting, he managed to break his collarbone three times in two weeks without putting on a ski.

Burton took a year off from school to groom and exercise Thoroughbred horses, working in Virginia and at New York's Aqueduct Racetrack. He enrolled at New York University, and after graduating with a degree in economics, he moved to Vermont to pursue his dream of modifying the Snurfer, the first commercial snowboard, made by Brunswick. In 1977, Burton Snowboards was born in his barn in Londonderry, Vermont.

Today, Burton is sole owner of the 550-employee company, which by most estimates controls 40 to 50 percent of a $400 million market.

Jake Burton's success is built on two basic principles: his love of snowboarding and his love of life. Early in snowboarding's history, Burton recognized its potential and believed it could be a major sport. Out of his passion for this pastime flowed a business and a way of life. Financial success wasn't Burton's only priority; he set out to build a legitimate snowboarding movement and became a staunch advocate for the sport.

"I THINK SUCCESS IS ENTIRELY REALLY ABOUT HAPPINESS. THAT'S WHAT IT'S ALL ABOUT FOR ME."

I grew up in the 1960s, a time when life was about having fun. I always loved sports. I wasn't a great athlete, but I was always a huge fan of athletes and watching them do their thing. I always saw myself getting into the sports business one way or another. That was one thing I was determined about.

I did some skateboarding as a kid. I was much more inclined toward individual sports; I was a perfectly good athlete, but I wasn't a great football or basketball player. I swam a lot as a kid and in college, but I was so undersized that I wasn't really equipped to compete, and I didn't win much. But I ski raced in high school, and that's when I think I started to do better and get more competitive.

My father was always there for me. He was a terrific counsel, a guy who really understands life. My brother was an incredible guy. I was constantly compared to him—though not always in a favorable way, since I screwed up from time to time as a kid. He was always there for me, too. He was captain of the high school football team, school president, and he went to Yale. But he got suspended from Yale for some kind of prank, and that put him in line to get drafted. But he didn't want to be in the army, so he enlisted in the marines. He was sent to Vietnam, where he was killed. I was twelve years old when he died; he wasn't even twenty. Then, when I was seventeen, my mother died. I think losing those two people in my life so quickly made me incredibly independent and self-sufficient.

It wasn't a materialistic time when I grew up. A buddy of mine ran a landscaping business, and I saw that he had plenty of dough, so I thought, "Wow. I should get in on that." This guy was very successful, so I approached his younger brother and we went into business together. We did very well, considering how young we were. But I realized pretty quickly that a partnership wasn't right for me; ultimately, I needed to do my own thing. The idea of working for myself got my entrepreneurial spirit going.

I started working for a very small company, as a kind of business broker. People were selling successful small companies to larger corporations, and I would interview these entrepreneurs. I didn't realize that starting a manufacturing business was a lot tougher than starting a landscaping business. I had no idea what I was getting into when I left to start Burton. If I had, I probably would have thought twice. But the entrepreneurial experience I'd had, coupled with what I'd learned interviewing all these successful business owners, gave me a false sense of confidence—which was probably what I needed to make the plunge.

It was a simple equation: I knew how to ski; I understood snow. But I really wanted to surf. And I didn't have a surfboard, so surfing had an incredible allure for me. When I saw this new thing—surfing on snow—I immediately gravitated toward it. I developed a passion for snowboarding, and I was convinced it could become a sport.

In those early days, I used to load up the station wagon with snowboards and go out to try to sell them. Sometimes I would come home with as many boards as I'd left with. At that point in time, my tank was low. I remember just lying in bed one morning not wanting to get out of bed. It was so discouraging. I came very close to bailing. The first couple of years were so rough that when I bottomed out, I was something like $100,000 in the hole. I think what I'm proudest of in the whole thing is my perseverance.

The thing that was really important to me wasn't even the financial side of it or the idea of establishing Burton; it was that I believed there was a sport there, and I knew I was right. I became so focused on that, and I think that's when things started to take off. At first, my goal had been financial success. But it wasn't until I got off that and it became something else—a kind of mission—that it all came together.

It took a while for people to catch up with snowboarding. We brought a demographic back to the mountain that hadn't been there in a while. Kids weren't skiing much then; ski lodges were building video arcades in their basements to lure them in. Once the kids jumped on, it was just a matter of time before people began recognizing the athleticism of the sport.

It was a lot of hard work communicating with the resort owners. We lobbied them hard, showing them what was going on. If they had issues, we'd try to talk them down and address the whole thing using common sense. I can remember making a presentation in Aspen and being told, "Sorry." They didn't want the snowboarders; the skiers complained too much about them. It was frustrating. But by then the sport had so much momentum that we just thought, "Your loss."

Now Aspen is hosting the X Games.

We went from being insignificant, not even a bug on the windshield, to being a kind of nuisance to the ski industry at the trade shows. Then, all of a sudden we were a threat—and then we were the heroes. It was such a weird transition.

I think you have to be so focused—like a racehorse with blinders on—to succeed that way. You just have to be driven. In my case I had a great idea, but that alone wouldn't have got me there. I was incredibly motivated, but that wouldn't have got me there. I surrounded myself with really good people. I think those three things combined were what led to the success. Too often you see people who have two of those three and it doesn't work. I saw people in snowboarding who were pretty motivated, who were right there with the same idea, but who just didn't surround themselves with the right people.

Some of it is out of your hands; it's just luck, timing. Of course, to a certain extent timing *is* luck. If I'd tried to do what I did ten years earlier, it probably wouldn't have happened. I think snowboarding eventually would have come around one way or another, but I think the timing was just perfect.

Today, I've got a lifestyle that's just incredible. I snowboard more than a hundred days a year. I look out at mountains from the window of my office. I travel all over the world. I went to Russia this year with some of the best snowboarders in the world. I work with a great group of very energetic, motivated, and capable people. I have an insane family, and we all love to snowboard together. I've got three boys—seventeen, thirteen, and ten. They drag me into the park and put a hurt on me.

I think success is entirely really about happiness. That's what it's all about for me. You just have to follow your passion. Not everyone is lucky enough to stumble on something that will take him to the level I've reached. But you can't go wrong if you're doing what you love.

• • •

CHAPTER 10

Don Hewitt

CREATOR AND EXECUTIVE PRODUCER (1968–2004), CBS NEWS' *60 MINUTES*

Television pioneer Don Hewitt is best known and most respected for creating the groundbreaking CBS News program *60 Minutes*, considered the most successful broadcast in television history.

Hewitt began his journalism career in 1942 as head copyboy for the *New York Herald Tribune*. During World War II, he served as a correspondent in the European and Pacific theaters. He began his career with CBS News in 1948 as an associate director of *Douglas Edwards with the News*, then served as producer-director of the broadcast for fourteen years. He later became executive producer of the *CBS Evening News with Walter Cronkite*.

In the 1950s, Hewitt directed one of Edward R. Murrow's most respected programs, the news documentary showcase *See It Now*. During the 1960 presidential campaign, he produced and directed the first face-to-face television debate, between presidential nominees John F. Kennedy and Richard Nixon.

In 1968, Hewitt created the newsmagazine program *60 Minutes* and in doing so established himself as both a masterful storyteller and a prolific producer. *60 Minutes* finished in Nielsen's top ten programs for a record twenty-three consecutive years.

After thirty-six years at *60 Minutes*, Hewitt stepped aside as executive producer in 2004, assuming new editorial responsibilities as executive producer of CBS News, lending his unparalleled experience and expertise to all facets of the network.

While Don Hewitt remains rather humble about his own success in life, he isn't afraid to boast about the enormous success of 60 Minutes, *the groundbreaking show he created almost four decades ago. When you've changed the course of television journalism history, perhaps bragging rights are in order. Hewitt had a vision—a big vision—waiting to be realized. The way Hewitt tells it, though, he failed his way to success. Only once he was freed from conventional expectations was he able to find his own way and create an entirely new kind of programming.*

"PEOPLE ALWAYS ASK ME FOR THE FORMULA FOR OUR SUCCESS, AND I TELL THEM IT'S SIMPLE—FOUR WORDS EVERY KID IN THE WORLD KNOWS: 'TELL ME A STORY.' IT'S THAT EASY. IN TELEVISION, IF YOU KNOW HOW TO COMMUNICATE WITH PICTURES BUT YOU DON'T KNOW HOW TO COMMUNICATE WITH WORDS, YOU'RE IN THE WRONG BUSINESS."

Even though *60 Minutes* is the most watched, most honored, and most profitable broadcast of its kind in television history, I have to admit that my success in television was the product of a large dose of luck and a small dose of wisdom—just enough to capitalize on the luck. As a college dropout, for reasons I was never sure of, I became at twenty the youngest war correspondent assigned to the Eisenhower headquarters in Europe. After that, everything seemed to fall in line.

Years later, I was stunned when I got a call from NYU saying they wanted to give me the Alumni of the Year Award. I said, "I'm a dropout!" They said, "No, it's all right. So much happened to you after you dropped out that we think you deserve this." I said, "I'm reluctant to admit that, but if you think so, it's okay with me."

I guess you could say I'm a competitive guy. I was captain of the track team in high school and never lost that hunger to be first. I can't think of a field in which being competitive is not a large part of anyone's success.

When I first went into television, I was working for an outfit called Acme News Pictures, an arm of the United Press that fed news pictures to newspapers. That's where I was when I got a call from a friend at CBS saying they were looking for someone with picture experience.

"What in the hell would a radio network want with picture experience?" I asked.

"Not radio, television," he said.

"What-a-vision?"

"Television."

"You mean you sit at home and watch people performing in a little box? They don't have that."

"The hell they don't," he said. "If you don't believe it, go over to Grand Central. They've got an experimental studio upstairs over the train station."

So I went—and I was flabbergasted at what I saw. Flabbergasted and mesmerized. I was a child of the movies who could never make up his mind whether he wanted to be the reporter in *The Front Page* or the producer in *42nd Street*. And I looked at the cameras and the microphones and the stagehands and the sets and the newsroom and said, "Oh, my God. In television you can be both of them. You can be the reporter and the showman." That appealed to me.

The other thing that really helped me was that when I went to CBS in 1948, all the talent in New York at the time—incredible people like John Frankenheimer, Sidney Lumet, Yul Brynner, Frank Schaffner (who directed *Patton* and *Nicholas and Alexandra*), and Bobby Mulligan (who directed *To Kill a Mockingbird*)—were leaving for Hollywood. I'm convinced that's nine-tenths of why I was as successful as I was: All the competition had left.

I became the producer of the *CBS Evening News*, but after a while I was removed because they didn't think I was a serious enough journalist to go on doing it. So I began doing documentaries. It was mostly very boring stuff, and I was kind of devastated that I had ended up in a job that bored me. That's when I came up with the idea of producing a television newsmagazine, because as good as the documentaries were, no one was looking at them. No one had the attention span to sit through an hour on one subject.

That's when I got the idea for *60 Minutes*. When I was directing Edward R. Murrow's *See It Now*, which was a very prestigious but not very watched broadcast, he also did another broadcast called *Person to Person*, where he interviewed celebrities. John Crosby, the reviewer for the *New York Herald Tribune*, described the two Murrow broadcasts as "high Murrow" and "low Murrow." A little light went on in my head. I said, "Oh, my God, that's the formula." Put high Murrow and low Murrow in the same broadcast, and you've got a winner. It's okay to look in Marilyn Monroe's closet if you're also willing to look into Robert Oppenheimer's laboratory. That was the formula for the success of *60 Minutes*—mixing people of substance and people of celebrity, just as *Life* magazine did in print.

60 Minutes just took off. It became one of only three broadcasts in the history of television that was number one five times. (The other two were *All in the Family* and *The Cosby Show*.) Am I proud that we spent twenty-three consecutive years in the top ten? I would be a liar if I told you I wasn't.

When all is said and done, telling stories is what it's all about. So it's your ear as much as your eye—and sometimes more than your eye—that keeps you in front of a television set. It's what you hear, more often than what you see, that holds your interest. And words, rather than pictures, are what *60 Minutes* is all about. People always ask me for the formula for our success, and I tell them it's simple—four words every kid in the world knows: "Tell me a story." It's that easy. In television, if you know how to communicate with pictures but you don't know how to communicate with words, you're in the wrong business.

Nine-tenths of my success came from picking the right people to do the job—people who had the same feel I did for what the public wanted. We needed to be serious but not too serious, to edit judiciously so we didn't ever bore anyone, and to choose subjects with universal appeal, whether it was Vladimir Horowitz or Robin Williams, serious subjects like the advantages or dangers of atomic energy, or light ones like how they made the movie *Casablanca*. I'm not an elitist—I think that probably played a bigger part in whatever success I had than anything else.

CHAPTER 11

• • •

Michael Milken

PHILANTHROPIST

Dubbed by *Fortune* magazine "The Man Who Changed Medicine," Michael Milken first became interested in medical research in 1972, when his mother-in-law was diagnosed with breast cancer. In 1982, he formalized his philanthropy in the Milken Family Foundation, which works with more than one thousand organizations worldwide, launching and supporting extensive medical research and education programs.

A decade later, after being diagnosed with prostate cancer himself, Milken founded the Prostate Cancer Foundation, the world's largest private funder of prostate cancer research. His most recent medical initiative is FasterCures, a Washington, D.C., think tank dedicated to removing barriers to progress against all life-threatening diseases. He is also chairman of the Milken Institute, a nonprofit, nonpartisan economic think tank.

At the same time he was pursuing his philanthropy, Milken became a Wall Street legend. He is said to have revolutionized modern capital markets, making them more efficient, dynamic, and democratic. By 1976, the financial theories he developed in the 1960s had been proven in the world's markets and today are considered mainstream.

Although he was once the center of a government securities prosecution that continues to provoke controversy, Milken is widely respected today as the father of financial innovations that have driven America's economic growth since the 1970s.

Michael Milken has devoted his life to helping others. In the first chapter of his life, he was a financial genius, a visionary who revolutionized the junk bond market. In the second chapter, he revolutionized the way we think about cancer—from researching its causes, to fighting the disease, to finding a cure. Milken's tireless philanthropic efforts continue to inspire and motivate him (and others) to keep fighting and working toward total eradication of cancer.

"I VIEW SUCCESS AS HAVING THE FREEDOM TO PUT MY IDEAS INTO ACTION."

I feel extremely fortunate to be part of the same community that my parents moved to in the San Fernando Valley many decades ago. Today, if the Valley itself were a city, it would be the fifth largest in the United States. It has lots of young, middle-class families and the kind of nurturing environment that makes you feel confident you can come up with new ideas. That feeling of community was there when I was growing up, and it's there today.

I'm still close with many of my high school friends. Many of them have been very successful in their careers. I was head cheerleader at a time when that was a prestigious position that involved community philanthropy. Sally Field was a song leader at the same time. In high school we created remarkable organizations that engaged in community service.

One of the events that had the most profound effect on my life was the Watts riot in Los Angeles on August 11, 1965, at the height of the civil rights movement. I was a student at Berkeley in the middle of the free speech movement. But that summer, when I came home from college, I learned that civil rights wasn't just a matter of where you could sit on a bus—it also meant access to capital. In a democracy and a capitalistic system, providing money to people based on their ability rather than the color of their skin would also advance civil rights. What happened that night in Watts really changed my life forever.

When I went back to Berkeley, focusing on business and finance became my civil rights movement. Doing my own credit work at Berkeley, I discovered that no one really understood credit—that the conventional wisdom was wrong. That eventually led me to Wharton and then to Wall Street.

I came out of Wharton with all these ideas and went to Wall Street, because that's where people made decisions on access to capital. I went to work for Drexel, then the leading white-shoe research firm in the financial world, whose people had financed the Civil War for the North, put up the money for the Panama Canal, financed the gold rush. Their ancestors had signed the Declaration of Independence. By using their research as the platform, I felt we could change the way people looked at credit.

In the late 1960s and early 1970s, when many firms were on the verge of bankruptcy, I was presenting my ideas to Wall Street, writing papers, building what became the largest trading group on Wall Street. I was in my mid-twenties.

In 1974, probably the most important year [up until 2008] in financial history since the Depression, everyone thought the world was coming to an end. New York City was going bankrupt. But I'd studied two hundred years of the history of credit, and I decided to take a different position. Our group took a positive view—that all the doomsday scenarios were wrong—and at that point we were alone in saying so.

In that period the stock market went down 50 percent, interest rates doubled, the banks rationed credit—and while it was hard to understand at the time, all of that laid the groundwork for today's market-based economy. Since then, our economy has evolved from one that was based on a few banks to one that, at least in the United States and parts of Europe, is a true market-based economy. That's essentially our financial structure today, and eventually it will be the structure for the whole world. It's what I call the democratization of capital—a process that spreads prosperity more evenly to people everywhere.

In the 1970s, I got the chance to apply on Wall Street everything I'd researched in the 1960s. My studies, my ideas, and everything I believed all came true during a very difficult economic period—and that gave me a feeling of personal satisfaction. We realized that we could create financial structures that would allow companies to survive, that would give companies access to capital, help them create jobs and build new industries. I consider the last thirty years of financial history a playing out of what was introduced in that 1974–1976 period.

Success, for me, was having the freedom to put my ideas into action.

It was also a period that changed my life. When my father was diagnosed with melanoma, I traveled around and visited almost every major cancer center in America, but by the end of 1976, I concluded that I wouldn't be able to save his life. Science couldn't move fast enough to save him. It was the first time in my life that I hadn't been successful at something I'd set out to do. And here the stakes were literally life and death.

My mother told me when I was very young that the definition of a problem is something that can't be solved by money. Nineteen seventy-six was the pinnacle of my financial career; I had achieved financial independence and my greatest career success. But I was powerless to help my father. It didn't matter that I had extensive contacts with thousands of companies throughout the world, that we'd been active in cancer research and had relationships with every cancer agency leader—none of this could save my father's life. That was what led me to dedicate most of the rest of my life to medical research.

In the 1970s, several of my relatives developed cancer. Most of them died, but not all: My mother-in-law was diagnosed with breast cancer in 1972, but she survived. All of this focused my attention on accelerating medical science—and that's why we formed the Milken Family Medical Foundation. I wanted to make sure that when my grandchildren look up the history of my family, they will note that my father had polio, but he died from cancer. Polio was a big thing for people like my wife and me, who grew up in the 1950s. When I talk to my children today, I have to remind myself that polio isn't really a word in their vocabulary. One of my goals is to do the same thing with cancer.

Even if we cured only 10 percent more cancers, it would be enormous progress. When you look at Lance Armstrong today or Scott Hamilton and thousands of others who have had testicular cancer, it makes me feel that all our efforts were worthwhile. The death rate from prostate cancer has dropped by 50 percent from where it was projected to be.

I try to talk to five people who have been diagnosed with cancer every week just to keep my focus and understand what cancer patients are thinking about today, not twenty or thirty years ago. I believe in my lifetime we will eliminate cancer as one of the greatest causes of death and human suffering. And, of course, it's not just cancer we're fighting: Our work with FasterCures is helping to remove barriers to progress against *all* life-threatening diseases.

Sometime in the mid-1990s, *Time* magazine wanted to put me on the cover for an article about prostate cancer, but I discouraged it. I went to see my friend Walter Isaacson at Time Inc. and told him, "You know, Walter, *Time* should get a cancer correspondent just like they have war correspondents. More people are dying every year in the United States than in all the wars of the twentieth century."

He didn't take my advice, but they did something smart—instead of putting me on the cover, they used General Norman Schwarzkopf, who was diagnosed with prostate cancer in 1993. Most of the major magazines—*Time, Newsweek, Fortune, Forbes*—started putting cancer-related issues on their covers around that same time. I think those stories really helped lay the groundwork for more cancer research.

I once said, "You're measured by your children and your children's children." I've had the great fortune in my life to be associated with thousands of world leaders. Many of them have families that do well, and many of them don't. I've always admired those who have been successful but who also have great families.

So, as I'm celebrating the birth of my first grandchild and my thirty-eighth wedding anniversary, I would tell you that thirteen years ago I didn't expect to be around, or to see any of my children marry, or to see any grandchildren, or to celebrate my thirtieth anniversary, not to mention my thirty-eighth.

I think one of my greatest successes is longevity.

CHAPTER 12

• • •

Brian France

CHAIRMAN AND CHIEF EXECUTIVE OFFICER,
NASCAR

Since its inception in 1948, NASCAR has been a family-owned business. Brian France grew up learning the ropes from his grandfather—William "Big Bill" France Sr., who founded the business and ruled it for three decades—and his father, Bill Jr., who preceded Brian as head of the company.

France's first major directive after taking over the company in 2003 was instituting changes to NASCAR's point system in an effort to create more excitement at the tail end of the season. In addition, France has been at the forefront of NASCAR's dramatic sponsorship growth, including a groundbreaking agreement with Nextel Communications, which began sponsoring the NASCAR Nextel Cup Series in 2004.

Before assuming his current position, France had a diverse career at NASCAR. He helped develop and manage the Weekly and Touring Series divisions and launch the Craftsman Truck Series. He took over NASCAR's marketing responsibilities in 1994 and opened NASCAR's New York office in 1997.

France was also one of the key proponents of NASCAR's new research and development center, a facility dedicated to improving the safety and operational efficiency of the sport. He founded NASCAR's Diversity Council, an organization comprising motor sports executives focused on encouraging greater diversity within the industry.

In 1999, *Sports Business Daily* named France "Sports Industrialist of the Year," and in 2006, *Time* named him one of their "100 People Who Shape Our World."

Brian France's unique vision and tenacity are in large part responsible for making NASCAR the nationwide phenomenon it is today. France saw NASCAR's potential early on; he recognized the loyalty of the sport's hard-core fan base and transformed that support into commercial success through unique sponsorship and marketing ideas. France led the way as the sport exploded onto the national stage, and he ushered NASCAR into a new era of growth and unprecedented success.

"I THINK THE DESIRE TO BE EXCELLENT, IN WHATEVER INDUSTRY YOU CHOOSE, IS CRUCIAL TO SUCCESS."

When I was fifteen years old, I worked at the dog track. I shoveled ice. I had paper routes. You name it, I tried it. I was an early Shaklee salesman. I did odd jobs throughout high school and college. I wasn't a great athlete, but I liked to compete. I played Little League baseball. I remember wanting to compete early on; I always remember having that strong desire to compete and excel, and I think that always translates to business. As soon as you figure out that you're not headed for the pro leagues in whatever sport you choose, you start reapplying that mind-set to business. I'm also a huge sports fan, so I follow coaches and other motivational figures to see how they approach things.

Sports help you—in part because they have a scoreboard. Life doesn't have an obvious scoreboard. There is one down the road, but if you pick the right career, the wrong career, the right job, the right city to live in, it can take a while to see whether your decision was good. In sports, you win the game or you lose. It makes you zero in.

My father was a major mentor, and he clearly led by example. He was a guy who got a lot of things done, so he was a tremendous role model for me. We were a great complement to each other. My dad specialized in the competitive side: racing rules, keeping the playing field even among all the manufacturers (Toyota, Dodge, General Motors), keeping the drivers and teams happy. He always had a tremendous ability in that area.

My dad let me work in the areas where I showed the most interest, and they happened to correspond to areas where we needed work: getting our television agreements in order, improving our marketing and licensing arrangements so that we could compete with the other sports. Getting our publicity machine ramped up to help us break onto the national sports scene as one of the top four or five sports leagues in this country. As I zeroed in on those things, my dad kept his hand on the competitive side, which was our bread and butter.

My first NASCAR assignment was on the West Coast. I had a little office in California and worked on the short tracks, which are the minor leagues of stock car racing. We wanted to make stock car racing a truly national sport, not just a regional one, and early on we had a lot of disappointments. I remember chasing a lot of big corporations to join NASCAR—and losing some important accounts or programs we were trying to sell.

Our success didn't happen overnight, but once things got rolling we did have a very fast run. It took a lot of hard work to gain traction. We were taking events to new locations and building new speedways, and whenever a new one came online, it would be very well received. The turning point came in 1994, when we went into Indianapolis, which of course had only open-wheel and Indy car races, never a NASCAR event. They have three hundred thousand seats in some huge stadiums, so we had plenty of internal debate: Was NASCAR big enough to draw a big crowd in Indianapolis and not be embarrassed? Branching out from the South was a huge deal, and people doubted we could do it. Well, not only did we sell out, but that's exactly how we reached critical mass. Soon we were building tracks in Dallas, Miami, all over the country—and NASCAR was just as dynamic and popular outside the Southeast as it was there.

People think it was a really smooth run, but we had obstacles along the way. Probably our most significant challenge was taking our television rights back and not only monetizing them smarter by getting a much bigger rights fee, but actually using new media to help grow the sport. We did the right television deal, one that got us on network television week in and week out, and handled things like our international rights as well. That was a hard thing to do, because at that time the tracks had managed their own television rights for twenty-something years. We had to convince them that it would be best if we spearheaded a single, unified strategy—that the money would all be allocated and flowed through in an equitable way. When we put that on the line, trying to convince a bunch of entrepreneurs that we could do it better than they could, it was a big risk—one that could have gone the wrong way.

Teaming up with Fox was the big breakthrough. It meant billions of dollars for the industry, which was pretty significant. But we always said that it isn't enough just to get the money. In our business we have to promote the events and the team sponsors, who are so important to our sport. So getting a network television deal, versus disappearing on cable, was really important to us. Getting the production and the promotions all right—not just part of it—was really important. Then, convincing our constituency that we *did* get it all, and got it smart, wasn't simple.

It's hard to convince some people that we didn't have to do some of the things we've done in the last five years to make things better. No one likes change. No matter how many people read books warning them that the world is changing fast, the reality is that change makes many people uncomfortable. So when we had to make changes—and we've made a lot of them to improve our position—we've had to persevere through some tough times. Once you get to the other side of the street, everybody's happy. But getting there, you have to be able to hang in there.

When you become the boss, some people will tell you to go slow, especially if you're not upside down in the business. Take your time, listen more. To some degree, of course, that's important. But you also have to lead. You have to take an approach people can get behind, especially if you intend to change a few things. My theory is that it's better to make a fast start. That doesn't mean you go out and do a bunch of things that don't need to be done, but it does mean that if there's a big decision to be made, you shouldn't defer it. Make those important big decisions early rather than later.

I have a fourteen-year-old stepdaughter and twins who are four months old. Somebody told me, and this is probably true, that you'll know if you've done something right with your kids when they get to be between twenty-one and thirty-one. That's when you can see that they're either going to have that desire to achieve—whether as a CEO, a world-class tennis player, or the world's best schoolteacher—or they're not. If your kid is thirty-one years old and he hasn't done it, he's probably not going to do it.

By thirty-one, I was rolling. I may not have had as much native ability as I'd have liked, but I always had the desire. I didn't necessarily have the wisdom in my early twenties to sort out milestones and where I should or shouldn't be. But I was trying to achieve. As for now, I can't always tell you that I'm hitting every mark, but I have some of my own goals. They're not written down, but I think about them often. The important thing is to put yourself in the position to have the freedom to do things on your own terms. Most people aren't in that position. Most people can't live wherever they want; they can't operate the way they want in their career. So putting yourself in that position as early as you possibly can is a huge advantage.

I think the desire to be excellent, in whatever industry you choose, is crucial to success. But I don't think success happens overnight. I'm around a lot of smart and successful people. And I've had a few moments of luck along the way. I'm not saying you have to have good luck to succeed, that if you don't, you're dead. You still have to have all the other things. But a little luck helps.

CHAPTER 13

• • •

Jason Binn

CHIEF EXECUTIVE OFFICER, NICHE MEDIA

J ason Binn started his publishing career as co-founder of *Ocean Drive* magazine in 1993. He then founded Niche Media Holdings in 1998, building what *BusinessWeek* calls "a fast growing empire" of upscale glossies that has cornered the regional publishing market with the country's preeminent local luxury magazines.

In 2006, Niche Media joined the Greenspun Media Group to become one of the largest networks of exclusive city-specific and custom publishing companies in the country. In 2007, GMG purchased The Ocean Drive Media Group and merged the operations under Niche Media. Currently Binn serves as CEO and founder of Niche Media, the umbrella for titles including *Art Basel Miami Beach, Aspen Peak, Bal Harbour, Boston Common, Bridgehampton Polo, Capitol File, CityCenter Las Vegas, Gotham, Hamptons, Los Angeles Confidential, Michigan Avenue, Ocean Drive, Ocean Drive Español, Philadelphia Style, Style: Palazzo/ The Venetian, Trump, Vegas,* and *Wynn.*

Through the development of a vertically integrated strategic model, Binn has successfully validated the concept of the controlled-circulation publication as a prized commodity in the eyes of consumers and advertisers. His "winning formula" (*BusinessWeek*) begins with magazines that chronicle and celebrate community leaders and local celebrities. Then, unlike most magazines that rely solely on newsstand sales and subscriptions for their circulation base, Niche Media works with some of the most highly respected data bureaus in the country to ensure that its magazines are delivered straight into the hands of the country's most sought-after readers—those with the highest disposable income.

In 2007, Binn was featured in *Crain's* "Forty Under 40" list of successful entrepreneurs, and in 2006, Binn was the only person within the magazine industry to be inducted into the American Advertising Federation's "Advertising Hall of Achievement."

Jason Binn always knew he wanted to stand out. A true visionary, he saw opportunity where others didn't and made things happen through pure creativity and tenacity. When he got started, he had no experience in media, no doors that would open for him automatically in publishing. So Binn created his own door, launching a new brand of high-end magazines, which soon had luxury goods makers clamoring for ad space and a loyal following in some of the wealthiest enclaves around the country.

"SUCCESS, FOR ME, MEANS BEING THE BEST AT WHAT I DO. THAT'S ALL THAT MATTERS. I ALSO THINK IT MEANS STANDING OUT AND MAKING A STATEMENT. BUT YOU CAN SELL 'THE SIZZLE WITHOUT THE STEAK' FOR ONLY A SHORT PERIOD OF TIME—SOONER OR LATER YOU'VE GOT TO COME UP WITH THE BEEF. YOU'VE GOT TO HAVE A SOLID FOUNDATION."

When I was young, I played a lot of sports—tennis, football, I did everything. I wanted to be the best at whatever I was doing, and I made sure I explored every possible option. Before I chose a camp, I looked at a ton of choices. When I went out at night, I did my research and made sure I showed up at the best place in town. When I applied to colleges, I submitted applications to tons of schools.

I always took life very seriously, and from a young age I was very career-oriented. Once, when I was just a kid, I looked up at my dad on the golf course and said, "Oh, my God, I have so many things to worry about. I have to tie my shoes; I have to learn how to tell time." To this day, my father loves telling that story. I never got caught up in going out and partying too much during school. I was thinking about tomorrow, aware that there was always more responsibility to take on, knowing I always wanted more. That's always been my attitude.

I've always wondered, "How can I be different? How can I create something new and exciting and original?" It was a difficult challenge, distinguishing myself as a young person yet knowing all along that to make it big, I was going to have to do just that. These days, when students come out of college looking for a job, the process is so hard, so competitive. I get résumés and e-mails all the time, saying, "I'd like to work for you; I love what your business is about." But there aren't enough hours in the day to call everyone. Now when someone uses a little creativity—sending a résumé with a creative little display or a .pdf file—or follows up with a call to my office, that's when I stand up and take notice.

Marketing, branding, and promotions have always intrigued me— that was my area of expertise. While at my first job at an advertising agency in 1991, I worked on the Crystal Light, Cool Whip, and Corning accounts. One of my accounts was up for review, and I was scared that everyone working on it was going to get laid off, so I quit. When my manager asked me why I was quitting, I said, "Because I thought we might be losing the account." Well, we ended up *not* losing the account, yet I ended up leaving anyway. My dad asked me if I'd have left my job if he weren't helping me pay my rent. I said, "No." He said, "Well, you're an idiot. If you don't get a job in two weeks, you're paying your own rent."

So I had to go get a new job. I picked up *Women's Wear Daily* and opened to the classifieds. I closed my eyes and pointed on the page and decided that whatever came up, that's what I'd go for. I touched it, opened my eyes, and said, "Oh, the Warren Group." I went over to the company, knocked on the door, and found out it was a dress manufacturer. I got a job—for $10,000 a year more than I'd been making—selling and marketing dresses on Seventh Avenue. My dad said, "You've got to stay there for two or three years. No one wants anyone who jumps around." So I stayed and had a great experience.

Back then I knew a guy I'd run into around town. One day he asked me what I did, and I told him I worked for a dress company. He said, "You should be doing a lot more. We should do something together." We were inspired and decided to head down to Miami and start a magazine.

Miami was a very interesting place back then. The place was full of fancy photographers like Patrick Demarchelier, shooting campaigns for Ralph Lauren and Revlon and the Gap there. Thierry Mugler and Claude Montana and the whole fashion scene were very prominent. Charlize Theron and Angie Harmon were modeling in shoots for *Harper's Bazaar* and *Vogue* and all the big national magazines. Gianni Versace was doing South Beach stories with all these great, colorful prints. Every ad campaign had these bronzed men—that was very much in vogue. There were a lot of successful businessmen and young kids going to college who wanted to wear those shirts and be in shape and tan.

For my generation, Miami was very significant. I see it as our Woodstock, our Studio 54. We didn't realize the significance at the time; we didn't know that five or ten years later what we had experienced would become a whole mind-set everywhere else. Supermodels were our celebrities, and fashion was as relevant as anything else in pop culture. Miami was the hideout, and we made ourselves the gatekeepers. That's what *Ocean Drive* was all about.

If I'd looked at and followed other media models, I wouldn't be in business today. There were peop. : who had messages out there about creating a community in their magazine, in the social sense. There were people out there who created brands around their names and their businesses—Marvin Shanken with the cigar community, Hugh

Hefner with *Playboy*, Forbes with business and finance, Jann Wenner with the music industry. They took their content, brought it to life, let their community take part in what they were doing, and became socially relevant. They created worlds.

But you can never be complacent about what you're doing. At the end of the day, I think you're only as good as your last magazine; you're only as good as your last party; you're only as good as your last launch. You've got to keep everything fresh and strong. The world is always speeding up, not slowing down—you need to stay relevant! Many magazines and media companies get fixed in a mode, always reaching out to a specific type of reader or individual. What makes our company, Niche Media, exciting is the fact that we're young, we speak to the young movers and shakers, but we speak to the older crowd as well.

Success, for me, means being the best at what I do. That's all that matters. I also think it means standing out and making a statement. But you can sell "the sizzle without the steak" for only a short period of time—sooner or later you've got to come up with the beef. You've got to have a solid foundation. Our formula for success has been to create local magazines that are nationally recognized.

It put a smile on my face when I ran into Mayor Bloomberg at the White House Correspondents' Dinner in Washington. He asked, "I've seen the magazines, and I've always wondered, 'Are these guys really making money?'" I said, "Yes." And he said, "I figured." That was very flattering.

CHAPTER 14

• • •

Peter Carlisle

MANAGING DIRECTOR, OLYMPICS
AND ACTION SPORTS, OCTAGON

Peter Carlisle is the driving force behind the success of Octagon's Olympic and Action Sports division. An expert at the forefront of the booming action sports industry for more than a decade, he has successfully transitioned his creative marketing strategies to emerge as the leader in the representation and marketing of Olympic and Action Sports athletes.

Carlisle oversees the career management of Octagon's clients through contract negotiations, endorsements, and licensing and merchandising opportunities. He has successfully created national partnerships between his clients and corporations including AT&T, Coca-Cola, Dannon, Disney, Hewlett-Packard, Lenovo, Nokia, Office Depot, Omega, Subway and VISA, among others.

His roster of clients includes fourteen-time Olympic gold medalist swimmer Michael Phelps, multiple medalist swimmer Katie Hoff, snowboarding gold medalists Ross Powers, Seth Wescott, and Kelly Clark, among others.

Carlisle has twice been named "20 Most Influential People:

Sports Agents" and is a member of the "Forty Under 40" Hall of Fame following three career "Forty Under 40" Awards by *Sports Business Journal.*

Carlisle began his professional career as an attorney. In 1997, he founded Carlisle Sports Management, a representation firm focused on Action Sport athletes, which was acquired by the international sports marketing agency Octagon in 2001.

A lawyer by training, Peter Carlisle wasn't fulfilled practicing corporate law and instead found a way to combine his law degree with his passion for sports. With foresight and a unique vision—along with an entrepreneurial spirit—Carlisle became a sports agent, representing athletes and helping extreme athletes in particular to draw national attention to their sport. Carlisle's idea of success isn't just about money and getting his clients on Wheaties boxes. Success is about furthering his clients' interests and helping them realize their dreams.

"IN MY WORLD, SUCCESS IS WHEN YOU FURTHER A CLIENT'S INTERESTS. IT'S AS SIMPLE AS THAT."

When I was a kid, I wanted to be an Olympic hockey player. I grew up in Maine and spent countless hours playing hockey on the pond behind our house. I was at the formative age of twelve when the 1980 Winter Olympics took place at Lake Placid; I watched every second of every U.S. hockey game and recall in vivid detail everything about the win against the Soviets. The idea of a dream against the odds, coupled with my obsessive interest in hockey at the time, left me inspired. I remember thinking, "I want to go to the Olympics." Honestly, that's the only time I can think of where I thought, "Hey, this is what I want to be when I grow up."

Now that the Games are such a big part of my life, I can easily trace it back to the role they played in my own household. As kids, my two brothers and I weren't allowed to watch television; it just wasn't a significant part of our home life. And yet for two weeks every four years, the TV remained on continuously. Our whole family was glued to the set. It didn't matter what sport was on; the magic of the Olympics transcended any particular sport, capturing some abstract notion of purity, hope, and dreams.

Beyond that surge of passion for the Olympics in 1980, I lacked any particular ambition as a kid. That's not to say I wasn't driven; it's just that I never applied that drive to any one particular activity long enough to make much progress. I guess you could say I was exceptionally well-balanced or impressively mediocre in an exceptionally broad array of interests and activities; you'd recognize my ambition only if your perspective encompassed the full spectrum of my interests.

Unfortunately, I brought this same scattered approach to my schoolwork. I didn't really focus on academics until my junior year in high school. When I applied to college, I had only two years of decent grades to show my academic capabilities. Despite the warnings of my guidance counselor, I applied to very good schools, figuring they'd see my potential. Instead, I was rejected from just about all of them. It was a huge blow. For me, it was easy to overlook the objectivity of the process and instead take it personally. Initially, I felt like a failure.

In retrospect, however, being rejected from the schools of my choice was a defining moment for me. Without that sense of failure, I probably wouldn't have dug so deeply to counter it. I realized that if I accepted their judgments, I'd be allowing them to define me. On the other hand, if I ignored them, applied myself, and proved them wrong, I'd be defining *myself* in the process. So that's what I did, and it was that moment that instilled in me the drive to succeed.

Now, as an adult, I thrive on that type of challenge and adversity. I feel I can focus as intensely as anyone, that I can outwork people to accomplish what I want. Whether that's actually true or not is secondary; confidence comes from the fact that I can't be convinced otherwise.

I finally settled on the University of New Hampshire, where I did very well academically. I say "settled" because that's what I did: I enjoyed my time there, but throughout the year and a half I spent there, I was on a mission to prove to the school that had rejected me that I was worthy of admission. My hard work and dedication paid off, as I was accepted to and graduated from Bates College.

While I had finally understood the importance of academics, I hadn't yet figured out what I wanted to be "when I grew up." By then, I knew that my dream of Olympic hockey wasn't going to come to fruition, but I hadn't found a new dream to replace it. In the spring of my senior year, I seriously contemplated taking a job as a tennis pro in a foreign country. Ultimately, I decided, being a tennis pro might be fun for about six months, but then it would probably get really boring. I didn't know what else I wanted to do, but throughout college I'd often been told I'd be well suited to law, and law school seemed like a fairly productive way to defer a long-term decision. So I headed off to law school. In retrospect, this was a good thing: If I'd entered the workforce younger, I would have lacked any real basis or perspective to know what I wanted to get out of law school. For me, getting a law degree was more an intellectual exercise than a professional prerequisite.

Over time, I found that what I really enjoyed about the legal profession was the business of law—the way you structure a law firm, or your own practice, by recruiting clients or small businesses and helping them grow. This idea—that there could be an entrepreneurial twist to a traditional practice of law—fascinated me, and it really pulled me in.

I'd always wondered how I could combine my passion for sports with the practice of law. I think everyone at some point does that, really strives to connect their passion with their profession. So I started to help some local athletes, mostly snowboarders, and started thinking about how to develop more marketing opportunities for these athletes.

After much thought and deliberation, I took a chance and formed my own company, funding it on my personal credit card. I figured I would spend half my time building this sports practice and half the time practicing traditional law until the sports practice had enough momentum.

I figured it would take three years for my company to become self-sustaining. But things worked out better than I had anticipated. Six

months after I founded Carlisle Sports Management, I had successfully transitioned all my legal clients back into a law firm and shifted
my focus entirely onto sports.

Now that I was fully invested in the world of winter sports, I began
to recognize that there was this convergence of forces in the field.
Studies were being published calling Generation Y the biggest demographic since the Baby Boomers and predicting how they would
transform our economy. At the same time, snowboarding was gaining
significant momentum and quickly becoming the fastest-growing sport
in the country. There was a lot of talk about it becoming an Olympic
sport, and I saw an opportunity there—a way into the traditional marketplace through the Olympics. I figured being associated with the
Olympics would make snowboarding appealing to mainstream media
companies, which in turn would be effective in reaching Gen Y. So it
all came together in my mind. But they were all separate at the time,
and it's not as though too many people were connecting the dots. In
fact, people said, "You're crazy to be doing this." But it seemed clear
to me that this was going to work. It just made sense. By nature, I'm a
fairly entrepreneurial and speculative guy, so I took the leap.

There's no better way to learn than having your own livelihood
depend on making a company work. I think it's a great advantage to
create something out of thin air. I believe it gives you a sense of confidence and helps you develop a stronger understanding of the business
than other people competing in your space. There are myriad argu-
ments as to why I shouldn't have done what I did, but once I succeeded,
the reward for taking those risks was a hard-earned confidence.

If I weren't comfortable with risk, if I weren't fueled by it the way I
am, my job would be two-dimensional compared with what it is. We're
trying things that have never been done, we don't know how it's going
to turn out, and yet the careers of our clients, or of a company's division, can be hanging in the balance with each new risk. Ultimately, the
only way to measure whether the risk was successful is for you, and
your client, to define success.

In my world, success is when you further a client's interests. It's as
simple as that. I know that may sound trite, but it's best to simplify

the formula by focusing entirely on the professional side of things—furthering the client's interests—and relegating my own business interests to a secondary position. If I do my job well for the client, and I'm successful by that definition, then everything else is going to fall in place. It may not always work out that way, but to me that's the only way to do it. If you focus too much on the business itself, then it's too easy to become distracted from doing your best for the client.

Before I do anything with a client—even before signing a new client—I have a very matter-of-fact conversation to determine their interests and goals, and I offer my opinion on the marketplace, past, present, and future. Before we can enter into a relationship, we have to be on the same page as to how we define success.

If an athlete comes to me and says, "Hey, I think I need an agent," generally speaking he has no idea what he actually needs or even what an agent really does. If he says he would like representation, I typically ask, "Well, what are you looking for in an agent? Why do you want representation?" Mostly they'll say: "I would like sponsorship." "I'd like to have an easier time participating in this sport." "I'd like to be financially independent." "I'd like not to have to put money on my credit card." "I'd like to stop borrowing money from my parents." "I'd like to stop stressing out as to whether I'm going to get funding." "Sponsorship would make my life easier." So generally that's why they come to us. They don't come to us and say, "Hey, I need someone to help steer my life." That's rarely the case.

For example, I first started working with Olympic swimmer Michael Phelps at a very young age. During the recruiting process, I asked him point-blank: "Is your objective to become as rich as you possibly can be, or is it something else?" He stated very clearly that his primary objective was to change the sport of swimming, to help bring it to another level. And that's the objective against which we gauge our performance.

I can't tell you how many times Michael has turned down opportunities for a two-hour speech and meet-and-greet where he might be paid $50,000. He rejects these opportunities all the time, more than many people would believe. But then he'll go and do something that helps the sport and get paid nothing. People who measure success directly by the number of dollars generated might say, "He's not as successful as he could be." But he takes a much broader view, and that's what guides me in doing my job.

I derive satisfaction from helping my clients achieve their goals, not just from making them money. Even when we're turning down ways to make significantly more money for our clients, I embrace their objectives and look for unique and creative ways to further those objectives. That, to me, is success, and as long as my clients enjoy it as much as I do, and maintain those same yardsticks for success, then I expect the rest of it to fall in place. When you can put an athlete in a better position than he or she would be without your help, that's valuable, that's successful.

What motivates me is taking pride in what I do. It is that sense of satisfaction you get from working hard and doing a good job. Simple as that. In my own mind, I feel content and satisfied and proud of what I've done, and that's enough to insulate me from what others might think about what I'm doing.

Success in business and in life isn't necessarily something you can achieve on your own. All along the way, there are people who influence, guide, and shape you, often without your even realizing it. My parents were role models in a lot of ways. My parents are honest, conscientious, and hardworking people. They were also never the least bit materialistic, which led me to find meaning beyond the superficial. It's very easy for me to make decisions that are right for me, because that's the way my parents are, and that's the way they raised me to be.

On a personal level, I'm thirty-eight years old now, I have a family, and I think I'm changing the way I define success. When I was eighteen, success was about achievement in sports. When I was twenty-eight, success was about achievement in business. Now my idea of success is more about balance. I have no problem grinding it out and doing whatever it takes to be successful, but now it all happens against a landscape of different priorities. It can be difficult balancing my immediate competitive focus with my longer-term goals.

I still want to do big things in business, but I also want to be able to apply that same level of focus to my kids' hockey games. Most important, I want to be a good husband and a good dad. If anyone could have given me a piece of advice twenty years ago, it would have been to value balance.

I am certain that my definition of success will continue to change. And I'm okay with that. I see it as just another natural progression in life and something I'll be able to pass along to my children, as my parents did for me and my siblings. My success will likely include helping my children find their life's passion.

I wonder what their 1980 Olympic hockey moment will be.

CHAPTER 15

• • •

Eric Anderson

PRESIDENT AND CHIEF EXECUTIVE OFFICER,
SPACE ADVENTURES

Eric Anderson is one of the leading entrepreneurs in the space industry and an outspoken advocate of commercial space transportation, private space exploration, and space tourism. Dubbed an "astropreneur" by *Wired* magazine, Anderson co-founded Space Adventures, Ltd., the world's premier space tourism company, in 1998, together with several former astronauts and leading visionaries from the aerospace, adventure travel, and entertainment industries. Since then, Anderson has sold more than $150 million in spaceflights, including those taken by the first and only five tourists to have flown to space: Dennis Tito, Mark Shuttleworth, Greg Olsen, Anousheh Ansari, and Charles Simonyi.

Under Anderson's direction, Space Adventures remains the leader in the space tourism industry through the continuous launches of commercial passengers to the International Space Station, the offering of a circumlunar mission, and future suborbital spaceflights.

Previously, Anderson was the principal and co-founder of Starport .com, later sold to SPACE.com. Anderson was also lead engineer and business development lead for aerospace software firm Analytical Graphics and held various consulting and research positions with NASA.

Eric Anderson has applied his entrepreneurial drive to his great passion: space travel. As a child, he dreamed of becoming an astronaut and seeing the world beyond our own; today, he is tapping the power of the market and the private sector to make that vision a reality not for himself, but for the good of the entire world. He is a true pioneer on this final of all frontiers.

"SUCCESS MEANS FOCUSING ON WHAT YOU REALLY BELIEVE IN, SETTING AGGRESSIVE OBJECTIVES TO FORWARD WHAT IS GOOD FOR THE WORLD AND GOOD FOR YOURSELF, AND THEN ACHIEVING THOSE OBJECTIVES."

I grew up in Littleton, Colorado, not far from the U.S. Air Force Academy in Colorado, which is only about half an hour south of my childhood home. I was interested in space from a young age, ever since we studied the planets in third grade. I read *Cosmos* by Carl Sagan when I was quite young, and I loved *Star Wars* and *Star Trek*. The whole idea of humans reaching out into the cosmos was just thrilling to me. It seemed like the one great frontier that was left to be discovered. I watched all the shuttle missions at NASA, and my dream was to be the first person on Mars. I wanted to be an astronaut, an explorer.

I had incredibly supportive parents. They gave me the lessons and the tools to succeed. They certainly didn't push me in any one direction; they wanted me to follow what I was passionate about, which I'm grateful for. My parents are proud of what I've done.

In high school I always did well, and I decided I'd go to a university where I'd have a good chance of becoming an astronaut. Unfortunately, my eyesight grew quite bad—so bad that I was unable to qualify for a pilot's license, which was usually a prerequisite to join the astronaut corps. So I enrolled at the University of Virginia and studied aerospace engineering. I thought, "If I can't be an astronaut, I may as well build rockets."

I was in the honors system at UVA, and while I was there I started interacting with some great people. I met a number of former astronauts through the university, and they told me what an unbelievable experience it was to go to space and how important space exploration was for the future of humanity.

One summer, I actually interned at NASA. I was accepted to the NASA Academy, an exclusive program that chooses only one student from each state. While I was there I met a lot of top-level people in the space industry. At the age of nineteen, I was getting the lowdown on what the space industry was like. I met several really interesting entrepreneurs who later became partners of mine—including Peter Diamandis, who started the X Prize Foundation, of which I'm now a board member, and others.

I realized that the resources of space are infinite. Things like energy and real estate are finite here, but not in space. All we need to do is find economical and safe ways to get off planet, and within the next hundreds of years the human race will be able to expand into a multiplanet existence, which will enable our species to have an enduring presence in the solar system. This is essential for our survival.

I also realized at the time that the problem was that for the last forty years, the governments of the world had been in control of spaceflight. Most people haven't thought about the fact that less than a decade passed between the first human trip into orbit—Yuri Gagarin in 1961—and Neil Armstrong and Buzz Aldrin's moon landing in 1969. In only eight years, humanity went from having no one in space to landing people on the moon. In the ensuing thirty or forty years, however, we have done very little. We've learned how to live in space, how to build space stations and go into orbit. But we've done almost nothing to make space travel accessible and commercially viable.

There are six billion people on earth, and a significant percentage of them, perhaps 10 or 20 percent, would love to go to space in their lifetime. And the one thing we need to open up space, to pursue all those long-term goals—securing all that energy, those resources—is the technology to take people there safely and reliably, the way we use airplanes today.

In starting Space Adventures, I wasn't inhibited by the status quo or the space establishment. I'm really just a kid. I'm only thirty-three years old, with a dozen or so years of experience in the business world. I was a good student and I'm a pretty smart guy, but I think my true asset was the ability to look at the landscape with a fresh pair of eyes.

People said, "You know what? You're right, space should be open to private industry. But it's impossible. You don't want to have to fight against NASA and the military." But I just didn't think of that as a deterrent. I said, "This is the way it should be—space should be open to all. So let's try to make it so." I was fortunate to find people who believed in me, a few key investors—and, eventually, customers. I think people were shocked that I was able to find someone who would pay $20 million to go to space.

There was a time, back in the 1970s, when Pan American was selling tickets to the moon for $10, to be redeemable in fifty years or something. They sold hundreds of thousands of them; it was a novelty. No one understood how big the market potential for private spaceflight would be. In the 1990s, I would tell people, "One day you'll be able to buy a trip to space for $100,000." People would say, "No one would ever spend that much money."

Then, in 1999 and again in 2000, we met with Dennis Tito. I told him about the International Space Station and the type of flight we could provide for him, and I said, "But, you know, this is going to cost $20 million." He said, "If you can provide it, I'll pay it." And *boom,* his spaceflight was one of the biggest media events of 2001. It put a marker on the map that there were people willing to pay $20 million to go into orbit. Suddenly, it completely recalibrated the market. Market prices are influenced by costs, but they're much more set by the perception of value. Once someone gets out there with a viable service or product, a market is created. Now, there are guys like Richard Branson and others trying to get into this industry on our coattails because there's a proven market. And I welcome them. I'm honored that they believe in the potential of this industry.

In the last forty-five years, fewer than four hundred and fifty people went into space. That's only about ten per year, on average. In the last seven years, we've put five private individuals into space. Over the next ten years, we'll arrange for literally dozens of people per year, maybe hundreds, to fly to space. We are going to create more astronauts in the next five to ten years than in all of history before us. And after that, the rate will really start to climb.

Twenty years from now, there may be one hundred thousand people who have been to space. We're reaching a point that recalls the moment when the first settlers came to the New World to open that new frontier. Of course it takes time, but we're doing it with a profit motive, with a sustainable business model that will endure beyond the cycles of NASA budget cuts or political changes. Once a business is sustainable, it will endure.

The other beautiful thing we've observed about this industry over the last ten years is that the market is elastic—which is an incentive for companies to reduce prices over time. If we can sell one person at $20 million, we can sell a hundred people at $2 million. The total size of the market increases as the costs and prices come down.

I tend not to think of what we've done in the past decade as being exceptional. I think 95 percent of our work is still ahead of us. Maybe that's one ingredient for success, and the other is insanity. I feel that where there's potential energy, we can transform it into kinetic energy. That is, if there are millions of people today who want to go to space and millions more who may not want to go themselves but believe it's important to open space to the private sector, those people represent potential energy. And that potential will eventually translate into dollars, resources, and success for us. Where there's a market, there has to be a way to service it.

Success, for me, means focusing on what you really believe in, setting aggressive objectives to forward what is good for the world and good for yourself, and then achieving those objectives. Overcoming obstacles is what I have been doing for years now. And it's been working so far.

Natural-Born Leaders

CHAPTER 16

• • •

Brenda Barnes

CHAIRMAN AND CHIEF EXECUTIVE OFFICER, SARA LEE CORPORATION

Routinely named one of "The Most Powerful Women in Business" by *Forbes* and *Fortune* magazines, Brenda Barnes is one of the most formidable leaders in business today. Barnes has been a member of the board of directors of the Sara Lee Corporation since joining the company as president and chief operating officer in July 2004. She became president and chief executive officer in February 2005 and was appointed to her current position later that same year.

From November 1999 to March 2000, Barnes served as interim president and chief operating officer of Starwood Hotels & Resorts. Before that, she was president and chief executive officer of PepsiCo North America from 1996 to 1998 and had been the company's chief operating officer since 1994. During her twenty-two years at PepsiCo, Barnes held a number of senior executive positions in operations, general management, sales, and marketing.

Before joining PepsiCo North America, she served at other PepsiCo divisions, including Frito-Lay as vice president, marketing, and Wilson Sporting Goods as business manager.

Barnes is an exemplary corporate leader who has achieved success on her own terms. From the beginning, she was competitive and a high achiever. In every job, at every level, she has brought her own ideas about how to make things work better. At PepsiCo, she was a model of corporate success, and even when she left Pepsi to spend more time with her children, she continued to hone her leadership and business skills. When Barnes joined Sara Lee, she proved a woman's career can withstand interruption without consequence.

"IN A VERY BROAD SENSE, I WOULD SAY SUCCESS IS BEING ABLE TO DO WHAT YOU HOPED YOU COULD DO."

I grew up in a pretty large family. I was one of seven girls. Our parents set an example of excellence; doing well in school was just something that was expected in my house. Education was considered to be of paramount importance, and we were taught to do the best we could on every assignment. But our parents never put pressure on us to become successful. Rather, doing your best and being a good person were what mattered most to them. Those are the values that they instilled in us.

One thing I'm very clear on is that people—both in their professional lives and in their personal endeavors—constantly have to make choices. My choices in work, school, and life have all been guided by that ethic I got from my parents of doing the best job I can and nothing less.

Many years into my career, when I was working at PepsiCo, I had a very personal choice to make. I had been at the company for twenty-two years, and at the time I was the president and CEO of PepsiCo North America. For a while, though, I'd been struggling with the fact that I wanted to spend more time with my children, who were ages seven, eight, and ten.

One thing I realized at that time is that despite your attempt to give everything your all, you just can't be successful at everything. There are not enough hours in the day. So I made a choice to leave PepsiCo and the day-to-day management of a multibillion-dollar business. Why? I had three young kids at home whom I loved and wanted to spend more time with. I was thriving in a job that I loved, but it was all-consuming. And luckily, I knew myself well enough that I just couldn't continue doing either halfway or part-time. So I chose to go cold turkey and walk away from my career—knowing full well that I might never work for a company again.

I had actually tried to do this a year earlier but had chickened out and allowed one of my bosses to talk me out of it. So obviously I wasn't really ready for it. A year later I *was* ready, but that didn't take away the concerns or fears or worries: *If I'm no longer the president of Pepsi-Cola, who am I?* It took me a long time to realize that what you do is not who you are.

Somewhat unexpectedly, I gained a whole new perspective on business—and life—during the time I was away. I learned so many things that I think made me much better at what I do.

In addition to the time I spent with my kids, I sat on several corporate boards and was exposed to the cultures of many different companies. I saw the strategic issues, the decision-making process, and how plans were executed. I became knowledgeable on corporate governance and what was required there; the dynamics of board committee structures and how work got done; what great companies did to be clear about their strategies and to translate their strategies into action.

I taught a class at Northwestern's Kellogg School of Management called Managerial Leadership and was surprised by how much I learned in return. I studied the topic myself, and I gained an understanding through the eyes of people in their twenties of what—and how—they think. I learned a lot in that process.

I also taught a religion class for a number of years, which gave me a different opportunity to interact with my own child.

So I made some interesting choices on how to spend my "time away" from corporate America. I also chose not to do too many things. I knew that I didn't want to overbook myself with projects and defeat the purpose for which I had left in the first place.

Looking back, I know I would make that choice—to become more involved in my kids' lives—a million times over, even if it meant I never had a full-time job again.

I also realized that society wouldn't exist if people didn't stay at home taking care of their families. All the work and support that communities get from the women and men who stay at home is so undervalued today. I saw all the work these people, most of whom are women, did for no pay because they had passion about making the schools better or supporting the local food bank or some other community interest. And yet, unfortunately, the whole parenting profession is looked down on; people who dedicate themselves to being parents often feel they have to make excuses for that choice.

I came to value deeply that role, which many women choose to play. They shouldn't be ashamed of that decision. There are so many talented women out there, and it's so hard for them to get back to work after a hiatus raising a family. Often they lack confidence; if their résumé doesn't run right up to the day before yesterday, they're not sure they have anything to offer. But that doesn't mean they aren't valuable and experienced: It takes as much skill to deal with school districts as it does to handle any business challenge. There are people in leadership positions in our communities—who, by the way, also don't get compensated for their time and effort—who will never be given credit for all they do.

I'm certainly facing a huge challenge in my career today at Sara Lee. Many people in the industry have doubts that I'll be able to turn things around. To prove them wrong, I have to let the people around me—our entire workforce—know what the metrics of success are and how to understand their individual role in reaching our goals. My scorecard is a public one—share price, earnings, market share, and sales volume—and Wall Street looks at it every quarter. They can see my progress, and they're not at all shy about letting me know how I'm doing, whether I ask or not.

I try to inspire my team through actions and not words, and I'm completely transparent in my management style. I try to instill confidence in the people around me so they can succeed. I think that to be a leader, you have to treat people with respect and tap into their true potential.

In a very broad sense, I would say that success is being able to do what you hoped you could do. I talk about this often with my husband and my family: Did you achieve what you wanted to achieve? Did you meet your own expectations on certain things? For me, am I as good a mother as I hope to be? I judge that by what kinds of kids I think I have. Did I achieve a career aspiration and demonstrate that I met that goal? It's all about your own expectations.

I wish I could say I had it all figured out, that I knew where I was going and had the path to get there. That is absolutely not the case. For me, the rule at any point in time, whatever I was doing, was simple: Did I do the best I could? Did I achieve my objective, and in a way that was better than what I or others around me expected? I can certainly answer "yes" about my choices so far, and as long as I can keep doing that, I will feel successful.

CHAPTER 17

• • •

Richard Parsons

CHAIRMAN OF THE BOARD, CITIGROUP

Richard Parsons was named chairman of the board of Citigroup on January 21, 2009. Previously, Parsons had been chairman of the board of Time Warner since 2003, where he had also served as chief executive officer from 2002 to 2007.

As CEO, Parsons led Time Warner's turnaround and set the company on a solid path toward sustainable growth. In its January 2005 report on America's Best CEOs, *Institutional Investor* magazine named Parsons the top CEO in the entertainment industry.

Prior to becoming CEO, Parsons served as the company's co–chief operating officer. He joined Time Warner as its president in February 1995 and has been a member of the company's board of directors since January 1991. As president, he oversaw the company's filmed entertainment and music businesses, and all corporate staff functions, including financial activities, legal affairs, public affairs, and administration.

Before joining Time Warner, Parsons was chairman and chief executive officer of Dime Bancorp and managing partner of the New York law firm Patterson Belknap Webb & Tyler. Before that, he was counsel to New York governor Nelson Rockefeller and a senior White House aide under President Gerald Ford.

Although he's been one of the most successful corporate figures of the last decade, Dick Parsons defines his own success by his interactions with those working with him or for him. Parsons is motivated to build successful relationships and then to inspire and lead those around him. He even measures his legacy in those terms, valuing his reputation among former colleagues, employees, and shareholders above more fleeting accomplishments.

"WOODY ALLEN SAID, 'EIGHTY PERCENT OF SUCCESS IS SHOWING UP.' I THINK THERE'S A LOT OF TRUTH TO THAT. YOU'VE GOT TO GET IN THE GAME, YOU'VE GOT TO SHOW UP, AND YOU'VE GOT TO TRY."

I think I was very fortunate to have parents who nurtured and directed and disciplined and inspired and guided me. Who knows what is really nurture and what is nature? Experts have been debating that for years. I look at my own circumstances, and the biggest differentiator for me, in terms of being able to succeed, was education. But I'm also a believer in birth order. As a second child, I was forced into the role of mediator/diplomat, someone who had to make it work for everybody—that's the nature of the second child position. Whether I was born innately with those skills, or developed them, or a combination of the two—which is probably most likely—I've spent my whole life developing a set of skills that turn out to be useful if you do what I do, which is working with people, trying to inspire and lead them.

But you also have to develop skills if you want to bring value to the marketplace, so getting an education and developing a skill base is an essential part of success. There, again, I credit my parents with directing me and my wife with keeping me on the path. I got married after I got out of college and went to law school, and it was my wife who really said, "You need to buckle down."

Woody Allen said, "Eighty percent of success is showing up." I think there's a lot of truth to that. You've got to get in the game, you've got to show up, and you've got to try. You're not going to win all the time, but the only way you can be assured of not winning is if you don't show up and try. I've been fortunate that most of the things I've showed up for and tried have worked.

I have only two real regrets, and they don't really relate to my career. They both relate to periods when I was in school. When I was in college, a friend wanted me to crew with him on a sail to Tahiti. It required me to drop out of school for a semester. I didn't do it; I should have. When I was coming out of law school, I had a stipend to go study in Edinburgh, Scotland, for a year. But I was so anxious to get to work and be productive that I passed on the opportunity. I probably should have done that. In terms of my career, though, I can't think of anything I honestly believe I should have done differently. My touchstone is that you figure out what you think is the right thing to do, you give it your best shot, and it either works out or it doesn't. I can't think of anything to which I didn't try to give my best.

I was never what you'd call mercantile—driven by money or fame. I've always been more driven by being accepted in a circle of colleagues or friends who are people whose company and high regard I value. Like most people, particularly when they get a little older and a little wiser, I tend to define success not around money or even status, but around the quality of my relationships with other people. At the end of the day, that's what's real and enduring and important. One's reputation is a real and valuable possession; being well regarded by those who know you is something in which I take a lot of satisfaction.

When people look back at me, I would like them to say, "He was a good man." That's what I say about my father—he was a good man. That's enough for me.

I think one's personal sense of security is very important as well. I'm a reasonably secure person; I'm comfortable with who I am. The transient trappings—money, station, whatever—aren't as important to me as being true to myself and enjoying the fellowship of people I regard highly. When I see people who've known me a long time, they always say, "Gee, you haven't changed at all." That's because I really haven't.

When it's time for me to leave Time Warner, I'd like to be able to say, and have others say, that we turned this company over in good shape and left it in good hands. And obviously part of that equation is having it properly valued in the market. I don't think it is right now; it's certainly not where we would like to see it. But if people would say, "He left the company in good shape and in good hands," that would be cool. And then, beyond that, I would like to do something that focuses on children and education. I'm oriented toward kids, so doing something to help young people get access to educational opportunity is something I could be passionate about.

I am always reminded of something my grandmother told me when I was a kid: "You reap what you sow in this world." I really do think that is the secret to leading a successful life.

CHAPTER 18

• • •

Allan "Bud" Selig

COMMISSIONER OF MAJOR LEAGUE BASEBALL

Bud Selig was elected the ninth commissioner of Major League Baseball on July 9, 1998, having served as interim commissioner since 1992.

A lifelong baseball fan, Selig followed the old Milwaukee Brewers minor league team and the Chicago Cubs while growing up. He became a Braves fan when the National League franchise moved to Milwaukee from Boston in 1953. In 1970, a team of investors led by Selig was awarded the Seattle Pilots franchise, which became the modern Milwaukee Brewers.

Selig served a dual role as president of the Milwaukee Brewers and chairman of the executive council until his appointment as commissioner. At that time, his financial interest in the club was placed in trust and he relinquished involvement in all matters dealing with the operation of the Brewers. The team was sold in 2005, ending Selig's thirty-five-year relationship with the club.

Despite presiding over the game during a troubled period that included a 272-day players strike in 1994 and 1995, Selig has been responsible for guiding the game through a significant renaissance. He's overseen the establishment of interleague play, the addition of the wild card system, and the validation of the All-Star Game by making it count for home-field advantage in the World Series. In 2002, Selig engineered a historic labor agreement with the Major League Baseball Players Association, paving the way for the players association and the clubs to reach a labor agreement without either a strike or a lockout for the first time in thirty years.

In 2005, the league and the players association announced a historic agreement to expand its drug-testing program to toughen its drug policy. The new policy, which included random drug testing and stiffer penalties for offenders, highlighted Selig's long-term effort to rid the game of illegal steroids and performance-enhancing substances.

Bud Selig's profound understanding of the role of baseball in American culture has allowed him to modernize the sport and make it more popular than ever. His great achievements have come with his success at leading groups past daunting obstacles: first leading a consortium that brought baseball to Milwaukee; then leading the Brewers to success; and finally, bringing together baseball owners and players and preventing another labor stoppage from hurting baseball.

"TO ME, SUCCESS IS WINNING IN A WAY THAT GIVES YOU PRIDE AND GRACE AND THE FEELING THAT YOU'VE DONE IT THE RIGHT WAY."

I was a good student as a child. My mother was a teacher, so I enjoyed school. My parents never had to push me to do schoolwork. By the time I got to college, I wanted to be a history professor; I truly believed that was what I was going to do. But my father, who had a very successful automobile dealership, wanted me to work in the family business. I was very proud of my father. He came to this country as a little boy and was very successful. He was a remarkable human being in every way. And after I finished college and my service obligation, I did go to work in the family business.

Growing up, I was just a fair ballplayer. The first time I saw a curveball, I knew I would never make it as a major leaguer. Nonetheless, I remained a big baseball fan and eventually fell into baseball management as a career—somewhat by chance.

By the time I was twenty-nine years old, I was the largest public stockholder in the Milwaukee Braves. It was a pretty good position to be in. Then, two years later, the Braves upped and left Milwaukee and headed for Atlanta, and I lost my investment. It was 1965, and the people in Milwaukee felt the same sense of outrage and loss that the Brooklyn fans felt when Walter O'Malley moved the Dodgers to Los Angeles in the 1950s. We got less publicity, but our baseball void was just as large as Brooklyn's.

I decided to take the lead and put a group together—a consortium to bring a baseball franchise back to Milwaukee. It was much, much harder than I thought it would be. I kept running into brick walls. I'd go to baseball meetings and was treated like I had leprosy, as though I came from a foreign country, not Milwaukee, Wisconsin.

Since I didn't have a team, I tried the next best thing—to bring exhibition major league games to Milwaukee. The local sports editor told me I was crazy, that I'd ruin Milwaukee's baseball chances forever. "What self-respecting fan would want to watch a major league game that didn't count?" he asked. Regardless of his opinions, I knew I was right and went ahead with the plan. The day before we put players on the field for our first game, we had sold out. I closed my eyes. I could see a sign in my mind that said, "Milwaukee deserves a Major League Baseball team." Fifty-one thousand one hundred forty-four fans attended. That's a number that sticks in my brain. Within a couple of years, my group was awarded the Seattle Pilots, a team that was coming out of bankruptcy, and we moved the team to Milwaukee, where it became the Brewers.

It took five and a half years, but those years taught me a lot about life—how to deal with and accept disappointment and how to be patient. I just never deviated from what I needed to do—and I think the ability to focus on a goal helped me in the long run to become successful.

John Fetzer, the owner of the Detroit Tigers, was my mentor when I first came into the game. He always referred to his club as the Detroit Baseball Club and mine as the Milwaukee Baseball Club. He taught me that on the field we want to beat each other's brains out, but off the field we're partners. He told me that you should never think about your own myopic interest, but to always think about the best interests of the sport. That's a credo I've lived by throughout my career in baseball. Mr. Fetzer was a great man: It was he and my father who had the greatest influence on me.

Baseball is a social institution, and with that comes social responsibility. And that's a privilege. In 1947, Jackie Robinson and Branch Rickey made history when Jackie first stepped on the field at Ebbets Field and forever ended the game's racial barrier. That came before President Harry Truman integrated the U.S. Army and before the historic *Brown v. Board of Education* Supreme Court decision, and it arguably changed the course of our country's social history. It was baseball's most important and most powerful moment.

When I became interim commissioner in 1992, I'd already been in baseball a long, long time. I knew that taking on the leadership position was going to be painful. Change is always difficult, and baseball is a sport that had never adapted well to change. The game had gone five or six decades without change at all, and I believe it probably was hurt by that. We were also in the midst of a thirty-year war with the [Major League Baseball] Players Association that resulted in eight work stoppages. It was owners versus owners, owners versus players, and in the middle of it all was the commissioner. It was just brutal. I knew that had to stop. I got the owners to band together. I know it sounds trite, but I had to convince all sides to act in the best interest of the sport.

We funded studies; we got the young fans to come back. After all, if a business isn't economically viable, you have no business. In our negotiations with the players association in 2002, we were finally able to alter the financial landscape of the game and introduce meaningful revenue sharing among the clubs, a competitive balance tax, and the debt service rule. Today, baseball is more popular than ever, because we've finally succeeded in accomplishing what we had to do from an economic standpoint—and, most important, we've sustained labor peace.

No one is more competitive than I am. When I owned the Milwaukee Brewers, I lived and died with every game. I had major league temper tantrums that my wife can tell you all about. I had always loved Vince Lombardi, the legendary football coach, but I believe his quote about "winning is not the most important thing, it's the only thing" misrepresents his legacy. The only thing he ever asked of his players was to give everything they could give. I love people like that. I'm extremely loyal to them.

Persistence—or tenacity, or whatever you want to call it—is important in achieving success. You have to believe in what you are doing, and you have to understand how best to attain your goals and do what is right. You may not see the results right away, but in time—sometimes considerable time—you'll see you did make the right decisions, and you did it the right way.

CHAPTER 19

• • •

Jill Abramson

MANAGING EDITOR, *THE NEW YORK TIMES*

J ill Abramson was named managing editor of *The New York Times* in 2003, making her the first woman to hold that post. Abramson joined the *Times* in 1997 as the paper's enterprise editor, based in Washington, D.C. She went on to become its Washington editor and then Washington bureau chief before relocating to New York to assume her current position.

Previously, Abramson worked at *The Wall Street Journal*. She served as the *Journal*'s Washington deputy bureau chief and investigative reporter, during which time she won the National Press Club Award for national correspondence for her political coverage of money and politics.

In 1994, Abramson coauthored *Strange Justice: The Selling of Clarence Thomas*, a finalist for both the National Book Award and the National Book Critics Circle Award.

As a child, Jill Abramson was encouraged by her parents to try new things, and she has followed that path ever since, from being an investigative journalist at The Wall Street Journal *to becoming the first female managing editor of one of the world's most influential newspapers, The* New York Times. *Abramson's positive attitude and her willingness to make tough choices have allowed her to lead by example.*

"I THINK THE KEY TO SUCCESS IS TO BE IN LOVE WITH YOUR WORK, WHICH I STILL AM. IF I LOST THIS JOB TOMORROW, I COULD BE HAPPY BEING A REPORTER AGAIN, BECAUSE IT'S FUN AND I LOVE THAT, TOO."

My parents did not put a lot of pressure on either my sister or me when we were growing up. I don't remember any anxiety over our grades or anything like you hear with kids growing up now. "Find something you love and do it well," they told us: That's what they thought was the secret to happiness outside of the purely personal sphere of life. They didn't tell us, "Play it safe," or, "Always be a good girl." I don't mean to suggest that they encouraged risky behavior, but if we thought something sounded interesting, they encouraged us to give it a try.

My father was a total sports fanatic and a pretty decent athlete himself. When I was in elementary school, my father would come home from work and change during the summertime and we would go over to Central Park. He would pitch to me for over an hour and have me hit, even though I was really pretty bad. In part, of course, it was just something fun to do together, but I know he also wanted me to see that if I was willing to give it a try, I would improve. For my father, the crucial thing was that I was willing to give it a go—that I would get out there and hit even when other kids were watching. That was kind of the spirit he instilled in me.

When I got into high school, I sometimes came up with things to do that were different. After eleventh grade, for instance, I found an ad in some magazine where they would pay you a pittance to go over to England and join an archaeological dig. My parents just said, "Fun—go do that." They weren't the kind of parents who structured my adventures: When I came up with something, they generally supported my seeking it out.

I have never had a very clear sense of where I wanted to go—a vision of the path from point A to point B to point C. I've worked at lots of different places. I had a job in the election unit of NBC News during the 1980 presidential cycle, and I liked that a lot. After Reagan was inaugurated, NBC cut back their payroll radically and I lost my job. I got on the unemployment line and did a couple of very marginal jobs, including—this might have been my low point—writing rhyming poetry for special occasions. I don't remember being absorbed with worry at that point, but I definitely had the sense of what it meant to go from having an NBC News pass with my picture on it, working at NBC headquarters at 30 Rockefeller Plaza, to standing on line waiting to cash my check.

Early on in my career I had two editors, Steve Brill and Al Hunt, who were extremely hard-charging, and I was definitely programmed to want to please those tough taskmasters. A little like my father, they encouraged me to jump into the deep end of swimming pools, where I'd never gone before, and do investigative reporting. As I got a bit of experience in journalism, I found I was good at it. I had to cold-call powerful people, whether they were lawyers or political figures, and try to dig out the story behind the story. There weren't a whole lot of other women journalists doing that, but I was willing to do it because it seemed exciting.

In 1984, Steve Brill was expanding his empire, starting Court TV and buying a number of legal publications. He bought a weekly legal newspaper in Washington and said, "Here, I've bought this. Run it for me." I was thirty years old, and I'd never run anything. I moved to Washington and became the editor in chief of *Legal Times*. That involved running a staff of thirty, including an art department, and generating a lot of story ideas. In the process, I discovered that that was another talent I had: I could write and report, but I also had the capacity to lead a staff and be a good editor.

My ten years at *The Wall Street Journal* were fantastic. It was a hard-driving place to work, but it was only five days a week. The Internet hadn't really started. I was doing enterprise journalism, so I really controlled a lot of my schedule. I didn't work wild hours most of the time. I worked in intense spurts, but I don't at all feel I missed the school plays or anything like that. When I look at some of the younger women here at the *Times* who are covering City Hall or the White House—and have little kids at home—I'm in awe of how they do it.

In 1997, I joined the *Times* in the Washington bureau. By then I knew how to incubate ideas, write some of them myself, get others to write them—and fostering that kind of investigative/political reporting was something they wanted more of when I came to the *Times*, and I was able to deliver that. That was a big reason for my success there.

I certainly thought there was a great chance that my career would be hurt when Howell Raines became executive editor in 2001. People who'd known me a long time in Washington would come up to me at events and ask, "How are you?" as if I had cancer, knowing I was having a tough time with him. There were some days where the atmosphere felt hurtful or destabilizing, but I think being able to come to work, to continue to do good work, to stand up for the Washington bureau and myself, was a crucial thing for me to have done. It was hard, but if you don't stand up, I think you lose in some way. During that whole period, I never sat home and worried, "Am I going to lose my job?" That's what I mean when I say I'm not averse to risk.

There have been periods in my career when I'd say I was flailing a bit, that I wasn't certain I was operating on all cylinders. But sometimes you look back on those periods and realize you were actually just seeking the next interesting thing. My first book, *Where They Are Now*, was about women of the Harvard Law School class of 1974, and when I wrote it I read a lot about women in the professional and corporate worlds and the things that can hold them back or make them successful. Looking back, I realize what an advantage that the places where I've worked have genuinely wanted to see women in the top jobs. I'm not sure the challenges I faced in taking my job at the *Times* are all that different from the challenges men in this job have had. When I first got here, I may have talked a little too much. That's how it is when you're trying to prove you've got the stuff, that you're knowledgeable enough to help direct all parts of the paper. I think I've calmed down since then.

It seems to me that one key to leadership success is mutual respect. I think people respect that I have good ideas, but they know I don't think mine are the only good ones. I'm blunt and direct without being a bludgeon. And I'm fiercely competitive about the news. I will not let this paper slag in the urgency with which it covers every area of the news, from sports to wars. I also get a big kick out of it. If you drive people hard, you also need to go over and compliment them, and celebrate their breakthroughs, and show that you're getting as big a kick out of it all as they are.

I do worry a little bit about money. Certainly when I attend events like Harvard reunions, I'm reminded of how much money my college peers have acquired in different, more entrepreneurial lines of work. My profession is one you don't enter if you're in it for the money. Much more important are our two kids—I'm devoted to them. At this point, my husband and I have almost succeeded in paying to put them through college. Cornelia is about to start medical school, so that's a bit of a big gulp. I don't look toward retirement and assume I'll be in financial comfort. I know that any money manager would be appalled by my portfolio. But I feel so lucky that I get to do something I love and that I've also enjoyed a robust family life where no one has had to make a terrible sacrifice because of lack of money. "So far, so good"—that's my attitude toward it all.

I think the key to success is to be in love with your work, which I still am. If I lost this job tomorrow, I could be happy being a reporter again, because it's fun and I love that, too.

CHAPTER 20

• • •

William Donaldson

FORMER CHAIRMAN, SECURITIES
AND EXCHANGE COMMISSION

William Donaldson served from 2003 to 2005 as the twenty-
seventh chairman of the Securities and Exchange Commission, the chief regulator of America's securities markets and chief
enforcer of the nation's securities laws. His tenure marked the greatest
period of activity since the agency's founding in 1934.

Before joining the SEC, Donaldson was chairman, president, and
chief executive officer of Aetna, Inc., and before that he served as chairman and chief executive of the New York Stock Exchange. Earlier in his
career, he was the co-founder, chairman, and chief executive officer of
the investment banking firm of Donaldson, Lufkin & Jenrette. The Associated Press named Donaldson "Businessman of the Year" after DLJ
became the first NYSE firm to sell its shares to the public.

Donaldson left DLJ to accept a presidential appointment as U.S. undersecretary of state under Henry Kissinger and subsequently served
as counsel to Vice President Nelson Rockefeller. Following that, he
was the founding dean and William S. Beinecke Professor of Management at the Yale (University) School of Management.

William Donaldson fulfilled his two passions in life—public service and entrepreneurialism—by leveraging the leadership skills he learned early on in life. Growing up in tough times, Donaldson was imbued early with the idea that if you want something, you have to go out and earn it yourself. This self-reliance became the mantra for the rest of his life. Donaldson relished entrepreneurial activity with partners, which allowed him to pursue his interests while motivating those around him. He was able to apply this talent throughout his life, achieving a triple crown of leadership— dominating Wall Street with DLJ, innovating in academia as founding dean of the Yale School of Management, and setting policy in the public sector as chairman of the SEC. For Donaldson, success had been not about the position per se, but rather about bringing excellence to everything he takes on and taking pleasure from the success of those around him.

"EARLY ON, I DISCOVERED THAT WHILE MONETARY REWARDS ARE A MEASURE OF SUCCESS, A PROFESSIONAL LIFE DEVOTED TO THAT END ALONE WOULD NOT, FOR ME, DEFINE SUCCESS. THE REWARDS OF SERVICE, LOVE, FRIENDSHIP, AND CONTRIBUTION WOULD BE PART OF MY BROADER DEFINITION OF SUCCESS."

I was born in 1931 in Buffalo, New York, grew up during the Great Depression, and was a young teenager during World War II. My father was hit pretty hard by the Depression, and we had fairly modest means.

Two strong influences helped to shape me during that period. The first was my father's oft repeated response to my constant requests: "If you really want it, go out and earn it, because I can't give it to you." As a result, I was always convinced that anything was possible—but only with the application of self-starting effort. The second influence was the day-to-day impact of the world war—whether it was collecting scrap metal for the war effort or knitting (yes, knitting) wool squares for blankets for our servicemen. That experience left me with a deep-seated sense of patriotism. I had great admiration, even hero worship, for the older brothers and younger fathers who had marched off to war. These larger-than-life men (back then, they *were* mostly men) were the leaders—both military and civilian—of our country during that period.

I had a pretty active school life, playing high school football and hockey while trying to study—mostly motivated by wanting to get into college and, of course, by chasing girls. But during summers and vacations, I put that earn-it-yourself ethic to work in multiple efforts, beginning with the proverbial lemonade stand and newspaper route, which gave way through the years to working in a gas station and other summer jobs from toiling in a warehouse to driving a truck. During my high school vacations, I led the formation of a "company," United Enterprises, which at its peak employed upwards of fifty teenage kids, painting houses, mowing lawns, performing just about every sort of odd job there was.

I got great pleasure from all that entrepreneurial activity in partnership with others—from the team play it involved and from the feeling of working toward a common goal—and that pleasure has stayed with me throughout my life. Success at that stage involved winning in sports, making a little money in our business pursuits, and the friendships that ensued. College expanded my horizons intellectually—but not as much as the new array of extracurricular activities, such as becoming publisher of the university's daily newspaper, playing ice hockey, and participating in other organized activities.

Joining the marines after college seemed like the natural thing to do, motivated as I was by the example of my older brother's generation—though I understood little of what the Korean War was all about. While in the marines, I was heavily influenced by the USMC [United States Marine Corps] leadership mandates and esprit de corps; these have clearly influenced the roles I've filled in later years, perhaps as much as the formal training I received in graduate business school.

Starting Donaldson, Lufkin & Jenrette was the ultimate entrepreneurial endeavor. This business of success, I guess, is hard to define, but I think for me it has meant living out that dream. Clearly DLJ was a great success—we were in the right place at the right time—and that gave me a great measure of satisfaction. Not only had we started a new firm, but everything we did in that firm we did in an entrepreneurial spirit: *If everybody does it this way, why not do it differently?* That was true in terms of the kinds of people we hired, in the compensation systems we created, in taking the firm public against the New York Stock Exchange's wishes, and so forth.

I was busily engaged at DLJ for a long time, fifteen years or so, but all of a sudden I realized that I'd been there a long time and if I wanted to do some other things, I ought to start thinking about it.

In the late seventies, Wall Street was really in trouble. Everybody had a tough time. So I sat in a room with Mayor [Robert] Wagner and Governor [Hugh] Carey and basically did the budget. The governor asked me to stay on and be the secretary, which is a governor's chief of staff, and I decided I didn't want to do that. I was pursuing some other things. Around that time, Kingman Brewster asked me whether I'd be interested in helping to start a new school at Yale. I told him I wasn't qualified, but I was a trustee of Yale and I'd look around and try to figure out what the school should be. I ended up doing that because it was an entrepreneurial experience. I thought my next undertaking was going to be buying a newspaper—I was trying to pry the *New York Post* from Dolly Schiff—but this Yale thing appealed to me. It was entrepreneurial in a different milieu. I learned a lot about being entrepreneurial in an academic institution.

I then decided I wanted to take a run at governor of New York. I was off and running, but then I decided I didn't want to do it—mainly because of the extreme right orientation of the Republican Party. You don't hit the nomination unless you're there, and I wasn't there. It took being out on the hump and running around and listening to all this stuff—listening to the guys telling me what I had to do to appease the Right. I just decided I didn't want to do it.

When I came to the SEC, I tried to bring some entrepreneurial spirit there. They were so demoralized when I got there. Even the deepest bureaucrats were thrilled to have some direction and somebody to say, "We're going to get something done."

It destroyed me to watch what was going on, and I wanted to do something about it. We had the power because of the Sarbanes-Oxley Act and because of the public disgust over corporate corruption at that time. The place was ready to have somebody new come in and try to do something with it. That was fun. At DLJ, our final corporate objective was to have fun. Our tenth corporate objective, which we put in all our annual reports, was to have fun. What we meant was working with good people toward good goals and really enjoying what we were doing—the thrill of teamwork and accomplishment and all that. If you're going to spend twelve hours a day working, you'd better enjoy it or do something else.

In my professional career, I've been driven by a strong desire to do a number of different things, all stemming from the knowledge that the world is filled with a wide variety of careers in both the public and private arenas, all of them worthwhile. We have only one life to lead, so it seems natural to apply one's experience to a number of challenging opportunities—that may be the surest way to make a real contribution, which is one part of my personal definition of success.

Monetary reward may be one measure of success, but I learned early that success could never come from devoting my professional life to that end alone. The rewards of service, love, friendship, and contribution each must play a part.

CHAPTER 21

• • •

Jeff Zucker

PRESIDENT AND CHIEF EXECUTIVE OFFICER, NBC UNIVERSAL

J eff Zucker was named president and chief executive officer of NBC Universal in February 2007. NBC Universal is one of the world's leading media and entertainment content companies, with assets that include the U.S. broadcast networks NBC and Telemundo; cable networks USA, SCI FI, Bravo, Oxygen, CNBC, MSNBC, and the Weather Channel; movie studios Universal Pictures and Focus Features; digital properties such as Hulu (a joint venture with News Corporation) and iVillage; an extensive array of international television channels in Europe, Asia, and Latin America; and theme parks in Hollywood and Orlando.

Zucker has spent his entire twenty-two-year career at NBC Universal. Before assuming his current position, he had served as chief executive officer of the NBC Universal Television Group since December 2005, with responsibility for the strategic development and operations of NBC Universal's extensive portfolio of broadcast and cable television networks. Previously, he served as president of the NBC Universal Television Group from May 2004 until December 2005. Before that, he had been president of the Entertainment, News, and Cable Group since December 2003 and president of NBC Entertainment since December 2000.

Before taking the helm of NBC Entertainment, Zucker spent nearly eight years as the executive producer of NBC News' *Today*, a position he was appointed to at the age of twenty-six, making him the youngest EP in the history of the program. Under his leadership at *Today*, the program became the nation's most-watched morning news show and the most profitable program on television.

He also served as executive producer of *NBC Nightly News with Tom Brokaw* in February and March 1993, a post held concurrently with his role at *Today*. He joined NBC in 1986 as a researcher for NBC Sports' coverage of the 1988 Summer Olympics and joined NBC News as a field producer for *Today* in January 1989.

Jeff Zucker's combination of skills—his unique vision, competitive spirit, and willingness to take risks—makes him a quintessential leader. Zucker distinguished himself early on, achieving unprecedented success as the executive producer of NBC's Today *show at a young age. His rise to the top has not been without challenges, yet this self-described "outsider" has an innate ability to leverage his skills to take on the toughest challenges of his career.*

"TELEVISION IS AN INDUSTRY WHERE SUCCESS IS MORE OFTEN THAN NOT MEASURED BY WHETHER YOU'RE NUMBER ONE. BUT IF YOU'RE SHOWING IMPROVEMENT AND MOVING IN THE RIGHT DIRECTION, THAT CAN BE A MEASURE OF SUCCESS AS WELL."

I started playing tennis when I was six years old and played tennis tournaments virtually every weekend of my childhood, from the age of six or seven until I was eighteen. My life revolved around tennis. I thought about it seriously as a career, at least as an adolescent. But then I stopped growing at about thirteen, and I realized my limitations.

From that point on, I became more practical. I dreamed of becoming a sportswriter, covering the Dolphins for the *Miami Herald*. I never covered the Dolphins, but I did write for the *Herald* for a couple of years.

My role models growing up were [Bob] Woodward and [Carl] Bernstein. The first book I remember reading was *All the President's Men*. I was ten years old. I remember finishing it and then reading it immediately again. I was interested in politics, and I thought the legal world was a way into politics. So I applied to law school.

Two things derailed my plans for law school. The first was that even though I did get into a number of law schools, I didn't get into Harvard Law School, where I wanted to go. Had I gotten into Harvard, I would have gone no matter what. I am thankful every day that I didn't get in. The other thing that derailed my law ambition was that on the day I graduated from college, NBC Sports offered me a job as the researcher for the 1988 Seoul Olympics—a job that was too good to pass up. I decided to wait on law school.

Being an Olympic researcher has always been one of the best and most exciting entry-level jobs in all of television. The fundamental responsibility of the job is to travel the world uncovering the future stars of the next Olympic Games, getting to know all the athletes who will be potential stars. So I was responsible for helping to decide which ones we would highlight—and, in the process, becoming as conversant in their lives as they were.

A couple of things appealed to me about that job. First of all, it allowed me to crisscross the world at somebody else's expense at a very young age. That was exciting. Second, it gave me the opportunity to help shape NBC's Olympics programming, by determining what athletes and what events we were going to feature.

After the Olympics, I spent a year at the *Today* show as a general field producer. Then, about a year later, Katie Couric arrived as the show's national correspondent. I became her producer for the next fifteen or sixteen months. Our relationship worked because I think Katie and I had a very similar outlook on the world. We had the same sensibility about things, and we clicked from day one.

I ended up becoming the executive producer of *Today* at the age of twenty-six. I was very energetic, very competitive, very innovative, and I think the combination of all of those things—energy, creativity, drive—served the show and me well and I like to think contributed to our success there.

In my current job, what appeals to me most is leading the turnaround of the NBC Universal Television Group, from what's been obviously two difficult years. That's the challenge, and I like challenges. At this point, I don't necessarily equate success with being number one. Right now, we're just shooting for positive momentum.

Throughout my career, my biggest obstacle has been that I've always been viewed as something of an outsider. When I came from the sports division to the *Today* show, I was the "sports guy." When I came from the *Today* show to the entertainment division, I was the "news guy." When I came to oversee the Television Group, I was the "network guy." I think I overcame those perceptions by working hard, doing a good job, and showing the people I worked with that I cared about them. I almost don't mind being the outsider; outside eyes are fresh eyes, and they give you a different perspective.

As we mature and go through different life experiences, though, I believe our definitions of success change. I used to measure success much more in professional terms; now personal success is just as important to me. Ultimately, success does have something to do with winning. Sports is an instance where winning is really the only success. Otherwise, why keep score? If I didn't win my tennis match, I don't think I succeeded, no matter how well I played. And television is an industry where success is more often than not measured by whether you're number one. But if you're showing improvement and moving in the right direction, that can be a measure of success as well. Success isn't *always* about winning; it's about accomplishing things that help people, help the company, and help you.

My personal definition of success would be winning with class. I think everybody defines success a little differently; there's no right or wrong for any one person. Everyone has a different level of success that satisfies him individually. With luck, that's a level of achievement that individual is comfortable with. You can be just as successful raising your children as you can be doing something in the workplace; both of those can lead to success, and both are equally important.

One principle I've held on to throughout my life is never being afraid to make a mistake, but never making the same mistake twice. I believe you can take risks and try new things and not be afraid and not be beholden to anything that's come before.

There's a degree of risk taking in everything. If you're not willing to put yourself out there and take a chance—to go for it, to win the match—you probably won't have the kind of ultimate success you'd wish for. If you're not willing to try something new on the *Today* show, to try a new kind of programming in prime time, you may never succeed in network television. It's not for the faint of heart; you have to take risks. I think you have to be willing to fail. But if you're not afraid of failing, then you probably never will fully succeed.

I believe in luck, of course. I think there's a degree of luck in all of this. But you've got to prepare for luck. You can't just count on it. Great preparation puts you in the position to enjoy that luck and succeed even more.

I was diagnosed with colon cancer when I was thirty-one, and battling cancer really gives you perspective. When the key is not fear of failure but fear of death, it makes you realize what is important—that it's only television, and you can't control everything. Nothing matters if you don't have your health.

There is a downside to success, of course. I think we live in a culture that likes to build people up and then tear them down. Success sometimes leads to jealousy; it can make you a big target and then force you to come to grips with it and learn how to deal with it.

My one success in life that stands above all the others? My four kids.

CHAPTER 22

• • •

Cathleen Black

PRESIDENT, HEARST MAGAZINES

Dubbed the "First Lady of American Magazines" by the *Financial Times*, Cathleen Black is the president of Hearst Magazines, a division of the Hearst Corporation and one of the world's largest publishers of monthly magazines.

Black manages the financial performance and development of some of the industry's best-known titles, including *Cosmopolitan, Esquire, Good Housekeeping, Harper's Bazaar,* and *O, The Oprah Magazine*. She also oversees nearly two hundred international editions of those magazines in more than one hundred countries.

In 2007 Black wrote *BASIC BLACK: The Essential Guide for Getting Ahead at Work (and in Life)*, in which she explains how she achieved "the 360° life"—a blend of professional accomplishment and personal contentment—and how women can seize opportunity in the workplace. The book reached No. 1 on the *Wall Street Journal* Business Books list and *BusinessWeek* Best Seller List, and No. 3 on the *New York Times* Business Books list.

Black made publishing history in 1979, becoming the first female publisher of a weekly consumer magazine, *New York*. She is widely credited with the success of *USA Today*, where for eight years (starting in 1983) she was first president and then publisher, as well as a board member and executive vice president/marketing for Gannett, its parent company. In 1991, Black became president and CEO of the Newspaper Association of America, the industry's largest trade group, where she served for five years before joining Hearst.

Black is among a handful of women that have appeared on *Fortune* magazine's "50 Most Powerful Women in American Business" list each year since it debuted in 1998. She has also been included on *Forbes* magazine's list of "The 100 Most Powerful Women" and *Crain's* list of New York City's "100 Most Influential Women in Business."

Cathleen Black is a woman who leveraged natural-born leadership skills to establish herself as a top CEO in the male-dominated corporate world. She thrives on competing against all comers in the workplace and refuses to accept the very notion of limitations. The corporate ladder was a natural for Black: Job titles helped her measure her progress in clear and unambiguous terms, and as she moved higher, Black found her new challenges and opportunities continually energizing. Black's relentless optimism, determination, and ability not to take obstacles too personally are the keys to her leadership style. Throughout her career, Black has challenged the status quo at every turn and continues to pave the way for future generations of women.

"THE KEY TO SUCCESS—AT LEAST FOR ME—IS RELENTLESS OPTIMISM, DETERMINATION, AND NOT TAKING THINGS PERSONALLY. I'VE ALWAYS TAKEN THINGS SERIOUSLY. INSECURE PEOPLE TAKE THINGS PERSONALLY."

I grew up on the South Side of Chicago. There were six houses on our block, three of which faced one another, and Lake Michigan was at the end of the block. So we had sort of a private beach. More important, there was a country club within walking distance. I spent practically all of my living, breathing hours outside of school there, horseback riding, playing tennis, swimming, and generally having fun.

I especially loved riding. The horse shows were my favorite. A girlfriend of mine once said to me, "Cathie, I'm a much better technical rider than you are. But somehow, when you're in front of that judge in the horse show ring, you look like you're riding on top of the world." So I guess I've never really been afraid of competition; I relish it. And yet I'm not consumed by it.

When I came home one day and told my parents I wanted to go to Marycrest College in Iowa, my father looked at me like I had rocks in my head. My father wasn't Catholic, but my mother was, and we children attended Catholic schools; we felt a lot of pressure to go to a Catholic college. I can remember my father saying, "Cathie, you don't want to do that." He always had a bigger vision for me; he felt I should be exposed to a larger universe, at least geographically. So I went to college in Washington, D.C., which was a great decision. Though I'm not sure I could have articulated it at the time, I think I began to have a bigger vision for myself during my time there.

The most transforming moment of my life came during my sophomore year, when I learned about the opportunity to spend junior year abroad, which I found very exciting. I remember saying to my father that I was tired of nerds, nuns, and girls. I had gone to an all girls' high school and was at an all girls' college. I wanted to spend my junior year abroad. So I affiliated with Loyola University of Chicago, which had an extension center in Rome with about a hundred and fifty kids from colleges all over the United States. For me it was a singularly unbelievable ten-month experience. I loved every minute of it. It was the first time I'd been in a college class with guys, and I loved debating with them. Everything was an adventure. We traveled every weekend, and we took long vacations, with a ton of kids piling into a car or hitchhiking. At the end of the school year, a girl from Mobile, Alabama, and I and another guy even hitched from Rome to Northern Ireland.

For me, these were the building blocks for a life that was going to be played on a bigger stage. I never really thought I would come back to Chicago. I was always attracted to the media world. I don't come from that world at all, but I was very drawn to New York. I was dying to have an apartment and a job and roommates. I couldn't understand why anybody wanted to go to graduate school or, God knows, why anybody wanted to get married at that time. For me, it was really an adventure. I had a voracious appetite for exploring life. Once, when she was visiting me in New York, my mother and I were talking about my life. She was a pretty traditional housewife. She said, "Honey, you want to get married?" I said, "I don't know what I want, but I want a really exciting life." She had this look on her face, and I guess that was sort of a slap in the face to her—as though she hadn't had the chance to have that life. But I just had this bug in me; I wanted my life to be really exciting.

My first job was in advertising sales at *Holiday* magazine. I loved it. It was no big deal, but it paid more per week than a comparable job at Condé Nast, one of our archcompetitors. My boss was female and about ten years older than me. After five or six months at the job, I remember thinking, "I can do this. I'm good at this. Someday I want Phyllis's job."

A couple of months later, she resigned. I went in and pitched our publisher for her job. He said, "Well, we're certainly considering you for it, Cathie." I said, "I have a pretty good idea of what Phyllis makes, and I would want to be paid the same thing." The man almost had a coronary on the spot. I got the job, and though I didn't get what she made, I got a hell of a lot more than I was making.

For women of my generation, it was much more looking at the person in the next office or the next level up the food chain, thinking, "I can do that job. I'm just as smart as they are." For our male counterparts at the time and for many years later—and some even today—that sense that they're competing not among their own crowd but across a very diverse group of competitive, capable people was a huge shock for them. "I've been here that long—I should be getting that job," they always thought. But all of a sudden there was a woman saying, "Well, guess what? I've been here that long, too." Or maybe, "I haven't been here that long, but I'm doing a better job than you are."

For women, I think it was much more sequential, looking at that next job. At twenty-four I wasn't necessarily thinking, "I really want to be the president of Hearst Magazines." I don't think, frankly, that thought ever crossed my mind. But I did think about being advertising director of *New York* magazine when I first joined the ad staff there. Then I went to *Biz*, and I wanted to be the ad director there. Titles were important to me—they were a kind of recognition of how you were holding up the masthead. Then you say, "I want to be a publisher. What do I have to do to become a publisher?"

I joined *USA Today* when it was about a year old. The idea of helping to establish *USA Today* as the nation's newspaper was a very compelling proposition. Al Neuharth, the paper's chairman, CEO, and founder, was determined that we could really make it successful. It was tough. We flew around the country constantly to meet with our advertisers and got beaten up by skeptical ad agencies, especially in New York, where the coverage was set by *The New York Times* and *The Wall Street Journal*. The toughest thing was that you had one negative headline after another about our newspaper. But you know what? Our clients loved us. They couldn't have cared less about *The New York Times* or *The Wall Street Journal*. They were in Cleveland, they were in Denver, they were in Dallas, they were in Chicago, they were in L.A., they were in San Francisco— where the whole world did not revolve around the *Times* or the *Journal*. They loved *USA Today*. They thought their ad was like a billboard, and we positioned the newspaper very quickly to take advantage.

Within about four years, we carried five thousand advertising pages!

The *USA Today* experience was especially transforming for me. Those David and Goliath situations make you work harder—make you wonder, "How can we outsmart the competition?"

Years ago, someone asked me, "You're in the media? How can you stand that?" I said, "How can I stand it? I *love* it. It's fun every day. It's different every hour. I'm with interesting, smart, creative people who challenge me all the time." Would I have succeeded in a cosmetics company or Disney or on Wall Street? Probably. But this is the route I took, and I've been very lucky.

• • •

CHAPTER 23

Gary Bettman

COMMISSIONER OF THE NATIONAL HOCKEY LEAGUE

Gary Bettman is the first and only commissioner in the history of the National Hockey League. Since his tenure began in 1993, total league revenue has grown from $732 million to $2.6 billion.

In 2005, Bettman presided over a bitter lockout that resulted in the NHL being the only professional sports league in North America to lose an entire season to a labor dispute. In resolving the dispute, Bettman and the league's board of governors modernized and revolutionized the economic system under which the league operates, creating a partnership with the players through a new collective bargaining agreement that makes a shared objective of increasing hockey-related revenue.

In concert with the hockey operations department and the competition committee, Bettman has been a driving force in implementing several changes to the rules and in adding fan-friendly game elements, including the "shootout," introduced in the 2005–2006 season, which guarantees a winner in every regular season game.

Before being named NHL commissioner, Bettman served twelve

years with the National Basketball Association (NBA), attaining the position of senior vice president and general counsel. Before that, he was associated with the New York law firm of Proskauer Rose Goetz & Mendelsohn.

For Gary Bettman, leadership is advocacy. From his early days at Proskauer Rose through his appointment in 1993 as the first commissioner of the NHL, Bettman has always seen his role as serving the best interests of his clients. Bettman's expertise in managing complex organizations—a skill he learned under David Stern at the NBA—has allowed him to unlock the potential of the NHL and increase revenue threefold during his fifteen-year tenure. During that time, he has faced difficult choices, particularly when he had to draw a hard line in the sand to save the sport by canceling the entire 2005–2006 season to make necessary economic changes to the league. Bettman's iron will comes from his understanding of the true role of the advocate: doing the right thing.

"SUCCESS MEANS BEING WILLING TO WORK HARD, HAVING STRONG VALUES AND PRINCIPLES YOU ADHERE TO, AND BEING WILLING TO LOOK AT THE BROADER PICTURE. IT'S NOT ABOUT YOU. IT'S ABOUT THE GREATER GOOD."

I didn't have a prototypical *Father Knows Best* family. Most of my childhood was spent in a single-parent home, which was more unusual then. My parents got divorced when I was four years old, and later my father passed away. My mother remarried eight years later. So I never got the traditional pass-through of sports history from generation to generation. Maybe that's why I gravitated toward expansion teams as a kid: the Mets and the Jets and later the Islanders and the Nets.

I went to lots of games on my own. I used to take the subway from Queens to Madison Square Garden and do my homework up in the rafters while I waited for the games to start. I also played sports in the schoolyard, the way all kids did, but when I was growing up, there weren't a lot of organized sports in the New York City school system. I moved to the suburbs halfway through high school, and I played soccer. But I've always loved hockey. There is no better sporting event.

Until I got to high school, I wasn't a particularly stellar student. No doubt my teachers would have accused me of being an underachiever. By the time I got to high school, though, I understood the importance of achieving goals, of working hard, of getting into a good college, of learning for the sake of learning.

I went to college at the Cornell University School of Industrial and Labor Relations. The Ivy League universities aren't generally known for big-time collegiate sports, but Cornell has been a perennial top ten national power in hockey. When I arrived there, they'd recently come off an undefeated season and a national title. Despite my desire to follow or create my own traditions when it came to the pro sports teams, Cornell had such a rich hockey tradition that it was easy to become a passionate hockey fan. I went to every game at Lynah Rink and slept out on "hockey line" for season tickets all four years at Cornell.

Cornell was great for me because as long as I can remember, I wanted to be a lawyer. (It was also great because it's where I met the woman to whom I've been married for more than thirty years.) I can't tell you precisely why I found being a lawyer so compelling. I think it was my mother's influence: Her father had been a successful lawyer in New York, and that was something I'd heard a lot about. I also guess the notion of looking at both sides of an issue—being an advocate, articulating positions—became more and more attractive to me. I debated in high school, and I always felt that I could hold my own in discussions, so it seemed to be the logical place for me to gravitate. You've got to have a passion for anything if you're going to try to be successful at it.

I enrolled in the School of Industrial and Labor Relations at Cornell—not so much because I was interested in the labor movement as because this was one of the best, if not the best, pre-law curricula any college offered. The courses were primarily the social sciences, focusing on collective bargaining, dispute resolution, and organizational behavior. One of the courses I took was a seminar in the management of complex organizations. I did my thesis on a well-chronicled and complex organization: organized crime!

After Cornell, I attended law school at New York University, and then I got my first job at a large law firm, Proskauer Rose. Subsequently, I was given the opportunity to join the NBA as a lawyer.

When I was at the NBA in the early 1980s, there was a real debate over which was the stronger sport, basketball or hockey. When I joined the NBA, the company had just twenty-five employees, including support staff. Sports was just emerging as a major entertainment business. Media, marketing, and licensing opportunities were all expanding: It was the beginning of the new era.

Every business has its own characteristics, its own assets, its own strengths. Probably more important than anything else, what I learned by being at the NBA and working with David Stern was how to manage an organization as complex as a professional sports league.

Sports leagues have the characteristics of most major entertainment companies, but they also operate with a board that's different from most corporate boards. The goals and objectives of a traditional corporation are to build the organization and drive profits and value for shareholders. In a sports league, the board has an objective—to grow asset value, become stronger, and put out the best product. At the same time, however, each member of the board—each team— is trying to beat every other member. And since each member has its own territory, the needs and opportunities are quite varied.

When I became commissioner, I believed that the sport's footprint in U.S. markets wasn't as large as it could be—that the sport wasn't being exposed as widely as it should be. I saw a huge opportunity for growth, using great players and a great game as the foundation.

As a lawyer, I'm always thinking about how to serve a client. You put yourself aside and do what the client needs, within legal and ethical boundaries, of course. You're an advocate for your client; you're passionate about your client. That's the way I've always approached this game and my role as commissioner, which has been remarkably challenging and exciting. My client is first and foremost the game—and the owners and the fans and the business.

It was particularly challenging, to say the least, in 2004–2005, when we had no choice but to cancel our entire season. Based on the prior ten years—particularly the prior five—I knew the game would have trouble surviving if we didn't fix our business problems. I believed we owed it to our fans, and to the game, to make things right. We'd been treading water for too long, and that was no longer good enough. If we were going to move forward at all, we had to have a more solid foundation. Our fans understood what we were doing; they wanted things fixed, too. It wasn't something anyone wanted to do, but we had to do what was necessary to accomplish our objective. You've got to believe in doing the right thing, and you've got to have faith in your convictions. What's the point in taking half measures? You can never be successful unless you give it your all.

Hockey has the best, most connected, most passionate fans in all of sports. They proved it when they came back to our game in record numbers. That first season back was all about our fans; it wasn't about growing the game, it wasn't about reaching out to new fans. It was about reconnecting with our fans, who'd stood with us and supported us.

I know not everybody views it that way. Some people look at the work stoppage itself and think, "We won, they lost." That's the way most people think about competition: You win and somebody else loses. I've never viewed it that way. Success is a win-win. I look at success as a matter of having important goals and objectives and working hard to accomplish them. When you can work hard to achieve the results consistent with those objectives, then you're having success.

CHAPTER 24

• • •

Jan-Patrick Schmitz

PRESIDENT AND CHIEF EXECUTIVE OFFICER, MONTBLANC NORTH AMERICA

Jan-Patrick Schmitz became president and CEO of Montblanc North America at the age of twenty-nine. His ascent to the head of the company in 2003 came at a pivotal point in the one-hundred-year history of the luxury brand. That same year, under Schmitz's leadership, Montblanc opened its largest boutique in the world on New York's famed Madison Avenue.

Schmitz began his career at Montblanc in 1994, honing his keen business acumen and innate appreciation for the luxury goods market initially as president and CEO of Montblanc Japan, then as head of global supply chain management at Montblanc's international headquarters in Hamburg, Germany.

Jan-Patrick Schmitz has always been driven to succeed, to do everything faster than anyone else. Hearing Schmitz tell his story, one finds it easy to understand how he knew from childhood that he would run a company someday. His leadership skills were innate, and he was driven to succeed at an early age. If you worked hard and played by the rules, he saw, it wasn't

about whom you knew, but about how much you knew. Schmitz was fo-
cused and stayed the course. He found his path naturally, and while he
(like his father before him) urges his own children to find balance in life, it's
hard to imagine him leading his own life any other way.

**"IN THE END, I THINK YOU'RE SUCCESSFUL IF
YOU'RE SATISFIED AND GRATIFIED BY WHAT
YOU'VE ACHIEVED, AND IF YOU TAKE TIME TO
ENJOY THE REWARDS OF YOUR SUCCESS."**

I always wanted to be a leader. As far back as the sixth grade, I
wanted to be the first and the best; not getting an A in every class
was simply inconceivable. My mother often reminds me that when
I had a class assignment, I insisted on signing my papers with my
name followed by the title "Director." It got me in a lot of trouble
with my teachers and generated a lot of phone calls to my house—
but I never gave it up.

I am self-driven to excel. My goal was to finish school at the head of
my class, to study economics at school, and to work in a management
position where I would be responsible and in charge. Ironically, during
my undergrad years, my father gently suggested that I slow down and
enjoy life, that I have some fun, find some balance, not get too focused
on my studies. At that time, I didn't want to hear him; today, I realize
that he was right and regret that I didn't take his advice.

I always believed that speed is important, so I completed my education faster than most others and graduated with an MBA, summa cum
laude, at age twenty-four.

I majored in corporate finance, in the belief that everything in business could be explained and driven by numbers and by logic. One of
my professors, a teacher of organizational behavior, opened my eyes
to a very different, yet crucial, perspective. He encouraged me to look
at the "emotional" aspect of business, which cannot be measured in
dollars and cents, units and percentages. Hard facts are important, but

soft facts—the human factor—should enter into every decision as an essential element of success. After all, only 20 percent of business is hardware—meaning distribution, communication, product, and other tangible assets. Roughly 80 percent of business is software—including people.

Being a good leader and being successful are obviously related. Like a ship, which can have only one captain, an organization can have only one leader to motivate and inspire, chart the direction, decide on the destination, and get everyone there in time. Ultimately, to be successful, leaders need to listen carefully, analyze issues, and understand requirements and opportunities. They must develop a conscious vision of their direction and work diligently to make it a reality. While the development of a business plan can be a lonely process, being able to deliver it requires the ability to empower and motivate the organization—your people—in order to get it done.

Early in my career, I was sent to Japan to meet with a senior manager of our joint venture partner. We were not receiving certain crucial reports from that operation. His command of the English language was very limited, and communicating with him was difficult. It was the middle of June—the rainy season, very hot and unpleasant. We sat in his tiny office for four days before he finally agreed to provide us the information in a timely fashion—but only if we agreed that the report headers would read "MB Division" instead of "Montblanc Japan." My initial, subconscious response was: "I don't care what you title them as long as you give us the information." We recessed, and I thought about it; when we reconvened, he was stunned that I denied his request. It was obvious to me that he didn't value our brand enough to develop our business and that if I agreed to his conditions, the problems would escalate. We needed to make a structural change.

After carefully analyzing our business model in Japan, I developed a precise understanding of what was needed there. One of my strategies was to build department store distribution. When I met with the senior director of one of the leading department stores, I presented my case. Being young, aggressive, and somewhat hungry, I explained why he should increase our representation and selling space. He made it clear that he wouldn't entertain my proposition. After that initial encounter, I met with him several times a year, from 1996 to 2002, and discussed the same issues. Each time, he turned me down.

Defeat is a painful experience, but it can also be a learning experience. For me, defeat only refuels my energy; it motivates me to go back, evaluate and analyze the obstacles, and try even harder the next time.

It took me some time to understand and appreciate the cultural ideology of "seniority and relationships" in Japan. The director of stores was senior to me, but I had not shown the required respect for him or the patience to build a relationship with him. After six years of meetings, wherein I developed and nurtured our relationship, I finally succeeded in convincing him to expand our business. I learned that not every culture does business in the same way and that we need to understand and accept cultural differences in order to make changes.

At the age of twenty-nine, I became chief executive officer of Montblanc Japan. I brought my family there—and brought change as well.

I followed three basic principles to achieve success:

First, listen carefully before forming your opinion.

Second, don't be afraid to make decisions. Decisions are often made without complete information; risks are to be expected, an essential part of achieving growth and success.

Finally, be persistent, remain true to your moral values, and stand your ground. It's like sailing: Strong winds will push you forward, but they can also take you off course. Only when you're strong enough to hold your course will you arrive at your destination.

How did I arrive where I am now, leading Montblanc North America? How do people achieve a leadership role? It surely requires certain skills and experience, but there's also the Darwinian theory that the strongest and the fastest will survive and advance. This is true for any business as well as for the individuals managing it.

Once you achieve what you set out to accomplish, whether personally or professionally, it is intensely gratifying—but it's a hunt that never really ends. Every achievement is just another step on the journey; every success is only the beginning of the next challenge.

I don't think I've taken a break—a "time-out"—since sixth grade. That doesn't mean I don't take vacations, but basically, I've never taken a mental sabbatical. I'm always "hunting" rather than doing something with no definite purpose. In sixth grade, my objective was to graduate at the top of my class (though I often wonder why that was so crucial for me at that age). Today, having come full circle, I'm teaching my children to find balance in their lives—that, yes, you should strive for excellence and achievement but also enjoy the journey along the way. In the end, I think you're successful if you're satisfied and gratified by what you have achieved—but you also take time to enjoy the rewards of your success.

Do-Gooders

CHAPTER 25

• • •

Craig Newmark

FOUNDER AND CHAIRMAN, CRAIGSLIST

What began as a small San Francisco Web site to inform friends about local events has in a few years become nothing short of an international phenomenon. Craig Newmark, founder and chairman of the online classified advertising site craigslist.org, is one of the few dot-com success stories with a happy ending.

Newmark, an eighteen-year veteran of IBM, started the site as a hobby in 1995. Four short years later, the list had surpassed a million page views a month, prompting Newmark to quit his day job and incorporate as a for-profit.

Today, craigslist's fifty million users click on an estimated thirty million classified postings each month at more than 500 sites in all fifty states and over fifty countries around the world, generating more than twelve billion page views. The privately held company makes all its money—some estimates put 2005 revenues in the neighborhood of $20 million—by charging below-market fees for job ads in ten cities and for brokered apartment listings in New York City.

In 2000, Newmark founded the Craigslist Foundation to provide knowledge, resources, and visibility to the next generation of nonprofit leaders. The foundation applies the spirit and values of craigslist.org to the nonprofit world; where craigslist.org is about "people helping people," Newmark says, the Craigslist Foundation is about "helping people help."

With an unwavering moral compass and a business plan based on "doing the right thing," Newmark is part of a new breed of social entrepreneurs shunning excessive profit in favor of social change. What distinguishes Newmark from the majority of dot-com entrepreneurs is his steadfast refusal to maximize his commercial success. From day one, he's refused to charge a registration fee and will not allow corporate advertisements on the site. Though he considers the word idealist "too big" for what he's doing, his faith in humanity and inherent trust in people continue to fuel the success of craigslist.

"SUCCESS, TO ME, MEANS DOING SOMETHING MEANINGFUL AND GETTING SOME COMBINATION OF SPIRITUAL, SOCIAL, AND FINANCIAL REWARD IN RETURN, IN WHATEVER MEASURE FITS WITH YOUR OWN VALUES."

When I was a kid, I wanted to go into paleontology and study dinosaurs. Being a kid who's into dinosaurs makes a lot of sense—what kid isn't into dinosaurs? How I got from paleontology to the next phase—physics—is something I can't explain. It wasn't linear. It was a discontinuity.

Actually, I really had no clear idea at all what I would end up doing. At first I was interested in theoretical physics, but theoretical physics means sitting around musing about the origins of the universe, string theory, and so on. That's a very confined academic life, and I realized that one day I'd need a job. Then I went into computer science and artificial intelligence, which is the concept of thinking machines. I was hoping to do significant work that was related to computer science, so I went into computer systems work. I really had no ambition. Even right now, I don't have much ambition.

I was very excited and passionate about physics and computer science. I still am, but these days it's all just expressed by reading books on cosmology and physics and quantum mechanics and complexity theory.

I can't really explain how my career progressed. It just sort of happened. I just kind of followed my muse—pursued stuff I was interested in. I wanted a practical career, and the computer systems work I did was challenging and rewarding. When I got out of school, I did some systems work for IBM in Boca Raton, but then I went into the IBM field, where I focused more on consulting. After that, I went to Charles Schwab in 1993, and I got more into systems architecture and the Internet. At the very end of my time at Schwab, I figured, "Well, I see all these people helping each other; I should do that a little." So I started giving people advice, helping them with technology problems.

At that point I started my contracting career, and that worked out pretty well.

I didn't have any significant early influences, nothing beyond my early childhood values from parents and religious school. The deal is that as things are rotated around in my life, I just come back to basics—the golden rule, do unto others as you want them to do to you. Treat other people well, and give people a break. I have a general sense of what is right.

Basically, I set my moral compass early on, and that dictated my future actions. But only in running craigslist was I asked to articulate what craigslist is about. I just rediscovered the values I've always been acting on. I just made them more conscious.

I had no real master plan for craigslist. It just came out of the work I was doing. There was no pivotal moment, no light bulb that went on, as when an inventor comes up with a brilliant solution to a problem after a lot of hard thought. Our commercial success has been a big surprise. As a result, I'm living fairly well. Not "crazy" well—I don't *want* to live that well. I have a small house that works for me.

We started with some cool events in San Francisco, and then people asked for more, and I followed through. Over time, I made it a real company. Now, as a team, we listen to people, we do what seems right, and then we listen some more. It's a culture of trust: I believe that people are overwhelmingly trustworthy. That's what helps me feel comfortable giving more and more control over our site to the people who use it.

People say that craigslist itself has had a big positive effect on the world. Maybe so, but I can't take any credit for that—because craigslist is run by the people who use it. What people do with craigslist is up to them; it's organic by nature.

When I was young, in my late teens and early twenties, I'd say I was somewhat idealistic, but in a half-assed way. But people grow, especially when they have to focus on the daily business of life, and I've found that following through with what I believe in has helped craigslist have an effect. Now it seems right to keep following through.

I got up early this morning, and I've already done an enormous amount of customer service. Customer service reminds me of what my values are, of what's really important to me. I like to take real action in my work, even down to the level of helping other people with job listings. In certain respects I'm kind of lazy, so I try to do things to persuade and help other people change the world.

Success, to me, means doing something meaningful and getting some combination of spiritual, social, and financial reward in return, in whatever measure fits with your own values. All of us decide which of those values is most important to us, but once you've decided that, you decide how much of those rewards you need.

For me, this means continuing what we've been doing. For example, recently we added a hundred new cities. I've already seen on blogs that people are excited about the new cities. We've helped people out a great deal; the site has built a great deal of "social capital," which is a term in common usage now. It basically means that craigslist—and I guess, to a lesser extent, myself—has a fair amount of respect as good guys trying hard to do the right thing, and now and then try to help out in other ways. And that feels pretty good.

I wouldn't use the word *idealism* to describe the kind of work craigslist is doing. To me, this isn't idealism. That's much too big a word. This is just trying to do the right thing every day.

CHAPTER 26

• • •

Richard Holbrooke

FORMER U.S. AMBASSADOR TO THE UNITED NATIONS / SPECIAL REPRESENTATIVE FOR AFGHANISTAN AND PAKISTAN

On January 29, 2009, Ambassador Richard Holbrooke was named special representative for Afghanistan and Pakistan in the new Obama Administration.

Previously, Holbrooke held the position of vice chairman of Perseus LLC, a leading private equity firm in New York, since 2001. Holbrooke served as U.S. ambassador to the United Nations from 1999 to 2001, during which period he was also a member of President Bill Clinton's cabinet. Prior to that government service, he had been vice chairman of Credit Suisse First Boston since 1996, and, a managing director of Lehman Brothers from 1985–1993. As assistant secretary of state for Europe from 1994–1996, he was the chief architect of the 1995 Dayton peace agreement that ended the war in Bosnia, for which he received the first of several Nobel Peace Prize nominations.

He later served as President Clinton's special envoy to Bosnia and Kosovo and special envoy to Cyprus on a pro bono basis while a private citizen. From 1993 to 1994, he was the U.S. ambassador to Germany.

Holbrooke served as the assistant secretary of state for East Asian and Pacific affairs during the Carter administration, overseeing U.S. relations with China at the time Sino-American relations were normalized in December 1978.

After joining the Foreign Service in 1962, Holbrooke served in Vietnam, including a tour of duty in the Mekong Delta for the Agency for International Development. He served in the Johnson White House in the late 1960s, focusing primarily on the war. He wrote one volume of the Pentagon Papers and was a member of the American delegation to the Vietnam peace talks in Paris.

Richard Holbrooke was destined to "make a difference." His father wanted him to make a difference through medicine and science, but Holbrooke was interested in history and wanted to make a difference through diplomacy. Holbrooke developed his own innovative approach to diplomatic problem solving, combining scientific methodology with an extensive knowledge and deep understanding of history. Holbrooke's diplomatic career provided him a front row seat to history, from Vietnam and the Johnson White House to the Pentagon Papers to Bosnia.

"FAILURE IS A GREAT TEACHER. PEOPLE WHO ARE TRYING TO LEARN HOW TO SUCCEED SHOULD STUDY FAILURE MORE OFTEN."

A life fully lived cannot be planned. Within general goals, you should be open to unexpected possibilities. As Louis Pasteur observed (and this was my father's favorite quotation), "Chance favors the prepared mind." When I look back on my life, it seems as if it had a clear flow—in T. S. Eliot's words, "The past has a different pattern." Kierkegaard put it even more clearly: "Life can only be understood backwards, but it must be lived forwards." At the time, of course, there was no apparent pattern.

With this in mind, let me begin with a close, enduring friendship that shaped my life, although at the time it was just a high school friendship. My best friend in high school was David Rusk. He was editor, and I was sports editor, of the *Scarsdale High School Maroon*. When my own father died in 1957, his parents, Dean and Virginia Rusk, became kind of surrogate parents to me. His father was then president of the Rockefeller Foundation, and I had never met anyone like him—a former assistant secretary of state, confidant of General [George] Marshall, and so on. In our senior year, Dean Rusk gave a breakfast speech to our class. "You should think about public service, perhaps in the Foreign Service, when you graduate college," he said. I knew what a diplomat was, but that was the first time I ever heard of the Foreign Service.

In 1961, Dean Rusk became secretary of state under a charismatic young president. It was the first time I had ever known anyone who was famous, and it made a big impression on me. At that point, my life goal was to be a journalist. I was editor in chief of my college newspaper, the *Brown Daily Herald*. My role models were Abe Rosenthal and James Reston of *The New York Times*. I worked for the *Times* in the summer of 1961 in New York as a news clerk. Even more memorably, I had been hired as a kind of a gofer for a week in May 1960 during the ill-fated Paris summit with Eisenhower, Khrushchev, and Harold Macmillan. In an act of bravado, the *Brown Daily Herald* sent me to Paris to "cover" the summit, and the *Times* offered me $10 a day to fetch coffee and save seats at press conferences for their famed reporters. The summit, so full of hope, collapsed on its opening day because of the U-2 spy plane incident, but that week in Paris was my first direct exposure to both great journalists and historic events, and it made a lasting impression on me.

My father, an idealistic refugee from Lenin's Soviet Union, had always told me that I had to make a contribution to society. He was a doctor, and he hoped I would go into medicine or medical research. He wanted me—even expected me—to win a Nobel Prize in medicine, chemistry, or physics; how astonished he would have been to learn that when I was nominated for a Nobel, it was for peace. If I was asked what his greatest lesson was, I would say that it was to be intellectually curious, to be interested in everything. And to try to make a difference. I was also taught by my father that intellect and ideas were more important than connections or networking or wealth or social position. I was always pretty intellectually aggressive (and, some might say, socially inept). I was told at an early age that ideas were what mattered most. It was a classic New York Upper West Side ethos, although I thought the whole world was that way.

I entered Brown on a math/physics Alfred P. Sloan National Merit Scholarship after doing very well on my SATs. I think I got an 800 in math—hard to believe today, when I can't remember any higher math. I did almost as well in English. I stayed in math/physics for only about three semesters, but science was an excellent discipline for other things. It gave me an understanding of scientific methodology, as well as an approach to problem solving, which I much prefer to the legalistic approach more common in Washington. I see science as dynamic; law is more static, more based on the use and meaning of carefully drafted words. So in my sophomore year, I switched my major to history. That combination, science and history, was critical for me.

My family could not imagine me being a diplomat. For one thing, my parents, who had fled Hitler and Stalin, were convinced that anti-Semitism ruled the world. They couldn't conceive of the possibility that somebody from a Jewish background could succeed in such a WASP domain. I vividly remember my Swiss-German grandmother saying, "It's impossible for you to be a diplomat." I said, "Why?" She said, "Because you're Jewish." I said something like, "What do you mean? I am an American." But of course my mother's family had been forced to flee Hamburg in 1933 in order to survive, after having been loyal Germans and successful businessmen for a century. (My grandfather had won the Iron Cross fighting for the kaiser in World War I.)

When I graduated in 1962, the *Times*—my first goal—did not offer me a permanent job. But because of the influence of Dean Rusk, I took the Foreign Service written exam and passed it. Then I went to Washington to take the oral exam in front of three old (they were probably in their mid-fifties!) Foreign Service officers. I expected weeks of delay, but to my amazement, they called me back in the room right after the interview and said, "We're going to offer you a job." With no other prospects, I entered the Foreign Service as a Class 8 officer at the tremendous salary of about $5,500 a year, in July 1962. Less than a year later, after language and area training, I was in Vietnam as part of our provincial aid program.

It's hard to reconstruct today what I was thinking forty-five years ago; unfortunately, I didn't keep a diary. But I had dreams. Like every aspiring diplomat of my generation, I deeply admired George F. Kennan, who was in many ways the greatest American diplomat of the twentieth century. I didn't understand anything about Washington politics or bureaucracies. But to be thrown into Vietnam at twenty-two meant total immersion. Today, a comparable assignment might be Afghanistan, which is where I would ask to go if I were entering the Foreign Service today. In Vietnam in the 1960s, we junior officers saw the most senior American officials under immense stress, not always doing well. And almost everything they believed and told Washington turned out to be wrong. I learned that our senior people didn't know what they were doing, or what was happening, in Vietnam. In that sense, it was a lot like Iraq today. My own career goal at that point was to be an ambassador or undersecretary of state. You couldn't aspire to anything higher than that as a career diplomat.

My first assignment was in the Mekong Delta. It was very nontraditional work, running the rural reconstruction program in a large province. This program was, more famously, known as the pacification program, and although it was based on sound counterinsurgency principles (security, political, and economic programs), it did not work; the South Vietnamese government was too weak and corrupt.

I was married in Saigon in 1964 and moved to Saigon. Our group of young (under thirty) professionals in Vietnam included Frank Wisner, John Negroponte (my roommate for one year), Tony Lake, Les Aspin, Peter Tarnoff, and, oddly, Daniel Ellsberg—an exceptional group by any standards. (Four of us reached cabinet rank, two more to the level of undersecretary of state and defense, and one became the center of a celebrated, and illegal, break-in that led directly to Watergate and the downfall of a president.) The journalists included David Halberstam, Stanley Karnow, Joe Kraft, Neil Sheehan, Johnny Apple, and many

others. They were all high achievers. We knew one another well, and
some enduring friendships resulted.

In 1964, I became staff assistant to General Maxwell Taylor and
then to Henry Cabot Lodge, who was on his second tour as ambassador to Vietnam. At the end of my assignment, the State Department
planned to send me to Vienna as an assistant refugee officer. I was
only twenty-four, but I refused the assignment because I wanted to
stay in Vietnam. I will always remember how negatively the adminis-
trative officer of the embassy in Saigon, John George Bacon, reacted
to this impudent challenge to a personnel decision. "You have a brilliant future ahead of you," he said, "but you will move faster if you
slow down." It reminded me of my favorite war novel, *Catch-22*, which
I always regarded as a book about Vietnam, not World War II.

In 1966, at the age of twenty-five, after over three years in Vietnam, I found myself working in the White House. That was, of course,
another turning point in my life. The first day I was there, Lyndon
Johnson met with us. It was an overwhelming experience. Our small
staff—I worked on a special Vietnam civilian reconstruction task
force headed by R. W. Komer, a presidential assistant—was sitting in
the Cabinet Room, facing LBJ. For some reason, the president started
talking about pork. He had apparently read a cable that said the Viet-
cong had cut Route 4 from Mekong Delta to Saigon and the price
of pork was therefore rising in the capital. He said, in that inimitable
Texas accent, "I know something about pork. When the price of pork
goes up, politicians aren't popular." He turned to his national security
adviser, Walt Rostow, and said, "You've got to get that road open."
Rostow said, "Yes, sir." I was sitting there speechless, amazed at this
strange performance, a kind of Kabuki theater. Rostow couldn't open
(or close) that road; it would open and reopen as the war ebbed and
flowed.

Then LBJ announced that he had this great idea. "In World War
Two," he said, "we had these civil affairs officers, who are now in the
reserves. We should call them back into the service and get them to
help with civil affairs, run Vietnam like we did Japan and Germany."
At that point, I raised my hand. LBJ peered at me over his glasses; he

seemed to be thinking, "Who is this punk?" I said, "You know, Mr. President, sometimes there are limits to what an American can do in a place like Vietnam." There I was, twenty-five years old, talking back to Lyndon Johnson! I must have been nuts. Johnson looked at me with that long, mournful look of his, his earlobes hanging down like a beagle's, almost to his shoulders. And he said, "Well, son, your job is to get rid of those limits." This, in its entirety, was my first conversation with a president.

Slowly, I came to realize that while the commitment to prevent a Communist takeover of Vietnam was valid at the beginning, as it had been in South Korea, the situation was substantially different. Local circumstances really do matter. I began to question our tactics, then our strategy, and finally the commitment itself. To be in your twenties and to know that your superiors don't know what they're doing, to try to figure out what to do about our biggest foreign policy disaster (until Iraq), was an intense educational experience.

My father believed in taking an empirical approach to problems. It could be boiled down to a phrase that Deng Xiaoping used much later: "See truth from facts." In Vietnam, those facts seemed clear: Our involvement there was not going to be a success. The idea put out by conservatives today, that Vietnam was lost because of weak-willed liberals and journalists, is simply wrong. To blame those who accurately saw the problem—I'm not talking about flag burners; I'm talking about serious national security experts and observers who felt the commitment couldn't succeed—is a recipe for further divisions at home and disasters abroad. The American effort was always dependent on the quality of the South Vietnamese government, and this concept—the very heart of America's strategy—was flawed. If the Saigon government had been better, then we—or, more precisely, they—could have succeeded.

Everyone who served in Vietnam came away with a different conclusion and different reactions. To this day, Vietnam still divides people, not only people who served, but also people who weren't there and don't know what it was like. But it is inaccurate to say that the war was lost because of fainthearted liberals. It was lost on the ground, by a weak and corrupt ally and a flawed American military strategy.

In 1966, my old boss, General Maxwell Taylor, introduced me to Robert F. Kennedy, then a New York senator. Bobby, as everyone called him, invited me to Hickory Hill, the famed house in Virginia that served as the de facto headquarters of the Kennedy government-in-exile. I played tennis, swam, and even played touch football. I was dazzled, of course; who wouldn't be, among such glamorous, exciting people? Bobby was my last political hero; I thought he could unite a divided nation. He asked me about Vietnam; I told him that things were going badly and that I was discouraged by my involvement in a war I no longer believed in after working on it for five years. He told me not to quit the government, but to stay and work for what I believed in. We never discussed politics. After he was killed, I had lunch with Michael Forrestal, one of Bobby's close advisers. Mike told me that they had suggested that I be asked to become a member of Bobby's campaign team but that Bobby had said no; it would risk my career, and he didn't want that. If things worked out, he told Forrestal, then we would see. That was another moment that affected my life: Had he asked, I would have gone.

By the beginning of 1968, I had worked in the Johnson White House, written a portion of what later became known as the Pentagon Papers for Les Gelb, who headed the then secret project for Secretary of Defense Robert McNamara. I was in the office of Undersecretary of State Nicholas Katzenbach, still working on Vietnam. (Gelb became one of my closest friends.) The year 1968 was tumultuous, probably the most tumultuous in recent American history. Averell Harriman, then seventy-seven years old, headed the American delegation to the Paris peace talks with North Vietnam, and he made me part of a very small delegation. The experience, while it ended in failure as time ran out on the Johnson administration, was one of the most important of my life. It taught me about negotiations under extreme conditions, at that point where domestic politics, internal bureaucratic warfare, and international diplomacy meet. Harriman's deputy was Cyrus Vance, later to be my boss when he became Jimmy Carter's secretary of state.

Here was a dramatic example of the past having a different pattern: My later work on Bosnia and my association with a future boss can all be traced back to Paris in 1968.

After the election, I went to see Henry Kissinger in the Nixon transition offices at the Pierre Hotel in New York in December, right after Nixon was elected by a very close margin. I had known Kissinger from his visits to Vietnam in 1966 and from the Paris peace talks, when he had been a consultant to the Johnson administration. He was the Republican most privy to the inside secrets of the Johnson negotiations. I was still in Paris with the negotiating delegation, but time was running out for LBJ. Peace in Vietnam would not come for another four years. As we chatted about Vietnam, I said, "Henry, I don't want a job in the Nixon administration." He was startled; he thought everyone coming to the Pierre wanted a job. He asked, "Why?" I said, "Because I don't think I can work for Richard Nixon."

Staying out of the Nixon administration was, as it turned out, another key moment. Some of my friends who did go in, like Tony Lake and Mort Halperin, ended up in bitter battles over Vietnam and Cambodia and were illegally bugged by the Watergate plumbers. Even John Negroponte, who was a close aide to Kissinger after Lake quit, had a huge argument with Kissinger and was exiled to a consular post in Greece. I was lucky to have had the instinct to stay out; I would not have survived and might have been swept up in the drama of Watergate. I went to the Woodrow Wilson School at Princeton for a year as a State Department fellow and pretty much did nothing serious. I was still a career diplomat, but Nixon was president. So I got this idea to do something completely different—to be a Peace Corps country director. With the help of my then boss, Nixon's undersecretary of state, Elliot Richardson, I was sent to Morocco, which turned out to be a terrific job and a timely change of life after seven years in Vietnam.

I had never run an organization before. Now I had two hundred people, Peace Corps volunteers, under me. I lived for two years in an Arab culture. I even celebrated Ramadan, not for the whole month but for several days, just to understand what it was like. (This was in August, when the days were longer and fasting longer.)

In the spring of 1972, I took leave from the Foreign Service and became managing editor of *Foreign Policy* quarterly for five years. That, too, was a strange sort of accident. I had turned down an offer to become the first managing editor of this new quarterly in 1969, while I was at Princeton. I recommended a brilliant friend of mine named John Campbell, who got the job. Then, in the spring of 1971, while I was serving as Peace Corps director in Morocco, I was on a visit to Nepal. One morning in Kathmandu, as I was about to leave for a weeklong trek near Pokaran, the telephone rang. It was Tony Lake, who had entered the Foreign Service with Campbell and me, calling from Washington. "John just died," he said. A few moments later John's wife, Brenda, called. It was an undiagnosed thyroid cancer. Would I come back to speak at the funeral? Of course. I found a plane to New Delhi, then to London, finally to New York. In a daze, I spoke at a service. After it was over, the co-founders of *Foreign Policy*, Warren Manshel and Samuel Huntington, approached me and said they had to speak to me privately—and I realized that I was going to be offered the job again. After a wonderful year and a half in Morocco, I was ready to try something new.

The five years with *Foreign Policy* were another great education in a wholly different area. I learned how to edit, produced a fine quarterly, had a few coups (an interview with George F. Kennan, on the twenty-fifth anniversary of the "X" article, made the front page of *The New York Times*), and met a lot of the national security establishment for the first time. I could write. And for the first time, I could get involved in the national political debate over foreign policy.

In the summer of 1976, Jimmy Carter asked me to come to Atlanta to coordinate national security issues for his campaign. This was my first political experience, and I learned a lot from it. After the election, President-elect Carter wrote me a lovely letter, then called me and asked my advice on personnel decisions. I said, "Mr. President-elect, I would be honored to serve you anywhere, but you have Asia, which has been messed up for years, and I would love to run the East Asian bureau." So I got the job of my dreams, assistant secretary of state for East Asian and Pacific affairs, and was able to expand my Asia experi-

RICHARD HOLBROOKE   167

ence from Vietnam to all of East Asia. A lot of people thought I was too young for the job; at thirty-four, I probably was, but we had a very successful run in East Asia for four years, establishing full diplomatic relations with China and accomplishing many other things.

In 1981, Ronald Reagan arrived in Washington. I was done with public service. I had been divorced and was broke, so broke that if I went to a restaurant and the bill was, say, $30 for two, I was scared that if I had to pick up the bill, I wouldn't be able to pay my AmEx charges at the end of the month. At that point, my early role model, Abe Rosenthal, offered me a job at *The New York Times*, but not at decent pay. Several people I checked with for advice, notably Clark Clifford, said, "Try your hand at business. Try to make some money." I said, "I don't know anything about business." And no one would offer me a job. But Jim Johnson, my brilliant Princeton friend who had been Walter Mondale's closest aide, said, "Why don't we form a consulting firm together?" So we created Public Strategies, which allowed me to get out of debt—and actually accumulate some money for the first time in my life.

I acquired a few clients early on. Our clients were good, but it didn't feel right. The Washington consultant game wasn't quite as nasty or corrupt as it is today, but it was essentially the same. I don't mean literally corrupt; I mean aesthetically, ethically unattractive. Jim and I had agreed never to do anything that required us to register or act as lobbyists. And we stuck to it, never approaching any government official on behalf of a client. We gave strategic advice—but still did not like the work.

My favorite client, from the beginning, was Lehman Brothers. They gave me an office to use when I was in New York (I still lived in Washington). It was actually three cardboard boxes with a phone on top of them in the office of a man who became another close friend, Vincent Mai. The consultancy with Lehman Brothers grew into a full-time job by 1985, when Lehman bought Public Strategies, and I could get out of being a consultant. I suddenly had what I considered real money for the first time in my life—enough money to feel secure, at least by my standards. If I had enough money to buy any book in a bookstore, I was happy and thought I was rich enough. That changed everything.

However, I worked with people on Wall Street who were crazed if they got "only" $2 or $3 million bonuses. I didn't understand that. What's the ultimate goal of money? To take care of your children, and then your grandchildren, and to live decently. Money doesn't interest me; it's what you can *do* with money that does. I'm interested in what you can achieve or contribute of significance.

Over the years, I've discovered that you usually can learn more from studying failure than from studying successes. When you study success, you don't really know what the ingredients of success were. Was it brute force? Luck? Skill?

Take the 1962 Cuban missile crisis. To imagine the same crisis in the hands of the Bush team is scary. But was it the great skill of Kennedy and his team that led to its successful resolution? Or was it simply that Khrushchev believed we were truly ready to use force that caused him to back down? This is not to take anything away from Kennedy's performance, which I think ranks among the top diplomatic achievements in American history.

Failure is a great teacher. People who are trying to learn how to succeed should study failure more often. And as they proceed with their careers, they should be sure that their minds are prepared, in case chance should strike. When it all came together for me, in the fourteen weeks of our shuttle diplomacy and the Dayton peace agreement that ended the war in Bosnia, I think I was finally prepared.

CHAPTER 27

• • •

Susan Smith Ellis

CHIEF EXECUTIVE OFFICER, (PRODUCT) RED

Susan Smith Ellis is CEO of (PRODUCT) RED, the groundbreaking initiative founded by Bono and Bobby Shriver that unites the private sector with the public's buying power in an effort to generate a sustainable flow of private sector funds toward the fight to eliminate AIDS in Africa. Since joining the company in 2007, Smith Ellis has focused the company's efforts on building the brand—also known simply as (RED)—creating value for current partners and bringing new brands into the (RED) partner community.

Before joining (RED), Smith Ellis was the executive vice president of the Omnicom Group, the largest communications holding company in the world, with companies operating in the disciplines of advertising, marketing services, specialty communications, interactive/digital media, and media-buying services. Smith Ellis was also president and CEO of Team Omnicom L.L.C., a purpose-built company created to manage the Bank of America business across the Omnicom network.

Smith Ellis was previously executive vice president at the Diversified Agency Services division of the Omnicom Group. There she was responsible for identifying acquisitions, ascertaining growth opportunities for the network-owned companies, and consulting with DAS agencies on various strategic and business initiatives.

Before DAS, Smith Ellis was an executive vice president at BBDO, the flagship advertising agency of the Omnicom network. During her tenure there, she worked across a number of blue-chip businesses to develop integrated marketing solutions for such clients as Visa, GE, Charles Schwab, Gillette, and PepsiCo.

Susan Smith Ellis has leveraged all the benefits of her career as an independence seeker to become a true do-gooder. At every step of her career, Ellis has picked up new skills and built new relationships. The broad network of ideas and people that she developed over the years is now being brought to bear on the fight against AIDS in Africa.

"EVERYTHING I HAVE DONE UP UNTIL NOW HAS PUT ME AT A TIME AND PLACE WHERE (RED) WOULD COME MY WAY."

I didn't know what I wanted to be when I grew up, and to some degree I still don't. I've always wanted to do so many things; I often wished I could have more than one life so I'd have time to do it all. I would like to be a general contractor. I would like to be a restaurateur. I'd like to be an architect, a rancher, and an interior designer. I'd like to live in Rajasthan.

I suppose the way I've managed to keep myself engaged is to find work that offered a fast pace, a lot of variety, and creative, fun teammates. I like to move from thing to thing; I always have. I'm not someone who would ever drill down and be expert in any one subject. I love people who do that. I love to know them and be around them, but I need a variable diet of ideas and things to do and people to see and meet. I need to have stimuli or I get bored, and I'm not at all good when I am bored.

I have always believed my "success" was unplanned and accidental. But when I look back now, I see a pattern of choices, and each of these built on the other to create a career. I never think of myself as being particularly successful. I am fortunate to live at an interesting intersection of media, business, politics, and academia. Therefore I am often in the company of people who are much more accomplished than I could ever hope to be.

I was the third of four children and the only girl, raised in Ridgewood, New Jersey. I've often joked that living with three brothers was brilliant preparation for the male-dominated world of business. My parents have been an important influence in my life. They taught me about love and loyalty, family, and the value of hard work for its own sake. We were always expected to work. I started babysitting for neighbors when I was twelve. I did chores. My parents were big believers that keeping four kids gainfully employed was a way of keeping us out of trouble. It was also a way of teaching us that making a living isn't always so easy. So I had the work ethic instilled early on.

My parents also inspired in us a sense that we could do whatever we put our minds to. It wasn't anything grandiose, just a belief that if you put your mind to something and were determined and if you worked hard enough, you could succeed at whatever you tried. It truly was a belief in the American dream. They were also utterly democratic: I never had the sense that I had to be deferential to people because of their station in life. I think this served me well, as it made me comfortable with people from all walks of life.

It was in college that I decided I wanted to be an editor. I thought it would bring me in contact with a wide range of people and ideas. I could be a dilettante in the best sense of the word. I also believed that being an editor would give me flexibility—it was something you could move in and out of, a lifetime skill that would give me freedom to have a family or travel, and that I could do as a career or on a freelance basis.

I also wanted to write, but I was reluctant to be so self-disclosing. So I thought of this as a way to be around writers and the whole creative process of book publishing. My first job was working for a publisher.

I was in the subsidiary rights department, in a very clerical job. Then I moved to editorial, where I also did fairly clerical tasks.

I befriended an acquisitions editor who gave me some manuscripts to read on the side. These were unsolicited manuscripts—the "slush pile," as it's called—so you can imagine how dreadful they were. My job was to read through them and write very nice "Gee, thanks, but we'll never publish your book" letters back. Later there was an opening in the marketing side, and I applied for the job and got it. I actually liked marketing; I didn't expect to, but I did. Over time, though, I found the pace quite slow and the process formulaic. I needed to find a different avenue for my marketing interests.

So I decided to try my hand at an advertising agency. I was living in Boston at the time, and I interviewed in Boston and New York. Pretty much everyone told me there wasn't a place for me. I was "too old" for the entry-level training programs (at twenty-seven), and my publishing background qualified me for one thing: publishing. All of the rejection made the elusive ad agency more appealing. I was determined to prove them wrong.

Through a friend I met Jack Connors, who owned the Hill Holliday ad agency in Boston. I interviewed with him, and he seemed to like me. He believed in hiring for talent and training for skill. Little did I know that the "training" would be on the fly. It was fabulous. It was an entrepreneurial company, and it was growing like crazy. Because they were entrepreneurs and it was small, if you had a spark of intelligence and were willing to go figure stuff out, you were thrown to the winds (and the wolves). So I stayed there for thirteen years, doing jobs that changed constantly. I lived and worked all over the world. I moved from Boston to London twice and spent months and months in Paris, Frankfurt, Sydney, and Hong Kong. I also traveled extensively to other cities around the globe. Over time I managed accounts, developed business, did mergers and acquisitions, creative oversight, turnaround—you name it. One great gift of working in this environment was having room to fail. We were all building the plane while we were flying it, so no one had a best practice or a right way to do something. It was learn-as-you-do, and it was exhilarating.

I was lucky to find someone who was willing to take a chance on me. What I learned from this man would fill a book. Living and working outside the United States helped me develop diplomatic skills and become a consensus builder. It was also where I learned how smaller markets had diversified into many marketing channels. Learning to make ideas work across media, markets, cultures, and geographies would later come in handy in my career.

When I was younger, I lived to work. It was what I did, who I was, where I made friends—a surrogate community of endless new faces and places. I woke up to London and went to bed with Hong Kong.

When I was thirty-nine, though, all of that changed. I was married and pregnant with my daughter, Caroline, and took some time off to devote myself to marriage and motherhood. Sixteen months after Caroline came our son, Jack, and any thoughts of returning to work were long gone. I married a writer, and during my hiatus I often helped him with ideas for his columns or helped edit his pieces. So I got to be an editor after all.

After a few years, I was asked to do a freelance project here and there, so I did keep my hand in ever so lightly. But once the children started school, I was restless. After a six-year hiatus, I thought I might look around. I was told over and over again that having stepped off the train, I could not get back on—especially at the salary and seniority I'd hoped to resume. I was pretty much toast.

Then a former colleague in New York arranged an introduction to Bonnie Lunt, who helped agencies hire talent. We met and talked, and she was much more encouraging about getting me hired back after my time away. A few months after we met, she called and asked if I'd be interested in talking to BBDO. So I met with the legendary Phil Dusenbury and Allen Rosenshine. That was heady stuff: They were men I'd admired from afar, at my little perch at Hill Holliday. We packed up and moved to New York.

During my stint at BBDO, I focused on developing ideas that could be communicated across multiple media channels. It was during this period that I persuaded BBDO to launch an interactive agency from scratch. That agency is named Atmosphere, and I take some pride in the fact that it's grown and prospered in the nine years since. I loved BBDO, but I found that the agency business no longer held my interest, and I began to feel there was something more for me to learn.

Through a series of meetings with Omnicom executive Tom Watson, I was offered a position within the DAS division of Omnicom Group. I was part of a management team that worked with a wide spectrum of communications, from public relations to promotions to branding and many more disciplines. During this time I was in a staff position, consulting on a variety of projects. It was, for a while, a perfect fit for a working mother. I traveled rarely, had selective client contact, and my work/life balance was pretty perfect. But I didn't feel that the "soft" art of consulting and facilitating was satisfying to me. I wanted to be on the cold, business and revenue side, and I started thinking about what I might do as an entrepreneur. But I never got the chance to find out.

It's only in hindsight that I can see how valuable this seemingly fallow time was. I was absorbing all things Omnicom: the companies, what they did, who did what well, who could best fix a problem, who could win a pitch. I was building a network and a knowledge bank that would later work to my advantage. So when I decided, after seven years, that it was time to try something new, Omnicom management had the foresight to offer me a change and keep me from looking outside.

I was promoted to executive vice president and officer at Omnicom Group, the largest communications holding company in the world. Oddly enough, even though Omnicom is a company with $12 billion in revenue, it's an entrepreneurial culture. All those years of being thrown into new situations served me in good stead there. Soon after this promotion, I led a team that won one of the largest global integrated marketing and advertising accounts in the business. I managed a team across multiple companies and disciplines in the network. We built a model where a centralized integration team manages and "subcontracts" Omnicom agencies on a retained and project basis. This gives us both the carrot and the stick to foster collaboration and playing by the rules of engagement on this account. All my collective experience put me in a place where I could drive revenue, manage a network of talent, and help build a brand.

And then, out of nowhere, I got a phone call asking if I would be interested in becoming the CEO of (PRODUCT) ^{RED}, the Bono and Bobby Shriver initiative to build a business where profits from partner brands would help fight the AIDS epidemic in Africa. I Googled everything (RED) that I could find—Bono, Africa, AIDS, and so on. I must have read five hundred articles on the subject. And I thought, "This would be great. This is something where I could apply my experience, and what I did would truly matter."

It was a long process, managed by Kleiner Perkins, and they were as thorough as their reputation. Eventually I was offered the job. When I told my boss, John Wren, the CEO of Omnicom, he was incredibly supportive and generous. During our conversation, he mentioned that larger statements of purpose should now be an integral part of any marketing communications effort. I think that's true. What we do, as individuals or as companies, is not just business. We're not just part of an economy. We're part of a society. And what we do matters beyond the boundaries of our immediate stakeholders.

(RED) is at the end of its start-up stage, the initial rush of enthusiasm and success. The challenge now is to make it a sustainable brand, one that continues to compel people to buy the (RED) product. It is the intersection of desire and virtue, and it's the most interesting marketing challenge I've ever encountered. Our success or failure has a measurable impact. If we grow and prosper, fewer people die of AIDS in Africa. It keeps you focused.

Everything I have done up until now has put me at a time and place where (RED) would come my way. I feel both exhilarated and blessed that every day I work with enormously talented, smart, and generous people who have embraced me. And I am still learning and growing.

CHAPTER 28

• • •

Gwendolyn Sykes

CHIEF FINANCIAL OFFICER, YALE UNIVERSITY, AND FORMER CHIEF FINANCIAL OFFICER AT NASA

Gwendolyn Sykes joined Yale as chief financial officer in July 2007, where she is responsible for the financial stewardship of the university, including budgeting, accounting, and transaction management, financial reporting, internal control, and the integrity of financial information.

A long-time public servant, Sykes previously held the position of CFO at NASA. She was appointed to her position overseeing the financial management and health of the $16 billion agency by President George W. Bush and confirmed by the U.S. Senate in 2003. That same year, Sykes was awarded the NASA Exceptional Achievement Medal for outstanding budgetary and financial management leadership of the NASA financial community.

Sykes was an analyst for the Department of Defense for a decade before joining NASA, and also worked in Congress for U.S. Senator Ted Stevens from Alaska, where among her responsibilities she coordinated activities related to protecting Alaska's vital fishery industry during the *Valdez* oil spill.

Gwen Sykes's family history of public service helped shape her priorities. It was never about money; it was about doing something that mattered. As CFO of NASA, overseeing a $16 billion budget, Sykes was hardly your average accountant. The key to her success there was her ability to combine her creative financial skills with her passion for the space program, to find the money to finance future projects. At NASA, Sykes was on a mission to inspire the next generation of explorers to reach for the stars; today, she does the same for the next generation of leaders at Yale University. Not a small ambition for the daughter of a small-business owner from Alaska.

"THESE ARE MY OWN PRINCIPLES FOR SUCCESS: ALWAYS BE ACCOUNTABLE, NO MATTER IF IT'S GOOD, BAD, OR INDIFFERENT. ENGAGE PEOPLE. UNDERSTAND PEOPLE DYNAMICS. UNDERSTAND THAT PEOPLE ARE THE MOST IMPORTANT ATTRIBUTE FOR MOVING FORWARD. AND EMBRACE ALL CHALLENGES, POSITIVE OR NEGATIVE."

I didn't know what I wanted to do when I was a girl. I thought I wanted to become a lawyer. Working in finance for organizations like NASA or Yale wasn't even on my radar screen.

I ended up nowhere near becoming a lawyer. My dad had his own business where I grew up in Alaska, and when I was a teenager, I eventually found that my allowance wasn't meeting all my needs, so I made it a point to work for my dad. Of course, he was very by-the-book, so he gave me a paycheck. My dad was really into math; we didn't have calculators in our household. But it didn't take a calculator for me to realize that my take-home pay wasn't anywhere near what I thought it would be. I told my dad he must have made a mistake. That was when he told me about taxes and other withholdings. That got me interested in math and money real quick, and from there I just kept on learning.

I come from a family background of public service. My dad was in

the military, and then he had a service supply company, doing service
contracts for the military and for individuals; he was also very involved
in local government. My mother was a nurse and a nurse midwife for
the state of Alaska. She would go out into the rural villages and provide delivery services. My sister is a public health nurse.

I'm sure that growing up in Alaska as the daughter of a small-
business owner and a former military man helped to make me the
competitive kid that I was. I was a little tomboy from Anchorage. I
did it all—hunting, fishing, and camping. I had an older brother, and
I followed him around quite a bit. I had Tonka trucks and played
basketball with the boys. So being competitive and getting right in
there with both the boys and girls was natural to me. As a woman,
some people might say I'm a little aggressive—and I think that's okay.

I played basketball in my sophomore or junior year. Our team was
known as the Bad News Bears, but, boy, we always lost with style.
We were such a great team, even though we had the worst record. We
always had fun. We played a good game, we played to our talents, and
we weren't really worried about losing. We were excited to play as a
team and be family at the end of the day.

What I learned from that experience—and it was further reinforced
when I came to NASA—is that life is going to present you with challenges. And if you have a solid team or a solid group working toward
a common good, doing the best they can, even though you may not
win, at least you know you tried your best, and you can feel good about
what you've done.

At NASA, we had our fair share of challenges. One of the biggest,
on the financial side, was implementing a new agencywide financial
system. We took ten different homegrown legacy systems and replaced
them with one common system.

In the past, government agencies may not have been very credible in the area of financial management. But taxpayers want to know
that the people at the helm *are* accountable and credible. They want to
know that their money is being used in the most positive and effective
manner. An agency needs to prove those two things, to make sure the
public knows what they're getting for their tax dollar, so that when

they see taxes being withheld from their paychecks, they know they're getting real value in return.

Wherever I work, I try to put people first. I do a lot of the management by walking around. When I came to NASA, there was a lot of decorum and strictness; if you worked somewhere else in the agency, you never talked to the CFO. I found that very strange. I'm very open—very communicative, very friendly. I hug a lot. When I say "People first," I mean on a personal level. That way, when other departments do their financial management—when they do the budget for NASA—they think of it as their product and they're proud of it. And in turn, I'm proud of them because they're committed to what they do.

As you go back over the history of NASA, most of its recent exploration has been in the lower orbit between here and the international space station. There's a whole new generation of young people coming up who will take exploration farther out into our solar system. Our next generation of explorers is in our elementary schools, junior high schools, and high schools as we speak. In the United States, our graduation rate in master's programs in science and engineering has fallen way behind that of our competitors in other countries. So we have to do something today to give incentives to the next generation of explorers.

A transformation is under way at NASA right now—something we call "Moon, Mars, and Beyond." At NASA, we managed a portfolio of $16.5 billion a year for space exploration. Once the international space station is completed, they'll return to the moon and use that as our platform for reaching Mars and beyond. They'll also develop a new crew exploration vehicle that will take us to the moon and possibly to Mars. Financing all this will be quite hard; you can't just bill a space vehicle to a credit card.

But NASA has a finite budget, so it needs to keep the public—that next generation of explorers—constantly aware of the possibilities. I have a young niece, and whenever I got photos of Mars from the Jet Propulsion Lab, I would e-mail them to her because I knew she was excited about Mars. We need to engage her at this hour, at this point in her life, to let her know that there is something she needs to be striving toward in science and math and exploration. That will be one sign of success for NASA, not only the fact that we got to Mars.

These are my own principles for success: Always be accountable, no matter if it's good, bad, or indifferent. Engage people. Understand people dynamics. Understand that people are the most important attribute for moving forward. And embrace all challenges, positive or negative.

CHAPTER 29

• • •

Tim Collins

SENIOR MANAGING DIRECTOR AND CHIEF
EXECUTIVE OFFICER, RIPPLEWOOD HOLDINGS

Tim Collins is the senior managing director and chief executive officer of Ripplewood Holdings L.L.C., a company he founded in 1995 to apply an industrial partnership approach to leveraged acquisitions.

Since its inception, Ripplewood has invested in companies with more than $20 billion of revenue and has led several of the largest private equity transactions ever, including the acquisition of Shinsei Bank—the former Long-Term Credit Bank of Japan—which was a pioneering transaction in the restructuring of the Japanese economy.

Previously, Collins managed Onex Corporation's New York office. In addition, he was a vice president at Lazard Frères & Co. in New York, and he worked with the management consulting firm of Booz Allen Hamilton Inc., specializing in strategic and operational assignments with major industrial and financial firms. Collins began his career in finance, marketing, and manufacturing at Cummins Engine Company in 1974.

While most people see Tim Collins as a world-class financier, he is at heart an altruist in the corporate suite. Although he has been extraordinarily successful financially, Tim Collins has always remained emotionally connected to the situations facing other people. As Collins's work has extended to major initiatives in other parts of the world, he has taken deep satisfaction in the knowledge that his capital projects will have a positive impact on people's lives—and may even help to support better and more progressive governments around the world.

"PERSONAL SUCCESS MEANS DOING THE BEST YOU CAN DO WITH THE GOOD FORTUNE YOU'RE GRANTED."

To be honest, I've never really had ambitions. In high school, I wanted to be a doctor. Obviously I'm not. My career evolved by happenstance, and whatever plans I had were quite different from the way things actually evolved.

I grew up in a small town in Kentucky. In 1974, the year I graduated from high school, I worked in an auto factory. Then I went to DePauw University in Indiana. Interestingly, two of the ten members of the Iraq Study Group—Vernon Jordan and former congressman Lee Hamilton—were there at the same time. I worked at Cummins Engine for a number of years; then I was a strategy consultant in Chicago. It was this collection of perspectives that inspired the investment approach we follow at Ripplewood today.

Twenty years ago, I came to New York expecting to work here for two years. I came for a job that looked like it would be interesting and to expand my horizons. I thought I would work in New York for a couple of years, save some money, learn something, and go back to Kentucky. I never made it back.

I have had so many interesting experiences. I started my own business and made controversial and highly successful investments that transformed Japan. Now we're doing innovative things in publishing in the United States and in banking in Egypt.

Before founding Ripplewood, I worked for another firm doing the same thing we do now: buying businesses, bringing in great managers, and making them more valuable. I went there because I had the opportunity to work for Felix Rohatyn, who was a renaissance figure on the scene. Felix was known not just as a great businessman, but also as part of the team that saved New York City from its fiscal crisis in the 1970s. Obviously, Felix was the most important guy in the business; I was the least important. I was in charge of copying, pretty low on the totem pole. But he was my mentor, in the sense that when I did a good job, he would pat me on the back.

I've had lots of interesting experiences in my career. When we bought the Long-Term Credit Bank of Japan, we got a call from the Japanese prime minister, who invited us to the room where they receive the emperor. He was grateful that we'd shown confidence in Japan and hoped it would help stop the crisis in the economy. It was terrific to be appreciated that way. And yet, just before that meeting, my third son was born—and to me, his birth was a much bigger deal.

I'm not addicted to making deals. I work out of a sense of duty. I have kids and I love to fly-fish, shoot grouse, and read books. I'm reasonably good at what I do, and I do it because I think it's important. The money is not a singular focus for me.

I am enormously self-critical. We've never had an investment lose money, but we've had a bunch of investments that could have done much better. We've had great returns, but they could always be better. I'm pretty critical of my own performance. To be frank, it's hard to look back and be anything other than grateful. Before I went to college, I worked eighty hours a week at the auto factory. All the guys there worked incredibly hard. I just happen to have been a lot luckier. I'm self-aware enough to know that I have been serially lucky.

I think that people who've had amazing success—guys like Yashiro-san, who ran the bank that we bought and is a truly remarkable guy—never do it for purely selfish reasons. They have a higher calling. I think that's true of men like Warren Buffett and Bill Gates. Many people who do amazing things have a passion that goes beyond money or their own careers. That has certainly been my experience watching other people.

I don't think I have a millennial calling. I have a daily calling, which is to do the stuff that I'm pretty good at—allocating capital, stepping into situations like the Japanese bank, the Egyptian bank, or the automotive industry, where bringing great, talented executives and capital can be a catalyst for creating better businesses, more jobs, and better customer service. And I've had some amazingly talented guys to work with—men like Ron Daniel, who ran McKinsey, and Harvey Golub, who ran American Express.

A long time ago, Felix Rohatyn told me, "One of the things you want to aspire to is being good enough at your business so that you can choose to do business with people you like." I agree with that. In our business, we've been good enough at investing that we have the luxury of doing it in situations where we can make a difference, not just make money. That is a great luxury.

I tell my kids, "We've had great luck, and with that comes extraordinary responsibility." I tell my kids they have to do three things: They have to make the world a better place, they have to work hard, and they have to love the Lord. If they do those three things, I'll do anything I can to help them. If they want to be moguls or playboys, they can do it on their own. I think my kids will be more likely to write a great book or teach a generation of students than to go into business—and I think that's spectacular. Those are lasting contributions. To me, personal success means doing the best you can do with the good fortune you're granted. If you do those three things, whether you're a painter or a poet or a politician, that's success in my book.

My dad used to say that people fall into two categories: those who are running from something and those who are running to something. I'm not running to anything, but I've got a sense of purpose and responsibility that comes with the kind of background I've had. If you've been incredibly fortunate, you have an obligation to pass it along.

CHAPTER 30

• • •

Roger Barnett

CHAIRMAN AND CHIEF EXECUTIVE OFFICER, SHAKLEE CORPORATION

Roger Barnett is the chairman and chief executive officer of Shaklee Corporation, one of the leading providers of premium-quality, natural nutrition, personal care, and household products. Founded in 1956, Shaklee is the number one natural nutrition company in the United States, with more than 750,000 members and distributors in the United States, Japan, Mexico, Malaysia, Canada, and Taiwan.

Before joining Shaklee, Barnett was the managing partner of Activated Holdings LLC, an investment vehicle for a private family holding company, controlling more than $2 billion in assets. Barnett began his career at the investment banking firm Lazard Frères & Co. He then organized an investment group to acquire control of Arcade, Inc., a fragrance sampling company, and became its president and chief executive officer. During his six-year tenure, Arcade was transformed into the largest sampling company in the world, expanding from a solely U.S. operation into a global business.

Barnett was also the founder, chairman, and chief executive officer of Beauty.com, which continues to be one of the leading Internet re-tailers in the cosmetics industry.

Roger Barnett has had an interesting debate within himself for his entire life: Do I dedicate myself to business and earn money, or do I devote myself to the public sector and try to have an impact on the common good? Or even more challenging: Can I possibly do both at the same time? That became Barnett's quest. As you'll see, the yin and yang of the issue made him uneasy, and his search to find the answer took a lifetime. He finally achieved a melding of the two that satisfied his dual urge. Barnett considers himself a "public sector entrepreneur," and few would disagree.

"I THINK THE DEFINITION OF SUCCESS, FOR ME, IS MAKING A POSITIVE IMPACT ON THE WORLD, LIVING YOUR LIFE SO THAT THE WORLD IS A BETTER PLACE BY THE TIME YOU'RE DONE. IF ALL YOU'RE DOING IN YOUR LIFE IS TAKING CARE OF YOURSELF, FOR ME THAT'S NOT A VERY SUCCESSFUL LIFE."

The world at large has always fascinated me. My parents exposed me to other cultures early on by sending me off to camp in a foreign country when I was six years old. When I was growing up, my parents gave me an option every summer: I could either work or go on a study program, as long it was something substantive. I always searched for programs that would take me as far away as possible to experience something new. I lived with a family in Japan and went to school there; I lived in the bush in Africa doing animal behavior research; I worked on a farm in the Middle East. In short, I tried to experience the world.

From those experiences, I learned that in America, Africa, Asia, Europe, and the Middle East, we're all people with the same funda-mental human needs. And that everyone deserves the opportunity to live a better life.

I had two role models in my life. One was my great-uncle, who founded a company and ended up giving away more than $1 billion to charity. He was a great entrepreneur. He loved business, but he loved the idea of building businesses rather than just making money for himself. At the end of his life, I spent the summer with him. Every day, some charity—a school or hospital or other organization—would come to his office and ask for money. That summer, I saw the impact somebody can have giving away substantial amounts of money.

The other role model was my mother, who has dedicated the last forty-two years of her life to public interest law, helping the poorest families, first in New York City and now across the United States, get equal access to the justice system. In my opinion, she is now the leading public interest lawyer in the country; she has helped countless people by devoting 100 percent of her time to making an impact.

With those two people as models, I had a choice: Do I go into the public interest sector, like my mother, and use my time to make an impact? Or do I go into business, like my great-uncle, make money, and use that money to have an impact? I chose to go into business first. I was fortunate enough to be successful, but along the way I got engaged with many different groups and communities across the entrepreneur/public sector divide. My principal activity, my day job, was making money. Then, after I sold the company, I took some time and said, "What do I want to do next?" After looking at many different industries, I found an industry and a company that would allow me to combine commercial success and public benefit in one undertaking. That company is Shaklee, the number one natural nutrition company in the United States.

You could say that there are two driving forces in my life. First, I've wanted to make a positive impact on the world. My other driving force is that I've always tried to excel at everything I did.

I think you can train yourself to focus your thoughts on success. I played a lot of tennis when I was little against my older brother and his friends. I wasn't the best athlete in the world, but I was scrappy and had a competitive spirit. I remember playing against bigger and older kids who were better than me, but I knew I could beat them. If there was a high-pressure point on the line, at the critical moment I would announce, "It's match point, and I'm going to win." Not yelling or bragging, just saying it loud enough so they could hear. People thought, "Who is this little kid?" Most opponents couldn't handle it, and they lost.

The difference between getting an A and a B in college, in my mind, was simply effort. Sometimes it would come down to six hours. I used to study with other students. They would go to bed at midnight, when there was still a lot more to be studied and learned. They got tired and lost their ability to focus; I pulled an all-nighter. In many courses, those extra six hours made the difference between an A and a B.

One of my goals was to be summa cum laude in college. To pull it off, I needed to get seven A's in my last semester at Yale. I don't think that had ever been done before—normally, you take only four or five classes per semester. But I took seven classes, and I pulled it off. When someone says, "You can't do it," that's a challenge I just have to accept. It's about hard work and perseverance.

It was my grandmother who gave me the gift of belief and self-confidence. She gave all of her grandchildren different nicknames, and she named me "Special." I could have asked her why, could have protested that I'm not really special, but she was my grandmother and I chose to believe her. Before I went to sleep at night she would repeat it to me, and I credit her with giving me self-confidence by making me feel I could do whatever I wanted.

Through the years, that confidence has helped me fight self-doubt and the doubts of others. People are always saying, "It can't be done." In every business I've been in, people have questioned whether it could be done. You have to have that unwavering sense that any challenge can be met. If you don't, you lose.

I have had my moments of doubt. When I went to college, I thought of trying out for the soccer team. I came from a small high school that wasn't known for its athletics, but I was considered a pretty good soccer player. That first week at college, I joined a pickup game right outside my dorm. One guy kicked the ball right by me. He was so good, so quick—he went by me like I was standing still. I thought, "Man, if this is a pickup game, imagine what the guys on the team are like." So I never tried out for the team. It turned out that guy was the center halfback for the North Carolina State Championship team; he'd also run the hundred-meter dash in the Olympics for a Caribbean country. He was a superstar. But I didn't know that at the time, and I let myself get psyched out, so I never even tried out. It would have been fun to see what I could have done.

It was in college that my world focus and desire to excel began to work synergistically. When I was in law school at Yale, a group of us built $6 million worth of low-income housing and then wrote a book about it. We tried to publish it as a model. We went to Congress and lobbied for a low-income tax credit so that it could be applied not just to nonprofits, but also to developers. We tried to use private sector techniques for public good.

I've always been fascinated with that approach—trying to leverage private sector techniques for public sector goals. I was sure I'd eventually have to choose, but I kept trying to combine the two, and I couldn't find a way. That's why I'm so excited today about Shaklee: I've actually found something where you don't have to separate the private and the public sectors. At Shaklee, we use financial incentives for a public good—to bring basic health to people all over the world and to give people the opportunity to earn an income. We're here to guide and direct this behavior until it becomes self-sustaining. It's been a long journey from the start, when I thought those two things—my public and private sector goals—would be separate, that a career in one would have to follow a career in the other. At Shaklee, I can do them both, and I think that's unique.

Wangari Maathai, who won the Nobel Peace Prize in 2004, is a Shaklee partner. She is the global ambassador of our Million Trees/ Million Dreams campaign. Dr. Maathai won the Nobel Prize because she paid people to plant trees. The money, the financial incentive, got people's attention, and they self-organized into groups to teach one another how to plant trees. Along the way, they also taught themselves how to take control of their own community and developed a governing structure.

Frankly, the person you should be interviewing is Dr. Shaklee, who wrote a book called *Thoughtsmanship* in the 1940s. Its basic message was, "Think positive thoughts. You'll achieve success if you change your mind-set to focus on positive thoughts." The difference between the top ten players in any professional sport and the next ninety is all in the mind. Physically they're all comparable. It's all a mental game.

Today, I think that virtually all of the seven hundred and fifty thousand members of Shaklee believe that the company's future will be greater than its past. And with that belief, we're succeeding and significantly outperforming the industry. In that context, I consider myself a kind of public sector entrepreneur—a role that requires the drive, vision, and charisma of a business leader but uses them to do something in the public interest rather than just make money.

I think the definition of success, for me, is making a positive impact on the world, living your life so that the world is a better place by the time you're done. If all you're doing in your life is taking care of yourself, for me that's not a very successful life.

Independence Seekers

• • •

CHAPTER 31

Christie Hefner

FORMER CHAIRMAN AND CHIEF EXECUTIVE OFFICER, PLAYBOY ENTERPRISES

Named one of *Forbes* magazine's "100 Most Powerful Women in the World" in 2005, Christie Hefner was at the helm of Playboy Enterprises from 1988 to 2009. Daughter of the iconic Hugh Hefner, Christie joined the family business in 1975 and worked in a variety of the company's businesses before being named president in 1982 at the age of twenty-nine.

During her twenty-year tenure, Hefner oversaw policy, management, and strategy in all areas of Playboy Enterprises. She is credited with ushering the company into the new millennium by significantly expanding its television business from the launch of its branded channel in 1982, making *Playboy* the first magazine brand to be successfully leveraged into television. Continuing the company's electronic expansion, Hefner took *Playboy* online in 1994, making it the first national magazine on the World Wide Web.

Christie Hefner always knew what she wanted to do with her life—to make a difference. When she was growing up, it was her mother, not her famous father, who gave her confidence. While at Brandeis, she decided she would have an impact on the legal and social structure of society—planning to launch a career in either law or journalism. After a "temporary" detour on the way to law school landed her a job with her father at Playboy, Hefner discovered the company's long history of social activism and realized that it offered a perfect forum for her to have an impact on the broader social and political world. Hefner took the reins at Playboy before she was thirty years old—accepting the challenge of turning around the business and leading it into the digital age.

"SUCCESS MEANS ACCOMPLISHING WHAT YOU SET OUT TO DO. FOR ME, IT MEANT TURNING THE COMPANY AROUND. HELPING THE PEOPLE AROUND ME SUCCEED HAS BEEN MORE SATISFYING THAN BEING THE CEO."

The most influential person in my life was my mother, who basically raised me and who gave me confidence that I could accomplish whatever I set my mind to. After my parents divorced, she remarried when I was about seven. Even then she was the dominant parent in my life.

After my mother remarried, we moved to Wilmette, Illinois, and I lived there for eleven years. I was cast as Sleeping Beauty in a French-language production in fifth grade, and I remained involved in theater through high school and college and six summers at the national music camp in Interlochen, Michigan. I also ran track in grammar school, and I don't know if it still stands, but for a long time I had the fifty-yard-dash record there. Then I ran competitively for a short time in junior high and played different team sports, including field hockey and basketball. It's important to me to do things well. That's why, for example, I don't golf. I don't have the time to do it well enough to enjoy it. Instead I bike, I play tennis, I ski, I scuba dive.

I think it's fair to describe me as a competitive person. I was academically competitive, from my time in grammar school through college, where I was awarded Phi Beta Kappa in my junior year at Brandeis.

I was interested in major social-political issues from early on. When I was in high school, I wrote a letter to the editor opposing capital punishment, and it was published in one of the Chicago newspapers. A group of friends and I also started an alternative newspaper. I was interested in working for candidates, and I did that before I was old enough to vote. But I didn't go down to Grant Park for the infamous 1968 Democratic convention—where there was a massive protest against the Vietnam War and the Yippies were arrested—because my mother, probably wisely, didn't think it was a safe place for a sixteen-year-old.

What was most important to me growing up was pursuing a career that would be intellectually satisfying and emotionally fulfilling. I was interested in shaping the legal and social structure of society. So the two areas of greatest interest to me were law and, by extension, politics and journalism. After I graduated from college, I worked as a journalist for a year. Then I decided to go to law school. Before I did, however, my father suggested that I move back to Chicago first to learn a little bit about his company. It was an intriguing offer: I saw it as a kind of junior year abroad, something that would be intellectually enriching and interesting but last only a limited time.

I didn't expect to stay at Playboy because I didn't see it as an opportunity to have an impact on matters of social justice, the way law, politics, or journalism would. Coming out of the late sixties and early seventies, when my generation was rebelling against the Establishment, I didn't believe that big business was consistent with my generation's values. But of course I found that there *were* people of high conscience and values in corporate America—people who were using their resources for good—just as there are people with no sense of ethics or social conscience in any field.

What I discovered when I came to Playboy is that it's had a long history of social activism from its early stages, particularly through its foundation. When I first came into the company it was doing very well, and I didn't have any particular goals for it. As they said in *The God-*

father, my father made me an offer I couldn't refuse: a chance to learn about a variety of businesses I might not otherwise be exposed to and a chance to work with my father. I think my father's motivation was much more personal than professional. Because he'd been away when I was growing up, he saw my working for the company as an opportunity for us to get closer. I saw it as an interesting opportunity that was too intellectually intriguing to pass up—but I didn't expect to stay, and I don't think he expected me to, either.

Then, in the early 1980s, the company got in trouble. It needed a restructuring and a change in strategy. And my father and the board gave me the opportunity to turn the company around. One of the key first steps I took was to form an office of the president with the then CFO. From the moment I became president, I felt a responsibility to save the company—to save jobs, preserve the value of the assets and the brand, and protect the shareholders' interests.

I have always been motivated to exceed expectations and be successful. Success means accomplishing what you set out to do. For me, it meant turning the company around. Helping the people around me succeed has been more satisfying than being the CEO. I don't know that there are strict rules for success, but I think there are qualities that are important: Drive, perseverance, self-confidence, high energy, and organizational skills are all traits that have been important to me.

I went to Brandeis, a liberal university, and I came of age at a time when business was at best something to be suspicious of. In the business world, however, I've learned otherwise. I wouldn't have stayed if it were a manufacturing business. I stayed because I discovered that this company was built around a great magazine and that it had a long history of social activism in both its pages and its philanthropy. Playboy has attracted a remarkable group of people who are intellectually curious and concerned about the world. And the diversity of businesses at Playboy means that it's always an intellectually challenging environment. I've never thought about leaving because the right position never came up—but also because I feel protective of my people, the shareholders, and the investors.

There have been challenges along the way. Our move online was a big bet, especially being a public company. In 1994, *Playboy* actually became the first national magazine to go on the Web—at a time when other magazines that were moving to the Internet were doing it by licensing their content to other providers, like CompuServe or Prodigy or AOL, rather than building their own independent Web-based businesses.

When the dot-com bubble burst, it took confidence in our business plan to stay the course until we became profitable. We also spent millions of dollars fighting for what ultimately became the definitive Supreme Court decision protecting the rights of cable programmers and distributors, based on a ruling that the standard for speech in cable would be not the more limited broadcast television standard, but the more expansive standard applied to print and online.

It was one of those situations where you win one round, and the government appeals, and then you lose a round, and each step along the way you're wondering, "Should I keep spending all this money?" Your lawyers are confident, but they're also getting paid to keep fighting. When we ultimately prevailed, it became a very important piece of litigation—not just for us, but for the whole industry.

Playboy ended up being the ideal place for me. I actually spend quite a bit of time with both lawyers and journalists. The law part appeals to me because of its analytical elements, the journalistic aspect because of its creative elements, and the whole enables me to make an impact in the broader social and political world. And Playboy obviously has a strong point of view on a lot of issues I consider important.

CHAPTER 32

• • •

Bob Woodward

ASSISTANT MANAGING EDITOR,
THE WASHINGTON POST

One of the most respected and iconic investigative reporters in the newspaper business, Bob Woodward first gained national attention when he teamed with fellow *Post* reporter Carl Bernstein to investigate a burglary at the Watergate office building in the early morning hours of June 17, 1972. Their subsequent reporting on the ensuing scandal ultimately brought down the presidency of Richard Nixon.

Woodward has earned nearly every American journalism award, including the Pulitzer Prize, awarded to the *Post* in 1973 for Woodward and Bernstein's Watergate reporting. Their account of the investigation, detailed in their book *All the President's Men*, became a national best seller and was made into a popular motion picture.

Named one of the best investigative reporters in America by *The New York Times*, Bob Woodward has been the assistant managing editor of investigative news for *The Washington Post* since 1982. Woodward was the main reporter for the *Post*'s articles on the aftermath of the September 11 terrorist attacks, which won the Pulitzer Prize for National Affairs in 2002.

Woodward has written or co-written eleven number one nonfiction best sellers—more than any other contemporary American writer.

Bob Woodward discovered his calling largely by accident. He was heading to law school but took a summer job working at The Washington Post *and fell in love with journalism. A self-described "failure" in the newsroom at first, he wasn't deterred by early missteps. Instead, they made him only more determined to stick with journalism and learn the trade he'd fallen in love with. Watergate proved his gift for investigative reporting and set the course for the rest of his career.*

"IT'S HARD TO PUT A DEFINITION ON SUCCESS, BECAUSE IT'S MORE INTERNAL THAN EXTERNAL. DO YOU LIKE WHAT YOU DO? DO YOU ENJOY DOING IT? WHEN YOU SEE PEOPLE ON THE SIDEWALK, SOMETIMES IT'S HARD TO TELL WHO REALLY HAS INTERNAL SUCCESS. THAT'S WHAT'S MORE IMPORTANT THAN EXTERNAL."

When I was growing up, I wanted to be a lawyer—probably because my father was a lawyer and a judge. He had a law firm in the small town where I was raised—Wheaton, Illinois, outside of Chicago. But my life changed during the summer of 1970 when I was getting out of a five-year hitch in the navy. I was actually planning to go to law school in the fall, but I was bored that summer. I thought, "I'm going to go to school for three more years before I do anything?"

So I walked into *The Washington Post* and said, "I would like to be a reporter." They gave me a two-week tryout. I failed. I wrote a bunch of stories that weren't any good. I didn't know how to be a reporter yet. The editors at the *Post*, of course, discovered this right away. They said, "See, you don't know how to do this." I said, "Thank you very much. Because I've learned that this is what I love and want to do." So I went away for a year and worked for a weekly paper in Montgomery County, Maryland. Then I was hired back at the *Post*.

What I like about reporting is the sense of immediacy. You go into work and you're dealing with topics that are relevant, important, what people are talking about on the Metro or at the water cooler. Our job is to find out what's really going on and make some sense of it—to dig beneath the surface, if you can.

By definition, there is almost no routine in news. And in that way, it's unique compared with any other profession. A doctor or lawyer will have patients who may have routine illnesses or legal problems. The first question in the news business is always, "What's *not* routine? What's new? What's unexpected? What's surprising?"

Two editors had a big impact on my career. First there was Harry Rosenfeld, who gave me that first two-week tryout at the *Post* and later became one of our key Watergate editors. Probably more important was Roger Farquhar, a former state editor at the *Post*, who hired me at the *Montgomery County Sentinel* when I worked there in 1970–1971. There were only four reporters there, and Roger kind of turned me loose and taught me about news—how to press on things, how to look at records.

I'd been at the *Sentinel* only about six weeks when Roger assigned me a story on Maryland's attorney general and some money he'd given his old law firm for work on defunct savings and loan institutions. When the story came out, the attorney general was so enraged, he drove from Baltimore to Rockville, Maryland, and stormed into the office. I thought he was going to have a heart attack. Roger said, "Well, you made the attorney general mad," and he smiled. I was a little frightened, quite frankly. But Roger backed me up. We had the facts. It was all true. *The Washington Post* had to follow up the story. And it was a good lesson—that journalism might be scary sometimes, but that's the job.

Watergate began as a beautiful day in Washington. I was awakened and called in by the city editor. I think the editors at the *Post* that morning said, "Who would be stupid enough to come in on this beautiful morning?" And my name came to mind instantly because I'd worked there only nine months. I was the least experienced reporter, making less than any other. But I generally worked two shifts, because I loved it. I had spent five years in the navy doing things I didn't like, and I really liked this.

During Watergate we made some mistakes, and Carl Bernstein and I thought we might have to resign. One mistake involved the president's chief of staff, Bob Haldeman. We said something about him that was true, but we attributed it to grand jury testimony, and the person hadn't given that grand jury testimony. Ben Bradlee, the executive editor, said, "We stand by our story." That was the *Post*'s statement. Bradlee asked us to find out why we got it wrong. When we checked back with our source, he said he would have identified Haldeman if he'd been asked, but he hadn't been asked. In retrospect, that just shows how inadequate the investigation was. It reflected the ongoing cover-up. But at the time, it was scary to make a mistake like that.

Watergate was risky, but we were protected by the editors who quizzed us and delayed stories; Bradlee in particular wouldn't run some things. After all, as reporters, we were still young; if this all fell apart, we could go on to do something else. *The Washington Post*, on the other hand, had its credibility on the line. The company had recently gone public, and because of challenges to a number of FCC television licenses the paper owned, its stock was in the toilet. We reporters dig around and write the stories, but it's the people who have to edit them and publish them—Bradlee and the publisher, Katharine Graham— who took the real risks.

In all these years of reporting, one thing I've learned is that you never know the whole story. There are always surprises. Even as I look back on Watergate all these years later, there are still things we don't know. Whenever I talk to people about it, I realize that we didn't connect the dots many times—that our coverage was actually quite cautious and conservative given what we know now. So the lesson is, Be aggressive, but stick to the facts. You're never going to know the whole story, maybe not even half of it.

It's hard to put a definition on success because it's more internal than external. Do you like what you do? Do you enjoy doing it? When you see people on the sidewalk, sometimes it's hard to tell who really has internal success. That's what's more important than external. The most important thing is to stick to the present, the moment you're working in. When we started working on Watergate, if somebody had come up to us on the first day and said, "This is going to take two and a half years and define part of your career and life," I would have said, "You're kidding." So you never know.

I've just finished my fourteenth book. I still work at the *Post*. I'm sixty-three years old, and I still like it. Howard Simon, the late managing editor of the *Post*, gave me a good piece of advice: Make sure you stick to the daily business of getting information. Don't worry about whether this story is as good as the last story or where your career is going. Direct your energies toward the current work.

I describe reporting as pulling a thread on a sock perhaps to see what unravels. The oldest story in government is when officials don't tell the truth—or don't tell the full story—and the same is true today. When you know that, it's a great incentive—because if you can get a piece of what really happened, or the whole true story, that's news.

CHAPTER 33

• • •

Bert Fields

ENTERTAINMENT ATTORNEY

Bert Fields is one of the nation's leading entertainment attorneys and a partner at Greenberg Glusker, a full-service business and entertainment law firm. For more than thirty years, Fields has represented the industry's top performers, directors, writers, producers, studios, talent agencies, book publishers, and record companies. His clients include DreamWorks, MGM, United Artists, The Weinstein Company, Tom Cruise, Warren Beatty, Dustin Hoffman, Jeffrey Katzenberg, David Geffen, Jerry Bruckheimer, The Beatles, Madonna, Sony Music, and many others. In addition, he has represented such major authors as Mario Puzo, James Clavell, Tom Clancy, and Clive Cussler.

Over the course of his career, Fields has represented virtually every major Hollywood studio and talent agency, and he has tried many of the landmark cases in the entertainment and communications industries. Fields' practice is international in scope and extends beyond the field of entertainment, having represented such diverse clients as Arizona cotton farmers, Las Vegas hotels and casinos, real estate developers and regional shopping centers, clothing designers, manufacturers, boxing promoters, and investment firms.

Fields is the author, under a pseudonym, of two novels. His third book is a biographical work on Richard III published under his own name. His fourth book is an analysis of the Shakespeare authorship question.

Bert Fields is a real fighter who has never lost a case in which he was the lead counsel. Competitive on all courts—legal and tennis—Fields is a renaissance man with a wide array of interests who still remains motivated each day by his love for the law.

"I TEND TO SEPARATE SUCCESS INTO PROFESSIONAL AND PERSONAL SUCCESS. I CONSIDER BEING ABLE TO WRITE BOOKS A MATTER OF PERSONAL SUCCESS, BECAUSE IT BRINGS ME A LOT OF JOY."

The first thing you need to succeed as a lawyer, of course, is intelligence. Stupid people do not usually succeed at the law. But it takes more than just intelligence. I think it takes a lot of courage—guts. I tell young lawyers that they are going to experience very bad times in the courtroom—and that the ability to keep battling back is one of the main things that separate successful from unsuccessful lawyers.

I think law requires a competitive nature. When I play tennis—and I'm a bad tennis player—I'm the kind of person who goes rolling on the court to get every ball. But judgment is also very important. There are many, many lawyers who are bright, full of courage and competitiveness, but have just appalling judgment. Those are the main factors, and I guess I would say, immodestly, that I have them on the plus side.

I get a great kick out of the legal process. I usually say luck doesn't have much to do with it, but I'm lucky enough to have chosen a profession that I love doing. I don't ever plan to retire, even though I'm seventy-seven. I suppose at some point I won't be able to do it anymore, but I don't feel like I'm anywhere near that point yet.

I was an only child, and my parents treated me as a very special person, a prince. I went to high school in New Mexico, in a small town where my father was a surgeon stationed in the air force. I played football in high school, and I think that contributed to my ability to keep pushing on despite pain and adversity.

I attended Harvard Law School, and probably my proudest accomplishment was being on the *Harvard Law Review*. It was a fantastic experience, not least because it helped my writing enormously. That experience taught me to write—to be economical in my writing and to make sure every sentence was clear. The analysis I learned there probably exceeded the analysis I learned in any class.

I had no idea what kind of law I wanted to do when I graduated from law school in 1952. I went into the air force and tried court-martial. Once I defended a case and got an acquittal for an airman who was accused of burglarizing the deputy base commander's office. The base commander, outraged, put through a court-martial on me for excess zeal in defending my client. I was very worried about that. The process went on for two or three weeks, until the Eighth Air Force Headquarters threw out the charge. Things like that harden one.

When I came out of the air force, I thought I was sort of a hotshot trial lawyer. That's all I wanted to do—try cases. I tried cases for people in the entertainment business, and I started getting a lot of referrals. I became an entertainment lawyer by geography—being in California—and by accident. It certainly wasn't by design.

Successful entertainment lawyers are generally very bright people, very media savvy and tough-minded. The qualities that make one a success in that field are not that different from what they would be in the oil and gas field if we practiced in Houston or up in Silicon Valley doing high-tech law work. I think the qualities that allow one to rise to the top are pretty much the same. Once in a while you come across somebody who gets there by being very social, but it's an extreme rarity because the people in business want somebody skilled to be a lawyer or do contract work or litigation. I have become friends with some of my celebrity clients over the years, but that's just because I like them. I don't think I ever got a client by socializing. I don't tend to make lunch appointments unless that's the only way I can meet with somebody.

I have never lost a trial for which I was lead counsel. Back in 1956, when I was a young assistant lawyer to a much more senior lawyer, we lost the case. But since then I haven't lost a trial. Still, I don't go around saying that. I have lost motions, and in at least one instance I can recall, I lost a motion at the very beginning of a case that knocked out the case. This is what I mean by judgment: You don't go to trial unless you've got a significant chance you're going to win.

I tend to separate success into professional and personal success. I would choose the same profession even if they paid me in apples or gold medals or stars on a blackboard. I just love the process. I don't mean to say I don't enjoy the money; I do. It brings me a lot of very nice things that I otherwise couldn't afford. But I would still be doing this if it didn't pay off.

I consider being able to write books a matter of personal success, because it brings me a lot of joy. I don't do it for the money or good reviews or to sell a lot of books; I do it because I really like it. And, as with the law, I just love the process. Right now I'm writing a book on Queen Elizabeth I. I became fascinated with her while I was writing a book about Shakespeare, so I decided I would write about her. Of course, a lot of people have written about Queen Elizabeth, but I'll take the same kind of approach I took to Richard III and Shakespeare—a puzzle-solving approach, because there are a lot of issues and puzzles surrounding Elizabeth.

I enjoy writing history books so much that I probably will keep doing that instead of writing my memoirs. I would have to leave a lot out of my memoirs because of the limits of attorney-client privilege. There is some autobiographical stuff in my novels: As I told my wife, the law parts are for the most part based on actual records. The sex parts I made up. She thinks it's just the opposite.

I'm going to give a chair to Harvard Law School, so that a hundred years from now there will be a Bertram Fields Professor of Law. That's a kind of remembrance I'd like. Of course, I'd like my family to remember me fondly. And I'd like the people I knew and practiced law with and did deals with to think back on me as a person they respected and liked and even laughed with. That's about as well as I can do for immortality.

CHAPTER 34

• • •

Anna Cheng Catalano

FORMER GROUP VICE PRESIDENT, BRITISH PETROLEUM

Named one of *Fortune*'s "Most Powerful Women in International Business" in 2001, Anna Cheng Catalano is one of the most experienced voices in the petroleum industry, having held a variety of positions in her more than twenty years with Amoco Corporation and British Petroleum.

Cheng Catalano held the top marketing position at BP, responsible for repositioning the company's marketing profile. After the launch of BP's brand in 2000, Cheng Catalano was a key driver of the company's "Beyond Petroleum" program.

Before that, she had been president of the Amoco Orient Oil Company in the mid-1990s, establishing and managing Amoco's first downstream refining, marketing, and transportation business in the People's Republic of China. Her understanding of Chinese societal and business culture, coupled with strong Western operational management experience, provided a unique blend of skills necessary for commercial success in the PRC. Cheng Catalano was one of the few Amoco executives to gain a senior role at BP after the two oil companies merged in 1999, assuming the role of BP's group vice president for emerging markets, with responsibilities for Asia, Africa, Latin America, Eastern Europe, and the Middle East.

Anna Cheng Catalano always followed her own path and set her own goals, regardless of the obstacles in her way. In her wide-ranging career in the oil industry, Anna followed the opportunities and deftly learned to adapt in a male-dominated industry. Anna's drive for independence motivated her to take on new challenges within the corporate arena. When she saw the limits of the path she was on, her drive for independence also became a liberating force and allowed her to stop proving herself and take on something entirely new.

"I ONCE HEARD THAT SUCCESS IS GETTING WHAT YOU WANT AND HAPPINESS IS WANTING WHAT YOU GET. I REALLY LIKE THAT. TO ME IT'S IMPORTANT TO FEEL YOU ARE DOING WELL AT WHAT YOU WERE MEANT TO DO."

My parents are Chinese immigrants. Dad's home is a place called Ningbo, and he made it over in 1949. My mom is from Szechuan, the place with all the spicy food. They came to the United States with graduate school fellowships to the University of Texas at Austin, leaving China shortly before the Communist takeover with nothing but the clothes on their back and every expectation of going back.

My dad is a research scientist. He did postdoctoral work in New Mexico, then in Princeton, and ended up working for the Midwest Research Institute in Kansas City, where I grew up. Three of their four girls, starting with me, were born in Kansas City. I spoke Chinese at home, so English is my second language.

My parents had the challenge of raising four girls in a midwestern city that didn't have a lot of Chinese people. They really wanted us to know about the country they came from, about our ethnic background, so we spent a lot of time at the dinner table talking about China and Chinese philosophy.

My parents are Buddhist, with a very strong Confucian philosophy of life, so we spent a lot of time talking about values and what's important and examples of people who did good things and people who did stupid things. There were a lot of life lessons passed out at that table, along with the normal "What did you do in school today?" There was also a real focus on academics. I suppose that's par for the course for most Asian families. And after we came home from school every day, we spent time reading and writing Chinese. My mom took us through all the Chinese textbooks up through high school. I even learned how to write Chinese calligraphy with a brush.

But I also had a typical American middle-class childhood, wanting to do things every middle-class American kid wanted to do. When I was seven or eight years old, I wanted to be an astronaut. The morning after Neil Armstrong landed on the moon, I thought, "Man, *I'm* going to the moon." My room was filled with posters of the solar system, and I dreamed about getting a moon rock.

I think deep down my parents were always hoping that at some point they would be able to take us back to China. I think for a long time they were thinking, "We want to go back to our country." I truly believe they had every intention of going back. By the 1970s, my dad had spent many years working in America, including working on projects for the U.S. Army and the National Institutes of Health. He had developed a strong reputation in his field of study. He and my mother had made many good friends and had comfortably adjusted to "life in these United States." One day, he proclaimed, "You know, this country has done more for me than any other country in the world, and I think I need to become a citizen." My parents became naturalized citizens soon thereafter.

My parents were pragmatists; they knew the world was filled with prejudice. When they first moved to Princeton, they weren't allowed to buy a house in certain areas because Chinese people weren't welcome there. So my parents were aware of the underlying prejudice that exists in any country where you're a minority. But they were also very progressive. They strongly valued education, and they believed that girls could do anything boys could do. One day, when I came home from school crying because people made fun of the way I looked, my mom said, "You're a girl, and you're Chinese, so you're going to have to work twice as hard. But if you work twice as hard, you're going to learn twice as much." That was likely the best piece of advice I ever got; I've carried it with me throughout my life.

The decision to attend college was never optional for me or any of my sisters. You weren't considered finished with your education until you had a college degree in your hand! I chose to attend the University of Illinois at Champaign-Urbana, which gave me a chance to be on my own rather than staying close to home as many of my high school friends did. It turned out to be a great decision in many ways.

I didn't see myself going into business until I was in college. My parents don't have a commercial bone in their bodies! They're brilliant scientists, but we seldom talked about bank accounts or investments, and I didn't grow up learning about money. Then again, my dad developed cancer drugs that save people's lives—so the world was far better off having him put his efforts toward medicine.

During my first summer after my freshman year, I was lucky enough to land a job at the Amoco Pipeline office in Kansas City through the father of a good friend who was division manager. It was just routine office work, but the environment suited me perfectly—I loved the people I worked with and the family orientation. When I graduated with a degree in marketing in 1982, I took a permanent job with Amoco. My first assignment was in North Dakota. It immediately occurred to me that being a woman was going to be a little tougher in the oil industry. In fact, the first territory that opened up while I was in training went to someone who started out later than me—because, I learned later, the sales manager at the time didn't want a woman in his group.

Nonetheless, I enjoyed my first assignment, which involved selling tires, batteries, accessories, and motor oil. It was the first time I was really on my own, doing my own job. I'm sure it was also the first time Amoco had a female sales rep in North Dakota.

I remember going into a little town there once, walking into a coffee shop, and hearing people exclaim, "Oh, my goodness. It's the Amoco lady." Being the Amoco rep was a big deal in North Dakota. We had 40 percent of the market at that time, as well as a refinery, so it was a big company. For a twenty-two-year-old fresh out of college, being the Amoco rep was pretty cool.

The culture at Amoco was well-defined, based on years of a proven format of training and developing people in sales and marketing. One of the lessons I learned early on by observing my colleagues was never to turn down a new assignment. Amoco was a company that gave you loads of opportunities if they believed you had talent. I think I moved roughly thirteen times during my career. I took any job they gave me, and I worked my tail off.

Part of being successful in any business environment is learning how the game works—the unwritten rules, as a friend of mine calls it. One of the first things I had to do was learn to golf. I had never picked up a golf club—with my upbringing, are you kidding?—but I realized the golf course was where real business happened. Given the fact that I worked predominantly with middle-aged men, I also had to learn all about sports. I was always more of a casual spectator—hardly sophisticated enough to carry on the Monday morning water cooler conversation beyond five minutes. So every Monday morning I'd read the paper and figure out who won all the games, so I'd be able to hold my own with the guys.

During my career I witnessed my share of harassment, obnoxious comments, and all those things you read about in the papers. I worked in a male-dominated industry surrounded primarily by guys who were a generation older than me. Women of my generation in business had difficult choices to make. It was important to pick your battles and not put yourself in a place where you could feel compromised. I adopted a belief, rightly or wrongly, that there is a fine line for women between being a bimbo and a bitch. I learned quickly that a woman who's too assertive runs the risk of being called a bitch. I also learned that if you were the last one leaving the cocktail party at the company meeting, you put your reputation at risk, given the usual sorts of characters who were the last to shut off the lights. I was careful in choosing my battles because the men resented women who took on all the battles. And women who took on none of the battles never got promoted.

One of the hardest things I had to fight—perhaps more internally—was the worry that every time I got a promotion some people would claim I got it only because I was a woman. I remember asking the company vice president once how to handle people like that. He gave me some great advice: "If you know in your heart you deserved the shot, and you can continue to prove your skills, after a while, it's their problem. You have to stop making it your problem." And he was right. As long as I knew I deserved the promotion, I stopped trying to make excuses for why I got it.

In 1994, when I was pregnant with my second child, my name came up regarding Amoco's plans to open a downstream office in China. Apparently, in the course of discussing possible candidates, one person said, "We can't ask Anna to go because she's expecting a baby." Someone else said, "Why don't we ask Anna?" I'm so grateful that someone chose to ask me rather than making the assumption on my behalf. When I was asked, I told them, "As long as my child is born healthy, count me in. I'll go." So the first time I set foot on mainland China, my son was three months old. We were there for almost two years; I met relatives I'd never known before. It was an incredible experience, both professionally and personally.

I remember sitting around the table when I was about eight years old and all the other kids were outside playing. I had to sit at home going through textbooks, learning how to read and write Chinese. I've spent a lot of energy cursing my parents because I didn't get to have a normal childhood. But it all paid off when I got to Beijing.

It was nice to be named one of the top women at a Fortune 50 company. My parents never dreamed they would have a daughter who would do something like that, so it was neat for them. But those lists are mainly to give your mother something to tell her friends about. They're so subjective, and there are so many fabulous people I know who make huge differences but who never get mentioned in those lists, so I don't put too much credence in them.

In 1999, Amoco merged with BP, and the company headquarters moved from Chicago, Illinois, to London, England. With that move went the familiar culture to which I had grown accustomed and many of the people I'd grown to know and love over the years. The BP experience was great—we lived in London for five years, where I served as the company's first group vice president of marketing. But eventually I learned, through formal and informal ways, that I wasn't seen as being someone who was going to be sitting at the top table. And that's fine—every company has its prerogatives—but I always believed that my professional choices were in my hands. As someone who had never turned down a move, the thought of striking out on my own was scary. But I trusted my heart and knew I had the support of those who mattered most in my life. It was the first time in my career that I really felt I didn't have to keep climbing to prove anything to anyone. You spend a good part of your life trying to prove you're good, and then you reach a point in your life where you think, "I'm done proving myself. Now I actually need to figure out if there's something else I'm supposed to do."

At different stages in my life, I feel I've been successful at different things; it's actually very important to take the time to listen to that little voice inside your head that says you actually should be doing something different. I once heard that success is getting what you want and happiness is wanting what you get. I really like that. To me, it's important to feel you're doing well at what you were meant to do. As an executive, it's easy to measure yourself by how others treat you. That's not always positive, either. Too often people change their styles, their beliefs, and even their values to please others. I think that's dangerous. The most important thing to keep in mind is to be true to yourself and your convictions.

I made a promise that I would always be true to myself, and I wouldn't be someone I'm not. There are a lot of people who go through life doing something just because they feel it's expected of them. They run the risk of being unfulfilled, whatever others may believe about their success. It's important to not live someone else's dream.

CHAPTER 35

• • •

Bobby Flay

CHEF, RESTAURATEUR, AND FOOD NETWORK HOST

Bobby Flay's culinary versatility and larger-than-life personality are evident in the immense success he's achieved as a critically acclaimed chef, restaurateur, award-winning cookbook author, and television personality.

Flay discovered his culinary identity at the age of seventeen, working as a cook at the famed New York theater district haunt, Joe Allen's. This eventually led Flay to study at The French Culinary Institute where he earned the first "Outstanding Graduate Award" in 1993. He now serves there as Master Instructor.

Flay parlayed his immense talents into a string of wildly successful restaurants—Mesa Grill, Bolo, Bar Americain, Bobby Flay Steak—as well as a number of best-selling cookbooks. He has launched and starred in a variety of critically acclaimed and fan-favorite cooking shows on the Food Network, including the Emmy Award–winning *Boy Meets Grill*. Flay is also Food Correspondent for CBS News' *The Early Show*.

At the age of eighteen, Bobby Flay discovered the one thing he loved to do—cook. A brief stint on Wall Street cemented Flay's disdain for a job that he wasn't passionate about—and led him to pursue his life's work as a chef and restaurateur.

"MY IDEA OF SUCCESS CHANGES AS I GET
OLDER. WHEN I FIRST STARTED COOKING, I
THOUGHT I WOULD FEEL REALLY SUCCESSFUL
IF I COULD OPEN A RESTAURANT ONE DAY.
MY GOAL WAS SIMPLE THEN—JUST OPEN MY
OWN PLACE. THEN AT SOME POINT YOU HAVE
FIVE, AND THEN YOU START THINKING ABOUT
WHAT YOUR NEXT GOAL COULD BE."

I'm a New York City kid, born and raised in Manhattan. I went to every Catholic school in New York, and since I wasn't into academics at all, sports really saved me. I played basketball and baseball, and I ran track, which is basically what kept me in high school. I had no real aspirations growing up. My greatest wish was to hang out with my friends every day. I didn't have any sense of what I wanted to do, and I was a terrible student, so college wasn't really a big concern of mine.

In a sense, it was an accident that I got interested in becoming a chef. My dad was an attorney for a long time; then he went into the restaurant business—as a partner, not as a cook. Before my mom retired, she was in the pharmaceutical/cosmetic business. When I got out of school, my father said, "If you're not going to go to school, make sure you go get a job. There is no choice here." So when I got my first job in a restaurant, I wasn't setting out to become a chef; I just needed to work. I worked in the salad station of a Broadway restaurant called Joe Allen's, a famous hangout for theater people, actors and producers. I had just turned eighteen.

Then something sort of miraculous happened. About six months into the job, I remember waking up one morning thinking that I really liked it. I was actually looking forward to going to work every day. It went from being something I felt I had to do to something I really wanted to do.

About a year after I started at Joe Allen's, I enrolled in the French Culinary Institute. I was in the class of 1984, the school's very first class. By that point I was very much into cooking, but I was still very young. I worked in a bunch of restaurants for three or four years, until I was about twenty-two—that turned out to be my apprenticeship. But I actually got burned out a little bit. After working for four years in a kitchen, I was tired of it. All my friends had gone to Wall Street and were making a ton of money, and I was making $250 a week.

So I left the restaurant business for six months and I worked on the floor of the American Stock Exchange. I was a clerk in what they call the wires, which is basically the grandstand that overlooks the floor of the exchange. I had four phones in my ears, and I had to know all the hand signals, and I was yelling and screaming down to the brokers on the floor. It was quite a scene. But I hated it—because there was no creativity to it. Everybody was stabbing each other in the back to make the next nickel. It just wasn't for me. So I decided to go back to cooking.

One day, someone on the floor of the exchange told me they knew someone who was looking for a chef to open a restaurant in California. I applied for the job and was hired, and I spent the next year out in California. The restaurant was very successful, but the person I was in partnership with wasn't a very good businessperson. So after my paycheck bounced a number of times, I finally said, "If you bounce one more check, I'm getting on a plane. I'm not trapped here, just so you know. I'm five hours from home."

Sure enough, another check bounced, and I stuck to my word and got on a plane and came home to New York. Then I became the chef of a restaurant called Miracle Grill. At the time, the East Village was anything but a restaurant destination—this is back when you needed weapons to go down there. But slowly, slowly, people started saying, "This is a find in the East Village." I was there for about three years, and I started getting a little bit of a name. Then I became partners with a guy named Jerry Kretchmer, who owned Gotham Bar and Grill, and together we opened Mesa Grill.

I actually learned a lot about southwestern cuisine from a guy from California who moved to New York. He was the first good chef I worked for, and he really taught me about good food. I lean on his cooking philosophies even today. He opened a restaurant called Jam along with a couple of other restaurants. He was the first person to bring California cuisine to the East Coast. So I was always around all those ingredients—the corn, the fresh-dried chili peppers, the chipotle, all those things.

There's no magic to the restaurant business. It's a lot of hours, a lot of hard work. You just get up in the morning and you go to work. I'm always at the place I feel needs me the most. Yesterday we were changing four or five dishes at one of my restaurants, so I was there, working closely with the staff. Later that night I went to Mesa Grill, to check up on a couple of things I wanted the kitchen to work on.

When you become successful, it doesn't get any easier. In fact, I think it gets even harder. You can't rest on your laurels when you become successful. My philosophy is, if you're not moving forward in this business, you're not just standing still, you're actually going backward. You're regressing. That's how fast-moving it is. I tell my kitchen staffs that if all we do is try to keep the food as good as it is, it's only going to get worse. You always have to try to make it better so that the quality and consistency remain. In the restaurant business, you can never think, "Okay, we've got it now. Now we can kick back." *Ever.*

My latest New York restaurant is Bar Americain. It's less risky from a cuisine standpoint. But it's the way I like to eat now—celebrating regional American food, with a brasserie feel. If you don't pay attention to the old dishes and you take them for granted, they get tired. But there's something about revisiting them that works.

I'm often asked about cooking at home. It's like the old cliché where people wonder if the shoemaker has time to make shoes for his own family. My food at home is way simpler than it is at the restaurants. I think you'd hear that from almost any chef. My wife always jokes about what a messy cook I am. If I'm making a one-pot dish, I'll need fifteen pots to do it.

My suggestion to amateur chefs who are entertaining is to keep it really simple. If you want to try something new, start by adding one new element to what you already know. If you're making three dishes, do one that's new to complement two that are tried and proven. That way, you know at least two are going to work. Go slow. Don't try to be a hero.

If you're considering a career in the kitchen, I would definitely advise going to culinary school. Then start researching the kinds of food you want to learn. Seek out a job with a chef—someone you like, respect, and want to work with. Do that for at least a year, then go on to the next job and the next one. After working with at least three chefs you admire, step back and see where you are. You won't necessarily have your own style yet. You're going to be using other people's styles, but that's okay. You learn and then you experiment and adapt. That's how you get inspired.

I always have the next goal, and I try to meet it. Even though I've had some successes, I try to look for the next challenge. My idea of success changes as I get older. When I first started cooking, I thought I'd feel really successful if I could open a restaurant one day. My goal was simple then—just open my own place. Then at some point you have five, and then you start thinking about what the next goal could be.

Today, I would say my idea of success would be to have a more normal life. Seriously. That's a true goal. That's a very different goal from having five restaurants. But think about it: The first goal allows the second goal to be even a possibility.

I'm married now, and I have a great wife. I have a ten-year-old daughter from a previous marriage. And I'm probably going to have more kids. You have to make room in your life for that stuff. You have to find the happy medium where you can afford to enjoy your life but at the same time enjoy it. My ultimate goal is to be able to do both of those things successfully.

CHAPTER 36

• • •

John "Jack" Bergen

SENIOR VICE PRESIDENT, CORPORATE AFFAIRS AND MARKETING, SIEMENS CORPORATION

Jack Bergen is responsible for all external and internal communications, as well as integrated marketing and brand advertising, for Siemens USA, a $20 billion diversified electronics and engineering company.

Before joining Siemens, Bergen served as president of the Council of Public Relations Firms, the first trade association representing the public relations industry. Bergen joined the council from CBS Corporation, where as senior vice president for corporate relations he played a key role in the transformation of the Westinghouse Electric Corporation into CBS—widely recognized as one of the most successful restructurings in corporate history.

Earlier in his career, Bergen was president of U.S. operations for the public relations firm Hill & Knowlton and director of strategic communications at General Electric.

A Vietnam veteran who also led military units in Europe and Korea, Bergen served as an army ranger and paratrooper, a strategic planner in the Pentagon, and chief speechwriter to Secretary of Defense Caspar Weinberger during the Reagan administration.

Jack Bergen has always been motivated by taking the road less traveled. This need to succeed beyond what would have been expected of him propelled Bergen out of the Bronx and onto the world stage. Bergen's outstanding military career, along with his determination to bring discipline and energy to each challenge, set the stage for the example of leadership he has shown in the corporate world.

"THE KEYS TO SUCCESS INCLUDE ENERGY, PERSISTENCE, AND BRAINS. YOU HAVE TO LIKE TO COMPETE AND ENJOY BEING GRADED. YOU NEED TO TAKE RISKS. RISK ENERGIZES ME. YOU NEED BRAINS TO SCOPE OUT THE SITUATION, WHETHER YOU'RE A QUARTERBACK OR IN BUSINESS. AND YOU DON'T GIVE UP."

Growing up relatively poor in the Bronx defined me. The drive to escape shaped my future. If you were Bronx Irish, you became an accountant, fireman, policeman, or insurance salesman. I wanted to do something different, and to do that I knew I needed to break out of the neighborhood.

I've always worked. I used to deliver groceries for Gristede's, the grocery store chain. It was important for me to get lots of customers, lots of deliveries, and to be the top person with the most tips. I don't know what motivated me. I just wanted to keep score. I didn't enjoy seeing anybody else lose; I just liked to test myself against others and to do better than I did the day before.

I also sold hot dogs at Yankee Stadium. Each day, they would give bonuses to the three kids who sold the most hot dogs, and I was always in the top three. The joy came from competing with myself rather than the other guys. There was a defense mechanism there, a certain sneakiness about it. You didn't want to beat the other guy too badly because that could bring out more competition.

I played basketball and football and ran track in high school. I was never a great athlete, but I always played. I took joy from playing, from the satisfaction of competition.

My dad was a great baseball player; in fact, he quit high school and tried to make it to the majors but never did. I didn't want my dad to come to my baseball games because I knew how good he was, and I would have been embarrassed if he saw me strike out or drop a fly ball. So I never told him when my games were, and I think it probably hurt him. He was a good guy; he wouldn't have made me feel bad about it. My biggest disappointment as a kid was my inability to shine in the one sport all kids in the Bronx played: stickball.

I went to a Catholic school, and the nuns made a big deal about competition for grades. So I made sure to come out top of the class, all A's.

I think success comes with taking the road not taken—just as the old Robert Frost poem says. From the time I left elementary school, I always took the road not taken. Almost everyone who went to my elementary school continued in our parish high school in the Bronx, but I went to Fordham Prep, a prestigious Jesuit school. That was my first step in escaping the Bronx—leaving my parish school, a comfortable setting where I knew I could stay at the top of the class, for a different school. At Fordham I didn't make the top of the class, but I was in the Greek honors course, the toughest curriculum.

I always did the thing that looked a little bit harder. That way you don't have to fight so hard with the rest of the pack. If you take the tougher road and you make the team, it's a lot easier. Then you're in an elite situation, and people give you the benefit of the doubt. In the end, that was what allowed me to move up faster.

That's one of the reasons I tried to get into West Point. I lucked out because my track coach knew a congressman in the South Bronx, where few people wanted to go to West Point, and he put me on his list. After graduation, I went to the U.S. Army Ranger School, went to Germany, then came back, left my family, and went to Vietnam for a thirteen-month tour. I came home, went to grad school, and then went back to West Point for three more years to teach English and philosophy. I also taught the first black studies course at West Point. Then it was off to Korea, and when I returned I took a staff job in the Pentagon.

I'll be honest: I've never had a passion to be one thing in particular. I never really knew exactly what I wanted to be. I did have some disappointments—not being able to play baseball or being forced to go back and redo my marksman tests at West Point because I had never fired a weapon. But because I never had an all-consuming passion, I never had a moment when I was devastated that I'd pursued something and not made it.

At every point in my life, there's always been someone I learned from and wanted to do well for. There was a nun in elementary school. There was my roommate at West Point, Jim Powers, who was killed in Vietnam. He was a person with great values, whom I really admired and wanted to be like. Another was my first civilian boss, Tom Ross, a kind and wise man who helped me navigate the new corporate landscape.

Colin Powell was another. He was the military assistant to the secretary of defense when I was the speechwriter for Caspar Weinberger. Since we were the only army guys on Weinberger's staff, we got to be close, and I admired him tremendously as a person of integrity and quiet firmness.

With Weinberger, I learned the power of standing on your principles. In those days, the big issue was fighting for a bigger defense budget. No one in Congress wanted us to have the money we needed. I'll always remember those meetings: The congressional liaison guys would say, "You've got to have something in your back pocket to pull out as a compromise." Weinberger said, "No, I refuse to bargain over something so important." We got the budget.

I got my first big job break thanks to Powell. I had no real civilian skills coming out of the military. Powell called Tom Ross and said, "There's a guy here who's thinking about getting out of the army, and he wants to talk to you." I met him and was hired on the spot, even though I knew nothing about the business and nothing about corporate communications and public relations. Years later I asked him, "Why did you hire me?" And he said, "Because the day that Colin Powell called me, my wife had given me a hard time at breakfast about coming home so late every night. She said, 'You've got to get more balance in your life; you've got to get home earlier.' Powell had said, 'I want you to meet this guy Jack Bergen. He's a good guy, and he's made my day three hours shorter.'"

I lucked out again when I got to know Jack Welch after GE bought our company. It was his first acquisition, the largest in history at the time. I became the communications guy to help bring the two companies together for Welch.

People ask me, "How did you make it so high and so fast in the business world when you started out at forty-two?" I think it's because I had no fear of failure. It wasn't like the military, where if you screw up, somebody could die. There wasn't that kind of pressure. That was a very liberating feeling that allowed me to succeed.

The keys to success include energy, persistence, and brains. You have to like to compete and enjoy being graded. You need to take risks. Risk energizes me. You need brains to scope out the situation, whether you're a quarterback or in business. And you don't give up.

I've done many all-nighters at work. In combat you do it to stay alive, but in business it takes persistence. Many times I could have given up and gone to bed, could have just done it tomorrow. But I knew that if I did, I would have done a half-assed job. Still, you have to have balance: You have to have the ability to totally relax when you're not under attack by deadlines.

I am tough, but I'm not stubborn. I don't impose my will on everyone. I lead by example, and I bend a lot in order to win. I don't say, "Here are the five things you need to do to succeed." I don't preach because I know that others may have five different characteristics they feel are necessary to succeed. I'm always thinking about what's in it for the other people I'm working with or trying to influence. The key is to get outside yourself and find out what it's going to take for the other person to succeed. If you view life as a constant competition, there'll always be a person you're trying to convince or beat. But you'll show others there's a benefit for them, too.

That's the Bronx in me, still having its effect half a century later.

CHAPTER 37

• • •

Heidi Klum

SUPERMODEL / HOST AND EXECUTIVE PRODUCER,
PROJECT RUNWAY

Having graced the cover of every top fashion magazine in the world, Heidi Klum is synonymous with "supermodel." Her first big break came at the age of eighteen, when she won a national modeling contest in Germany. Klum went on to achieve international recognition and global superstardom in 1998 after landing on the cover of *Sports Illustrated*'s swimsuit issue, and she subsequently became the face—and body—of the hugely popular Victoria's Secret catalogs and runway shows.

Klum has successfully parlayed her modeling career into numerous entrepreneurial ventures, establishing herself as a smart and savvy businesswoman and earning herself a repeated place on *Forbes* magazine's "Top 100 Celebrities" list. She is the host and executive producer of the Emmy-nominated reality series *Project Runway*, called "the Prada of reality shows" by *The New York Times*. She has designed her own jewelry and shoe collections and is at the helm of a best-selling European clothing, accessories, fragrance, and beauty line.

Being a model was never going to be fulfilling enough for Heidi Klum. She was too smart and had too much personality to be seen and not heard. Klum was savvy enough to realize that if she wanted to stand out from the rest of the supermodel pack, she'd have to broaden her skill set. She began to explore new business ventures—acting, designing clothes, and creating and starring in television shows—that allowed her to showcase her brains as well as her beauty, and soon her success exploded.

"SUCCESS IS BEING AT PEACE WITH YOURSELF, LIKING WHAT YOU DO, AND HAVING A FAMILY. HAVING MONEY AND A SUCCESSFUL CAREER IS NO SUCCESS IF YOU DON'T HAVE LOVE AROUND YOU."

I always dreamed about being a dancer. I did jazz, ballet, and tap, starting when I was very young. I went three times a week, and I was really passionate about it. I was always the girl in the first row in the front, and I was always an achiever. I wanted to do my best. But deep down I knew I wasn't that good, even though I tried really hard. I could never do the splits far enough, and I could never kick my leg as high as all the other girls.

I was born in a small town in Germany. Growing up, my brother and I didn't have computers. We didn't have too many toys. But we were very arts-and-craftsy at home, always sewing and making things. We made clothes for our Barbies because we didn't have a lot of money. And if other kids had things we wanted, we would just make them ourselves. Once, when my parents came back from a trip, they brought us little crocodiles from Lacoste and we sewed them onto our sweaters because we couldn't afford the sweaters ourselves. We were inventive.

When I was seventeen, I saw this coupon in a magazine for a modeling contest, and I cut it out and entered it. It was a silly, spur-of-the-moment idea. I put on a bathing suit and my dancing stockings, scraped my hair up in pieces—which I thought was cute—put some makeup on, and my girlfriend took pictures of me on the couch.

It turned out that the contest was a much bigger deal than I'd thought. I had to drive five hours to Munich for the casting. I didn't even know what a casting meant at that time. It turned out the contest was going to be broadcast on television, and they needed to see if we could actually talk before putting us on the air. They asked us silly questions—"What do you like to eat?" or "What is your star sign?" They just wanted to see if you could answer or if you were too shy and quiet. Quiet doesn't make good television.

Then, all of a sudden, I was in the show. This time I went with my mom, and it was all very exciting. It was one of the biggest shows we had—like the Jay Leno of Germany. It was amazing. We had to learn how to do the catwalk a little bit, to present ourselves to the audience.

It was a six-month competition. Each week, they would show three girls and the viewers at home would call in to vote for the one they liked. Once you won the week, you had to win the month, and then finally the six girls who won the months all competed. I made it to the finale of the last six girls, and I won the thing. It was crazy. It was one of the biggest contests Germany had ever seen; the prize was a $300,000 contract—which was a lot of money in Germany in 1992. Actually, it's a lot of money now!

I had just turned eighteen. I used the money to buy my own apartment. I felt like I had already made it: If nothing else had happened, I would have gone to school and learned to be a designer. I never really thought I was going to make it big in this industry. Still, I always worked very hard. I went to more castings than they wanted me to; I was always the one who was pushy. I wanted to make the most out of my time. I never really thought, "Oh, maybe I'm pretty, but I'm not *that* pretty. I can't be prettier than all the other girls out there."

Around this time, Claudia Schiffer was really, really big, and so was Eva Herzigová. They'd come into the modeling agency, and I'd look at them, then look at myself, and I'd think, "I'm maybe three or four years younger, but I just don't look like that. They're so tall and skinny and amazing, with blond hair down to their butts." They just looked like Barbies—they were perfect. I looked in the mirror, and I couldn't imagine I was competitive with these people. In the beginning, I never got cast in runway shows: I was too short, too fat, not "rail-y" enough. I had boobs, I had hips, I had all the things you weren't supposed to have for the runway.

Still, I said, I'm not going to starve myself. I'm not going to change. I'm not going to get skinnier. So I started thinking about other opportunities. I started exploring doing television and commercials—being with clients where I could talk about the products. There weren't many girls who liked doing that kind of work. Most girls wanted to be cool, to be just a face, not to have to do *Access Hollywood* and *Extra* and all these things. But I loved it. I liked hamming it up in front of the camera, showing people how it is backstage, how we put makeup on, what the clothes rack looks like. I never minded doing that. And that helped me find my own way to the top, different from the way other girls did.

To this day, I don't think I'm better looking than other girls. I just think I was always more inventive. I knew I always wanted to do more than just catalog and photo shoots. I surrounded myself with people I thought would help me get to the next level. I always asked a lot of questions. Nothing ever fell into my lap. I think you have to make your own success. It doesn't always work out, and if it doesn't, go a different route and try different things. You have to see it as a kind of stepladder. If you can't reach what you want without getting onto that next step, then how do you get there? Figure it out. Read more; ask questions; see how other people did it.

For me, success means being really happy. Having a great family, to me, is the most I can ever wish for. Success is being at peace with yourself, liking what you do, and having a family. Having money and a successful career is no success if you don't have love around you.

I love that I have so many different things going on in my life, and that's what I thrive on. I always say I like a plate with different tastes. I don't want to eat the same thing every day. *Project Runway* is a great thing, and in Germany I do *Top Model*. I have a jewelry line, and I'm working with Birkenstock and all the other different things I do. If I had to focus on only one thing, it would be boring for me. I need to have all these different things to be happy.

I'm not a huge risk taker. I'm very German that way. I think about things a lot before I do them. I'm big on making schedules. I never think, "Let's see what happens tomorrow." I like to plan five to six months ahead.

I never fear failure because I always try my best. When I do a project, I give it everything. I might not be the best at a certain thing, but if I try my absolute hardest, then failure doesn't bother me—because I know there's nothing I could have done better.

If I had to do it all over again, there's nothing I'd do differently, and that's a great thing to be able to say. I'm pretty happy with the way things have turned out. Some things took longer to happen than others, but I think those ups and downs make you who you are. The more you work on things, the better you get.

CHAPTER 38

• • •

Sergio Zyman

FOUNDER, ZYMAN GROUP, AND FORMER CHIEF
MARKETING OFFICER OF COCA-COLA

Sergio Zyman is the founder and chairman of Zyman Group and the former chief marketing officer of the Coca-Cola Company.

During his tenure with Coca-Cola in the 1980s, Zyman reconceptualized the company's marketing strategy and boosted worldwide annual sales volume from nine to fifteen billion cases annually—the most explosive growth period in the company's history. His success prompted *Time* to name him one of the three key pitchmen of the twentieth century.

Zyman's legendary marketing career also includes tenures with PepsiCo and Procter & Gamble. Over the course of more than thirty years of hands-on marketing experience, Zyman has refined a set of proven principles for translating marketing strategies into positive business results. He passionately advocates a vision of scientific, process-based marketing as the path to higher sales and profits. The only definition of marketing success he upholds is "selling more stuff to more people more often for more money more efficiently."

In 1999, Zyman founded the Zyman Group, a cutting-edge marketing and growth strategy solutions company, named by *Inc.* magazine as one of the fastest-growing privately held companies in America.

Sergio Zyman's quest for independence has been the driving force in his life, giving him the ability to think about things in unconventional ways and to negotiate in unconventional terms. Growing up in Mexico, Zyman knew a conventional life lived on other people's terms wouldn't be enough for him; he had to blaze his own trail. Zyman's career has been fueled by an intense desire to control his own destiny. His immense success at the Coca-Cola Company underscores his marketing savvy and established him as a formidable competitor. Zyman is the ultimate consultants' consultant, advising leading brands around the world.

"TO ME, SUCCESS MEANT HAVING THE POWER OF KNOWLEDGE, THE POWER OF MONEY, AND THE POWER OF EXPERIENCE TO MAKE THE DECISIONS I NEEDED TO MAKE WHEN I NEEDED TO. IT WAS ABOUT POWER."

I lived in a very parochial environment. I was a Jewish guy in Mexico in a first-generation European household. The path was very narrow: Basically, you grew up, you went to school, you got a girlfriend, you got married in a big wedding, and your father-in-law bought you a house. Then you went to work for your father-in-law or your dad, you had a bunch of kids, and you were fat by the age of forty. It was a very clear and accepted way of life. But it wasn't for me. I wanted to do something totally different. I didn't know what it was, but I knew I wanted to travel and see the world.

I went to Europe with my mom for my bar mitzvah. We took a boat, but first we took a plane from Mexico City to New York. As we were sitting on the plane, we saw a guy with a button-down shirt and wingtips and a briefcase and a coat. He sat down and opened up his briefcase and loosened up his tie and untied his shoelaces. I got a look at this and thought, "Oh, my God, that is the life." Traveling on business on a plane and having a company take you around the world and do kinds of stuff like that. That became very romantic to me, being able to get into joining the world.

My father wanted me to move to Israel and get into politics. He really believed I could become the prime minister of Israel. He wanted to live vicariously through me. But that wasn't the sort of thing I wanted to do.

Getting out of Mexico was about opportunity. I didn't know what it was, but I thought I could do good; I thought I could be successful. I never planned to be what I am today. I always had an inferiority complex about it. I never thought I was going to be CEO of a company or anything like that. I just took advantage of the opportunities as the opportunities were presented to me.

When I started working at Procter & Gamble, success meant being promoted to sales training after serving as a staff assistant or a schlepper. Then success was surviving the three and a half months of training and becoming an assistant manager. After sales training, you had to perform. So those were the rules for success. I think that was the first time that being a success was important to me.

I think in order to win in business you have to be highly strategic. You have to be able to approach everyone you deal with in a planning mind-set. You have to understand what winning is. I find that in many cases, people don't spend time thinking about such things. When I was at Coke, I sat down with Bob Wright at NBC to negotiate our advertising for the 1996 Olympics. I knew Bob needed us to make a huge commitment or he was going to have a tough time getting other sponsors. I said, "How much do you want?" He said, "I need $68 million." I told him we wanted to spend only $45 million, but that he had a deal at $68 million. Wright wanted to know what I wanted in return. I said, "I don't know yet. It's your price, my terms." We paid the asking price, but we ended up getting about $100 million worth of media, morning TV, and all kinds of extras.

I did a similar thing with pro basketball. I went to see David Stern and convinced him we could help the NBA and make a hundred-year deal with him. Stern needed to expand the NBA. So we said, "Listen, we'll go build backboards in the inner cities. You don't have any business in any other countries—we'll take you international." And that's what he wanted. So it was a question of understanding what was important to them. I sealed that deal with him on a handshake.

Basically, I tried to stay ahead of everybody. I tried to foresee the behaviors of companies that were trying to change things. We changed the packaging of Diet Coke, knowing that Diet Pepsi would, too. By the time they followed us, we'd already changed it again. We did two designs at the same time. We never assumed any of our actions were going to last long.

I've developed my own rules for success. For me, success meant getting to the point where I could make the decisions myself. It meant having "screw-you money." I wanted to get to the point where I could say to an employer, "Screw you. I have enough money now, and I don't need you anymore." Today, however, success is knowledge, not just money. What do you know? How much do you know about the world? Do you know what's going on in India?

If you're not going up, you're going down. The question is, how far up the hill do you want to get? A lot of people have dreams of getting to the top of the hill, but they have no plan to get there. It's important to have a sense of what success is—whether it's buying a house, getting a job, or getting promoted. Unfortunately, most of us spend more time doing what we *have to* do than what we *want to* do. We try to succeed by conforming. A driven person's definition of success will change throughout his life. Once we achieve our initial goals, we start working toward the next level. That can go on and on forever—but it can also become a trap. Enough is enough. I know I've finally reached the point in my life where I don't have to prove myself to anyone. And there is no greater success than that.

CHAPTER 39

• • •

Vivian Banta

FORMER VICE CHAIRMAN, PRUDENTIAL FINANCIAL

Vivian Banta is one of the most respected women in corporate America. She has been one of *Fortune*'s "50 Most Powerful Women in Business" each year since 2000 and has earned a spot on *Forbes*'s "100 Most Powerful Women in the World" list every year since 2004.

Until she retired in 2007, Banta was a member of Prudential Financial's Office of the Chairman, with responsibility for the Insurance Division and its Closed Block business. Banta also had responsibility for Prudential's real estate and relocation services. She assumed the position in August 2002, having been with the company since 1998.

Before joining Prudential, Banta was executive vice president in charge of Global Investor Services at the Chase Manhattan Corporation. In this position, Banta increased revenue fivefold, and assets under her administration rose to more than $3.5 trillion.

Previously, she held the position of global securities operations and systems executive, and she began her career at Chase as vice president of global custody, international operations and systems, in 1987.

Vivian Banta's career—and life—epitomizes the maxim that it's the journey, not the destination, that counts. Her success comes from her strong sense of independence and her steadfast refusal to subscribe to anyone else's definition of success but her own. It's never been about any one particular position; instead, it's been about challenging herself and taking on new tasks that interest her. She looks at issues from multiple perspectives to find new kinds of solutions and is a perfect example of how you don't need to start with a specific goal in mind in order to achieve any success you wish.

"I DON'T DEFINE MY BUSINESS EXPERIENCES IN WIN-OR-LOSE TERMS. FOR ME, IT'S ABOUT BEING REALISTIC AND BALANCED. IT'S ABOUT MAKING TANGIBLE PROGRESS, ABOUT MOVING FORWARD AND DOING BETTER AS A GROUP. THAT'S SUCCESS."

I had no idea what I wanted to be when I grew up. I thought I wanted to be in business, but I didn't know in what capacity. I did not have a plan.

I ran for class president in junior high school. I ran quite a campaign! I went as far as riding around the school grounds in the back of a convertible, waving to people as I drove by. The funny thing is, I don't remember whether I won or not. I just remember competing for office. I also remember having a great time doing it and having a lot of fun. I didn't have to win—it wasn't do-or-die. The journey was more important to me than the result. I think that philosophy has been evident throughout my career.

An early disappointment in my professional career came when I was hired to go into an analyst training program at Bank of America. I didn't take the program seriously, didn't put the time and energy into it, and consequently I failed. But that turned out to be a very good thing for me. The lesson I took away is, "I do have to take this seriously. This is not a joke. It's not fun and games. I have to put energy, time, and effort into it if I'm going to make it work." Obviously, hindsight is twenty-twenty. Now I characterize it as a learning experience, but at the time it certainly seemed like a setback. I had never failed before.

I've also learned valuable lessons from examples set by others. Earlier in my career, when I was working for a bank that shall remain nameless, I was thrown into a position where all my predecessors had failed. The division had been put on the company's "watch" list, which basically meant that we were in serious trouble. And I was new to this business. One of the things I did know was that whenever there were serious problems, you had to send those problems up the management chain.

At the time, I had two bosses. When I explained the problems I was seeing to boss number one, his immediate reaction was to pepper me with questions, criticize me, and basically scare me to death. Then, when I explained the same set of issues to boss number two, his reaction was, "I understand what you're dealing with. How can I help you?" The difference between those two reactions was just unbelievably stark. Whom would you rather work for? I never forgot that lesson, and I draw on it all the time.

I don't define my success in win-lose terms. I actually define my success in being able to deliver tangible results that move the company or the business or whatever forward. Nine out of ten times you are not going to achieve what you set out to achieve. So for me, it's being more realistic and balanced. I wouldn't consider myself risk-averse by any stretch, but I would also say I have very good instincts. I have developed the ability to know when and how to do it, and I have a good batting average. At the end of the day, that's what's most important. It's not that my decisions are 100 percent right, but hopefully I get 80 percent right, and the ones I don't get right I can live with.

Earlier in my career, I defined success in very specific terms: "Can I get this job done?" "Can I achieve this particular result?" But I fine-tuned that approach as I got older. To me, success is about more than just achieving a specific goal; it's about being able to move the needle along multiple fronts and make tangible progress. I haven't had one all-encompassing goal in I can't remember how long. I set broader benchmarks for myself, and I try to get closer and closer to that benchmark on many fronts. Those fronts can be specific goals or initiatives or very amorphous notions—like trying to improve culture or morale.

I try to take my work seriously, but I don't take myself too seriously. I had a boss once who said, "For God's sake, Vivian, it's not a heart-and-lung machine. It's just a stupid bank." And he was absolutely right. It's not life and death. You can't take yourself so seriously that you start to believe your own PR, or you lose sight of what's really important. I think keeping things in balance is a good way to maintain success. It goes back to having a good sense of who you are, not overinflating your ego—being able to work with people, being sensitive, being ethical. All those things make a difference.

I have a wonderful life and a wonderful career. But there are so many people out there who don't have what I have, and as I look forward, I'd really like to find a way to give something back. I'd like to be able to work with young women in particular, to share some of my experiences and help guide them as a mentor. I'd tell them to find something that you love. I do believe that winners breed winners, and I do believe that if you find something that you love, you'll be good at it, and if you're good at it, you'll be successful.

CHAPTER 40

· · ·

Barry Weissler

BROADWAY PRODUCER

Barry Weissler is one of the most prolific producers in Broadway history. Along with his wife and producing partner, Fran, Weissler has won five Tony Awards—including one for *Chicago*, the legendary musical he brought back to Broadway in 1996. *Chicago* holds the record for the longest-running musical revival in theater history.

Weissler's other Tony Award–winning Broadway productions include *Annie Get Your Gun, Gypsy, Fiddler on the Roof*, and *Othello*.

A signature feature of a Weissler production is the rotation of celebrity replacements in leading roles—an ingenious strategy Weissler pioneered and perfected over the course of his career.

Barry Weissler discovered theater his freshman year of college and never looked back. Early success as an actor led Weissler to branch out, and as a writer, director, and producer, he has pursued his passion for the theater in nearly every aspect of the profession.

"I LIVE MY LIFE AS I WISH IT. I DON'T HAVE A NINE-
TO-FIVE EXISTENCE WHERE SOMEONE TELLS ME
WHAT TO DO OR RELEASES ME IF THEY WISH. I
CONTROL MY OWN LIFE, AND I SUCCEED OR FAIL ON
MY OWN TALENT AND ABILITIES. SO I ENJOY BEING
THE MASTER OF MY OWN SHIP. IF SUCCESS MEANS
ANYTHING, IT MEANS THAT."

I was the product of an Eastern European immigrant family. They were hardworking people with limited vision, and even though they cared for me and did the appropriate things any parents would do—clothing, feeding, and educating me—they never thought of helping me with intellectual pursuits or opening a window for me onto cultural events. For that, I was left on my own. In school, I had tremendous problems trying to comprehend and execute ordinary lessons; I was always on the borderline of literacy. I barely found one college in all of the United States that would accept me as an undergraduate without putting me through the normal testing, which I'm sure I would have failed. But luck smiled on me, and the college I chose helped open my eyes and took me down the road of literature and culture.

In the first half of my freshman year, I nearly failed out. The dean of the school warned me that if I couldn't raise my D/F average to a C or above, I was finished. I remember wandering around campus in a semidepression, left entirely on my own, with no idea how to solve my problem—when, purely by accident, I came upon the college theater on campus. I don't know what drew me in, but inside I went. The student actors were rehearsing *Measure for Measure*. I walked into that dark theater, sat down in the back, and watched. It was a comforting, welcoming experience. That moment was the beginning of my theatrical adventure.

After joining the college theater, I spent hours in the library devouring everything I could about the plays and characters we were working on. That was how I started reading literature. It was as if an electric jolt had activated some special mechanism in me: I became a voracious reader, reading seven days a week, sometimes staying up all night reading and thinking. In the second half of my freshman year, I made the dean's list and joined a history honors program. That one fortuitous moment when I entered the theater had changed my life.

When I started acting in that theater, I discovered that I had an ability to connect with the audience through my characters, and the reviews I gained were astonishing. One critic wrote ecstatically about my comic prowess—about how much fun I gave the audience and what a pleasure it was to have me as part of the acting ensemble. I was overjoyed that I'd found a way of affecting other people's lives. And it made me realize that the theater would become my life's work.

After college I moved to New York City, studying acting more seriously and working as an actor off-Broadway and on tour. The most I ever made was $50 or $60 a week, but the money was never important to me—it was the pleasure I gained from being in this industry and the feeling of accomplishment I enjoyed. Eventually, because I wanted more control in my choice of work, I turned to directing. This gave me an even wider scope of potential achievement.

At the beginning of my directing career, I was always apprehensive about going into a room full of actors and actresses—about using the right vocabulary, giving them the right motivation. I would stay up night after night working on the script, writing out every minuscule moment and move, so I'd always have notes to fall back on during rehearsals. This was a very difficult and intense learning experience for me. As the years went by and I became more experienced and confident, I stopped putting those little marks in my scripts and started directing from what was in my mind and my instincts. As my company became successful, I started managing more and more of our shows—which was the bridge that led me to producing, which eventually led to Broadway.

Every one of my projects is important. I simply want my work to have relevance and to touch the audience. My wife and I have undertaken projects that no one else wanted: *Falsettos*, a play about a married man who leaves his family for his gay lover, which revolved around the subject of AIDS; *Chicago*, which surprisingly no other producers wanted to mount on Broadway. For *Chicago*, we knew the music and lyrics were brilliant and that it was a performance-driven, not production-driven, piece. It became a very important theatrical event and a worldwide phenomenon. It translated so well all over the world. Whatever language the audience speaks, everyone understands the justice system, the conflict between the sexes. The themes are global, and the dancing and lyrics and music delight everyone, no matter what country they're in.

Then there was *Grease*, which we did in the early 1990s. Every critic in the world slammed it; I don't think we received one decent review. And yet it became the success story of Broadway and the road. We ran for four years, had two separate touring companies, and this taught me a great lesson: The public is more important than the critics. In the end, it's the public that decides if you're a success or a failure.

Confidence and good instincts come from experience. The more you work, the better you become, especially if you're driven by that primeval need to succeed, to better yourself. Some people are frightened that they won't attain success; others, me included, are driven by the fear that we'll fail, and we must succeed to stave off that potential failure. Even after the success I've attained, I still fear failure. But I'm also driven by the desire to please the audience, who have paid to come see my work. I take great pleasure in creating something that will touch an audience, take them on a wonderful journey, even change their lives a little bit. I want to create the right work from the right choices that can serve to give my audience a sense of joy.

Have I ever failed? Of course—in the theater, that comes with the territory. But over the years, I've learned how to handle it. I thought my first failures would destroy me and stop me from going on, but somehow I moved through them, became stronger because of them, and now I deal with the infrequent failures in a different way.

Yes, I've had great success, but I don't think what I enjoy about my work has that much to do with success. Of course I wanted to be successful in what I did, but it was the actual achievement that meant the most to me—learning my craft, acting, directing, and touching an audience. I like the word *achievement* much more than *success*. I live my life as I wish it to be. I don't have a nine-to-five existence where someone tells me what to do or releases me if they wish. I control my own life and succeed and fail on my own talent and abilities. I enjoy being the master of my own ship. If success means anything, it means that.

Another important aspect of my life is that I never reached out to do something theatrical for money; that was the furthest thought from my mind. I wanted to do good theater, and I was rewarded by having the public pay to buy my product. I hope I stay healthy and that everyone in my family stays healthy. I have many more productions I wish to do, and I certainly have no thoughts of retiring from this life. I don't know what I'd do if I couldn't continue my life's work.

Independents Who
Follow Their Dreams

CHAPTER 41

• • •

Brian Williams

ANCHOR AND MANAGING EDITOR,
NBC NIGHTLY NEWS

Brian Williams is the seventh anchor and managing editor in the history of *NBC Nightly News*, a position he has held since December 2004. His nightly broadcast represents the largest single daily source of news in America.

Williams is also the most honored network evening news anchor. He has received four Edward R. Murrow Awards, five Emmy Awards, the duPont–Columbia University Award, and the George Foster Peabody Award, the broadcasting industry's highest honor. Most of these awards were given for his work in New Orleans while covering Hurricane Katrina and its aftermath, and all were awarded to Williams in only his second year on the job.

Since joining NBC News in 1993, Williams has covered virtually every major breaking news event. As a veteran of political campaigns and elections, as well as the Middle East, he's traveled all over the country and around the world in the course of covering the news for more than two decades.

In 1994, Williams was named NBC News Chief White House correspondent, and covered virtually every foreign and domestic trip by President Bill Clinton until 1996.

For seven years beginning in 1996, he was anchor and managing editor of *The News with Brian Williams*, a live, hour-long nightly newscast on MSNBC and then on CNBC. Williams was the anchor and managing editor of the Saturday edition of *NBC Nightly News* for six years before becoming anchor of the weekday edition.

Before joining NBC News, Williams spent seven years as a correspondent and anchor for CBS in Philadelphia and New York, and before that he worked at WTTG in Washington. He started his career at KOAM-TV in Pittsburg, Kansas.

Prior to his broadcasting career, Williams worked in the White House during the Carter administration, beginning as a White House intern. He also spent several years as a volunteer firefighter in New Jersey.

His dream as a child was to be a network news anchor, but the odds were against Brian Williams from the start. Only three people in the whole world occupied the job he desperately wanted. But nothing deterred him— bad grades, failed jobs at small-market stations—or stood in the way of his dream. Williams is the personification of living one's dream, proving that once something is embedded in your psyche, few obstacles can derail you.

"WHAT ARE THE INGREDIENTS FOR SUCCESS?
TO ME, ABSOLUTELY NUMBER ONE IS SINGLE-
MINDED DESIRE. YOU HAVE TO BE WILLING TO DO
ANYTHING TO REACH YOUR GOAL."

I had a very deeply held secret. I grew up the archetype of the cold war–era kid, watching the black-and-white evening newscasts— mostly Walter Cronkite—believing that there was one job I wanted in the world. And there were only three of those jobs in the United States. It was the role of evening news anchor. I would have been content with numerous other professions, and God knows I tried them. But that one dream was something I kept secret all my life.

My family and friends say I was between six and eight years old when I started showing an interest in doing this for a living. I have no reason to doubt them.

I was a terrible student. My high school guidance counselor, seeing in me what others saw, sent me to a local community college, where the entrance requirement was a pulse. I confirmed their judgment, showing very little interest in my coursework. I was also volunteering as a fireman in my hometown in New Jersey, and the allure of waiting for the next run with the guys at the firehouse was much greater than that of higher education.

After a trip down to Washington with a friend, though, I caught an extreme case of Potomac fever. I was able to parlay some time in Washington into a White House internship and then into a job at the National Association of Broadcasters. There I met the manager of a small television station in Kansas. I begged him for an entry-level re-porting job and was hired. I wasn't great at it and couldn't live on the salary of $168 per week, so I moved back east. I had been in television a year.

After that first job went south, I couldn't get arrested. I spent days in the lobbies of television stations in the Midwest, hoping they'd screen the compiled tape of my work. I could not get them to give me the time of day. I lost an entire day off sitting in the lobby of a station in Mis-souri. I knew that the people I saw coming and going, looking at me sitting forlornly on the chair in their lobby, were the very same deci-sion makers I wanted just to screen my tape—yet they didn't make eye contact. Years later, after I became anchor of *Nightly News*, the station called to invite me to their fiftieth anniversary banquet. And I really did say to them, "You should have thought of that back when you kept me waiting in your lobby." I'm not usually the vindictive type, but back then it was all on the line for me.

There were times in my life when I thought all hope was lost. But I never gave up that dream in the back of my head. I returned to Wash-ington and took a series of menial jobs, thinking, "Well, okay. That was an experiment. They just don't realize I can do this." I had setbacks. I kicked around for a long time. There were times when I was so far from my goal that I could share it with no one. But I knew I could do it. I also knew it was about the most exciting thing to do in life—to be paid to travel and report the news of the day and see the world. I couldn't imagine anything I'd rather do.

Eventually, I got an inside job at a Washington television station—typing in the lettering on the screen. The boss there, the late Betty Endicott, put me on the air. She just said, "I think you would be good at this." I had to dig out the tapes of my previous work to prove to her that I'd done it before. And that launched me, because when I got back on the air in Washington, I got noticed at CBS. They hired me, and then NBC. Betty made what I call the last gut decision in television; there was no focus group, there was no consultant.

There's something interesting about the connection between being a fireman and being an anchorman—an endorphin-related common denominator. In both jobs, you have to have your boots next to your bed. You have to be packed and ready to go. I spent years responding to alarms, going to sleep with my pants connected to my boots on the floor next to the bed.

What are the ingredients for success? To me, absolutely number one is single-minded desire. You have to be willing to do anything to reach your goal. If life is a competition, I won my personal battle a long time ago, when I got the job I dreamed about as a young boy in front of the television set, watching the first color film of the Vietnam War. In this country, if you want something badly enough and you're willing to work harder than anyone else, then I don't see impediments. Luck mixed with hard work and a deeply held dream in the United States is a potent combination.

As a result, I'm not big on excuses. I tell this to a lot of students: You have to want it. If you chose television because it looked better than, say, farming or dentistry at your college career day, then you might as well go home, because you won't succeed. The work is too hard. There are a lot of people waiting to knock you down. But if it's all you could ever imagine doing, welcome to the best profession there is.

I awaken every day with the confidence of knowing that if it all went away tomorrow, I could support my family. There is nothing I'm not willing to do for a living. I've done a lot of it on my way up, and I don't count on any of this to be around forever. If it is, that's fine. I've already earned amounts beyond my wildest dreams. My wife and I regularly say that we have more than we need, so this is all gravy.

I find the self-made man or woman infinitely more interesting. Give me a self-made person and somebody who rolled out of bed on his twenty-first birthday to discover he had great wealth, and there's no question whom I am going to gravitate toward at a party—and whom I will get greater value out of knowing. I have worked for everything I have. I am a college dropout, and I'm not proud of that—but at least I can point to everything I have today and say, "I earned that."

CHAPTER 42

• • •

Mario Andretti

WORLD CHAMPION RACE CAR DRIVER

Mario Andretti is often called the greatest race car driver of all time, having proven himself a winner at all levels of competition. In his career he won the Indianapolis 500, the Daytona 500, the Formula One World Championship, and the Pikes Peak Hill Climb. In addition, he has won the Champ Car National Championship four times and was a three-time winner at Sebring. He has won races in sports cars, sprint cars, and stock cars—on ovals, road courses, drag strips, on dirt, and on pavement.

Andretti took the checkered flag 111 times during a career that spanned five decades. He was named "Driver of the Year" in three different decades (the 1960s, 1970s, and 1980s), "Driver of the Quarter Century" (in the 1990s), and "Driver of the Century" in 2000 by the Associated Press.

Though Andretti retired from full-time competition at the end of 1994, his family name continues to dominate motor sports today. Mario's two sons, Michael and Jeff, his nephew John, and his grandson Marco have followed in his famous footsteps and have each made a significant impact on the race car industry.

Today, Mario is a successful businessman off the track. His legacy continues with the Andretti Winery in Napa Valley, a petroleum business in California, several car dealerships, the Mario Andretti Racing School in Las Vegas, and the Andretti Indoor Karting and Games facility near Atlanta.

Mario Andretti was born to race cars. From the first time he saw a race car, the notion of becoming a professional race car driver never left his mind. On his way to becoming a racing superstar, Andretti had to overcome numerous obstacles, but he never let adversity get in the way. Instead he used it to fuel his dreams, and in the process he became the greatest race car driver of all time.

"WHAT MAKES ME A RICH MAN ISN'T THE NUMBER OF TIMES I WON. IT'S THE JOURNEY IT TOOK TO GET WHERE I AM. I LEARNED CHARACTER, COURAGE, RESOURCEFULNESS, PRIDE IN AMERICA, AND THE VALUE OF BEING EMOTIONALLY AND MENTALLY FIT. I LEARNED HOW TO ADAPT TO CHANGE. ALL OF THAT ADDS UP TO SUCCESS."

My twin brother, Aldo, and I were born in Montona d'Istria, Italy, in 1940. Montona d'Istria, which is now part of Croatia, is about thirty-five miles from the northeastern city of Trieste. My dad was self-employed; he made a decent life for us owning and managing seven farms.

The Second World War broke out around the time we were born. Even when it ended, there was no peace: The borders were still in dispute, as they always are following war. In 1945, Montona d'Istria was ceded to Yugoslavia as part of the postwar political settlement—and suddenly we were trapped inside a Communist country.

It was one thing for my parents to know deep down that they would never amount to anything under Communist rule—and quite another to make a move. And move where? We were a family of five, and any move would be into the unknown. We stuck it out for three years, hoping that the only world we had ever known would right itself.

But when things hadn't changed by 1948, we decided to leave Montona d'Istria, which was allowed as long as you didn't take anything with you. We left our home and our seven farms, which had already been nationalized. Our first stop was a central dispersement camp in Udine. About a week later, we were transferred to a refugee camp.

For seven years, from 1948 until 1955, we lived in the refugee camp in Lucca. There were about five thousand people living there, so it was very crowded. We lived in a large room with about twenty-five other families. Each family's quarters were separated by blankets.

More than anything, my dad wanted to get us the hell out of there. But it wasn't just "pick up and go." You had to submit a formal request for visas to the American consulate and then wait. Only so many people got visas. And when they reached a quota, that was it. So many people were trying to leave. Some were going to Argentina, some to Australia, some to Canada, all of them following their imagination. And some people stayed. Whatever you thought was your best bet.

My dad put a request in for U.S. visas, knowing full well that with the quota situation, it was likely to be a very long time before they were granted.

And it was then, while we were in Italy, that I started developing a love of car racing. One of my fondest memories is the sports car race called the Mille Miglia, a thousand-mile lap of Italy. One of the segments ran through the Abetone pass, near Florence. Every year my brother and I watched from the side of the road, and back home we talked about nothing else for weeks. We crawled under our blankets at night, mimicking the sounds of the cars, pretending we were race drivers on famous teams. We imagined the whole thing, just like we wanted it to be. Ask any kid, "What are you going to be when you grow up?" and you'll get an answer; well, I was going to race in the Mille Miglia, and I told everybody. And no one ever tells a child that his dreams might not come true.

While we were living in the camp, our passion for racing was sparked by our friendship with two guys who owned a parking garage in downtown Lucca. My brother and I would hang out there after school. In 1954, the fellows who owned the garage invited Aldo and me to go to Monza with them to watch the Italian Grand Prix. In those days, motor racing was more popular than any other sport in Italy. And the world champion at that time was Alberto Ascari, my idol. I was only fourteen, but I went to that race and the die was cast. I wanted to be a racer.

Now, while all this was happening, my dad was still determined to move us to America. We'd been in the camp for nearly seven years, and he was still waiting for word on our visas. We'd almost forgotten about it. Then, all of a sudden, our visas came through, and my parents told us we were moving to the United States.

On the morning of June 16, 1955, the Italian ocean liner *Conte Biancamano* arrived in New York Harbor. That was the day we began our new life in the United States—my parents, my sister, my brother, and me. We'd been in the refugee camp since I was eight years old; now I was fifteen. My dad had exactly $125 in his pocket to start our new life here. And none of us spoke English.

We settled in Nazareth, Pennsylvania, with an uncle, and we all got jobs. My dad worked at Bethlehem Steel. My brother and I worked at a gas station. My sister worked at a department store. And we pooled all of our money. My dad was determined to make a life for us, no matter what. Two years later, we had a house and a car. We weren't rich—far from it. But I'd say my dad rode the wave of change very well. Instead of being victims of change, we became victors.

I don't think you're born with the passion to succeed or the strength to overcome adversity. But somehow—like my father—I was intensely driven. So was my brother.

A few days after we arrived in America, while my brother and I were working at the gas station, a pickup pulled in towing a race car. Could there be a racetrack nearby? we wondered. Sure enough, there was a half-mile dirt track just a mile up the road.

Aldo and I checked it out. There was a lot of speed. And it looked *very, very* doable to us. Suddenly we had a mission—a new passion for life. Maybe America wouldn't be so bad after all.

Now, how exactly do you become a racer? First you need your own car. And there are only three ways to obtain a car: Steal it, which was against our principles. Buy it, except we didn't have *that* kind of money. Or build it yourself—that was our only hope.

So we set out listening to anybody who had even the slightest knowledge of race cars. We found out about engines, shocks, spring rates, suspension, chassis setup, and on and on. We built a 1948 Hudson Hornet into a Sportsman stock car. Four years after arriving in America, my brother and I were both racing. He would drive one weekend, and I'd drive the next. That's how it began for me. And after tasting victory, I never settled for anything less. My manic pursuit of this career began.

The sad part about this story is that it didn't work out for my brother, Aldo. He had two very serious accidents. As a result of the last one in 1969, he was hospitalized for several weeks and suffered such severe facial injuries that we no longer looked like identical twins. While my career was flourishing, it was the end of racing for Aldo. He had worked just as hard as I had. And he had wanted it just as bad. It's hard for me to put into words how tough this was. Today my brother is a successful businessman, but for twenty-five years he watched from the sidelines as I fulfilled the dream we both had. There was no jealousy or bitterness with him. He cheered me on. And the memories that make us smile now are the good ones as well as the bad.

Our experiences taught both Aldo and me some valuable lessons. First of all, life is not always fair. Just because you work hard doesn't mean you'll be paid back in kind. Setback and defeat and dreams that don't come true are part of living a full life. You have to be able to pick yourself up and brush yourself off every day. Really big success is built on adversity, failure, frustration—and the way you deal with turning it around.

It's no secret that I loved crossing the finish line first. My first love was driving a race car. I did it for almost forty years, and I loved it from the first day to the last. I cared about nothing else. In fact, I was totally possessed. But what makes me a rich man isn't the number of times I won. It's the journey it took to get where I am. I learned character, courage, resourcefulness, pride in America, and the value of being emotionally and mentally fit. I learned how to adapt to change. All of that adds up to success.

CHAPTER 43

• • •

Bernie Brillstein

FOUNDING PARTNER, BRILLSTEIN-GREY
ENTERTAINMENT

Bernie Brillstein began his Hollywood career in the William Morris mailroom in 1955. In the decades that followed, the talent manager and television and movie producer was largely responsible for some of the most successful movies, television shows, and entertainment careers in Hollywood history.

Brillstein first honed his skills as a talent manager, signing and developing unknown talent like John Belushi, Dan Aykroyd, Gilda Radner, and Jim Henson. As his clients rose to television stardom, Brillstein launched the Brillstein Company in 1969 and became a "packager," bringing together all elements of a project such as writers, directors, and stars. His first big package was *Hee Haw*; he followed this with *The Muppet Show* and *The Muppet Movie*, capitalizing on Muppeteer Jim Henson's genius and ability to diversify into all media. *The Muppet Show* was launched on network television at a time when a network show starring puppets was simply unimaginable. Brillstein was also involved in the launch of NBC's *Saturday Night*—known today as *Saturday Night Live*—and a number of blockbuster films drawing on the *SNL* talent pool, including *The Blues Brothers*, *Ghostbusters*, and *The Cable Guy*.

In 1991, Brillstein partnered with Brad Grey to form Brillstein-Grey Entertainment, one of the most successful management and production firms in the industry. After being tapped to head up Paramount Pictures in 2005, Grey divested ownership of the company; Brillstein later sold his half of the firm and served as consultant and founding partner. In 2007, the company—whose client roster includes Hollywood A-listers Brad Pitt, Orlando Bloom, Adam Sandler, and Jennifer Aniston—was renamed Brillstein Entertainment Partners.

Bernie Brillstein passed away in August 2008.

Bernie Brillstein was a product of the golden age of New York. He discovered he had the gift for spotting and nurturing talent as a teenager hanging out at the Copacabana, Club Somoa, and Stork Club. He fell in love with the entertainment business at an early age and never considered any other career. For Brillstein, his work was his passion, his relationships what he cherished most. In the cutthroat entertainment business, Brillstein was recognized for his loyalty and integrity, and the people he represented—an eclectic mix including Jim Henson, John Belushi, and Lorne Michaels, to name just a few—became his West Coast surrogate family.

"MY SUCCESS IS ALL ABOUT HONESTY, INTEGRITY, FOLLOWING THE TRADITION THAT WAS THERE WAY BEFORE YOU, AND BEING A PART OF A CLUB THAT NOT MANY PEOPLE ARE IN—THE CLUB OF PEOPLE WHO HAVE MADE A WONDERFUL REPUTATION IN A BUSINESS THEY LOVE AND WHOSE WORK MAY HAVE SOME STAYING POWER."

I actually had a wonderful childhood—with the exception of the fact that my mother was a mess for twenty years. Back then, doctors prescribed things so that women would shut up. So she was in bed for twenty years. My father was in the millinery business—women's hats—on the West Side of New York. He was president of the millinery synagogue, so he ran all the births, weddings, bar mitzvahs, everything. He was like the coordinator of life for most of the people we knew. I never heard that phrase before, but that's good—"coordinator of life."

In those years, my father *was* the Copacabana. He was the center of Thirty-sixth to Thirty-ninth streets and Sixth Avenue to Fifth Avenue. In those four blocks—and it might even have gone over to Seventh—everyone went to him. He made his life, which could have been pretty mundane, very exciting. It's amazing what people can do in four blocks.

My uncle, who was a comedian named Jack Pearl, and his wife, Winnie, who was a Ziegfeld girl—they were the East Side of New York. They were the 21 Club and the Stork Club and Bergdorf Goodman. It was a completely different lifestyle. Fortunately, I liked both. I like the grittiness of the Copa and all the jazz joints on Fifty-second Street. My father knew the people who had the Club Samoa, which was a bust-out joint where girls used to dance with you and make believe you were going to fuck them, which of course you never did. When I was thirteen or fourteen—this was right after the war—my best friend, Norman, and I would come from Madison Square Garden to the Club Samoa after the basketball game, and they'd have a club sandwich and a Coke waiting for us. We'd see the girls, then they'd get a cab and send us home. But it was great to see as a young kid. It was fantastic.

My uncle, who was a big star in those days, took me into every theater for nothing. He had a pass for Yankee Stadium that said "Jack Pearl and Guest." He'd take me in to see every show. We'd stand in the back and watch the first act, then go to another theater and stand in the back. It was fantastic. I got to know everything and everyone in that world.

As a young kid, I thought I was the king of New York. I walked into a club and knew I was home. When a performer walked on the stage, I knew in the first five minutes if they were going to be good or not. I could smell it and feel it. I still wish there were nothing but live entertainment. It's better than anything else.

What was I going to be when I grew up? Not a doctor: I don't like the idea of opening people up and seeing their small intestines. I don't think I could handle it. The tedious work of being a lawyer is not for me. I can't even stand in an editing room more than twenty minutes before I go crazy. But this freedom to go anywhere in the world and say, "This guy has talent," or, "This woman has talent" —what a wonderful thing to do.

When I came out of the army in 1955, I went to work in the William Morris mailroom. I thought that's where I could learn the business. Lo and behold, I was good at it. I know that sounds obnoxious, but I didn't go around the halls saying, "Hey, I'm better than you." I just tucked it into my brain and thought, "I can do this, easy. Not a problem." And after eight years I knew I didn't want to be there, so I left and went into my own management business with someone who had just left MCA.

In 1967, I came out to California, because that's where the television business was. I couldn't sign any big stars, so I started signing writers, producers, and directors no one else was signing. I went where I could succeed. Little by little, I built up this business.

If you don't have instinct for the business you are in, you can't do it well. What I love more than anyone else is finding people who are unknown. Jim Henson was unknown. Lorne Michaels was unknown. I loved making them into what I thought they were capable of. Did I know that Jim Henson would become a world-renowned genius? Of course not. But I knew he had great talent. And I knew Lorne was great. Did I know *Hee-Haw* would be a hit? No, but I knew people loved country music. With all the comedies I've done, *Dangerous Liaisons* was the best movie I was ever involved in. Everyone said it was Christopher Hampton, a great writer. Stephen Frears, a great director. I knew it was the story—which was about fucking in French clothes. It's not genius.

Probably my biggest disappointment in the business was when John Belushi died. I certainly never did drugs with him, but I knew he did drugs. We hired a trainer and a security man to watch him, but it wasn't enough. John had a great life. He loved being at Martha's Vineyard. He had friends everywhere. He loved the good times. So the real tragedy was that my best friend—not a client—died. I was disappointed in myself for not doing whatever else I could have done.

The business I do is built on trust. I have no contracts with any of my people. Why would you ask someone to sign a contract? You have to read thirty pages. After I've represented someone for a year or two, I couldn't ask him to sign papers. They know I'm working for them every day, and I know they're going to be great once I get them the work. If they're doing well, why would they leave you?

I'm proud of where I ended up. I'm really proud of who I am. Today, I can go into any restaurant and be recognized. I have a great reputation among my peers. My success is all about honesty, integrity, following the tradition that was there way before you, and being a part of a club that not many people are in—the club of people who have made a wonderful reputation in a business they love and whose work may have some staying power.

To me, success used to mean being able to call someone and knowing your call will be put through. Today, success means that I can buy the best health care. What else is more important when you get old?

• • •

CHAPTER 44

David Carey

GROUP PRESIDENT, CONDÉ NAST

D avid Carey is group president at Condé Nast overseeing the
company's properties that reach a business and executive audience, including *Condé Nast Portfolio*, *WIRED*, *Golf Digest*, *Golf World*,
and their related event and digital platforms, including wired.com,
portfolio.com, golfdigest.com, Reddit, and Ars Technica.

Most recently, Carey led the startup *Condé Nast Portfolio* and portfolio
.com, which debuted in April 2007 and generated headlines worldwide. With a foundation of blue-chip advertisers from multiple
categories, the simultaneous print/digital launch of *Condé Nast
Portfolio* was the most anticipated media launch in many years.

Previously, Carey was the vice president and publisher of *The New
Yorker*. Under his leadership, *The New Yorker* staged a remarkable turnaround as a business. The magazine's total circulation broke the million mark for the first time, the subscriber renewal rates reached an
industry high of more than 80 percent, and advertising revenues more
than doubled. As a result, in 2002, *The New Yorker* posted its first profit
in eighteen years.

Carey was the founding publisher of *SmartMoney*, a joint venture between *The Wall Street Journal* and The Hearst Corporation. Under his direction, *SmartMoney* reached profitability in just two years, and was named by *Advertising Age* as "Magazine of the Year." At Condé Nast, he served as the publisher for the re-launch of *House & Garden* in 1996.

In January 2001, Mr. Carey left *The New Yorker* to serve as president and CEO of Gruner & Jahr's Business Information Group. He returned to *The New Yorker* in July 2001.

David Carey was named by *AdWeek* as the industry's "executive of the year" in 2004, and in 2005 he was named by *Folio: Magazine* as a member of its "Dream Team" of publishing executives.

David Carey caught the entrepreneurial bug early on, running a media business out of his college dorm room while serving as publisher of the campus newspaper. For Carey, excitement comes from taking on new business challenges—whether it's resurrecting flailing magazines or building new enterprises from scratch. Carey is always on the hunt for the next challenge. He embraces risk and chaos and looks for the opportunity to make his next bold move.

"I THINK SUCCESS MEANS THAT AT THE END OF THE DAY, THE WEEK, THE MONTH, YOU CAN LOOK AT WHAT'S BEEN ACCOMPLISHED AND KNOW YOU PLAYED A KEY PART IN MAKING IT ALL COME TRUE."

I grew up in a middle-class family in Southern California, where my father worked for a local grocery store. As a kid, I was always taken with the story of entrepreneurs—those who beat the odds and became successful on the basis of their own ingenuity. Those are the people who always had an enormous impression on me.

In the dictionary under "Jewish mother" there's a line drawing of Janet Carey, so for better or for worse, her only son could do no wrong.

My parents were always incredibly supportive with all their children, and it was wonderful to have that as a foundation. I was given enormous amounts of love, encouragement, and internal support, and that gave me a great degree of confidence.

As a kid, I used to read *Architectural Digest* and occasionally *The New Yorker* and *Los Angeles* magazine. I was always taken with the style and intelligence of these magazines, how well they were put together, and the whole environment they created. They offered a glimpse into a world much different from Long Beach, California.

I was the publisher of the college newspaper at UCLA. The *UCLA Daily Bruin* was my first test in media innovation. We took over the campus phone book. We had our own miniconglomerate, with a staff of sixty, a big daily newspaper, and more. The paper received the award for best college newspaper in the nation.

My intense involvement with the newspaper made me much closer to a B student than an A student. I basically had a full-time job while in school; balancing the two at times was complicated, and sometimes I made choices that favored my work over my studies. In college, I became fascinated with Christopher Whittle, who had started his career in college in Knoxville doing student marketing and campus publishing; he eventually bought *Esquire* and became a celebrated entrepreneurial publisher. To me, he was bigger than Bruce Springsteen. I knew everything there was to know about him; I was a total groupie. After college I moved to New York, without a job in hand, and camped out on Whittle's doorstep. A few weeks later, they hired me.

I consider all of business to be just a set of intellectual puzzles to solve. It's like a Rubik's Cube. And as you become quite adept at solving that particular puzzle, you want to get a harder one. What's the new game you do with the numbers? There are different levels of it. You master the first level . . . and then, instead of just redoing the first level, and even though it would be easy to do that, there's something you relish about taking on a bigger, even more complex puzzle.

I always had an aptitude for business. I like to see the marketplace vote with their dollars. That's the only thing that validates my ideas. When I was publisher of *The New Yorker,* the magazine was initially in a very stressed state. Its editorial side was always first-rate, but it was losing money. On the one hand, it was wonderful to be in that incredible position with a magazine I'd always admired. On the other, I knew it was going to be a tough road—and it was, for a time, because the magazine's business needed to be restaged.

I had done two magazine launches before arriving at *The New Yorker*. In launches like *SmartMoney* and *House & Garden*, you start with nothing. You have no history to measure yourself against. *The New Yorker*, on the other hand, was a great brand—perhaps the most important in the entire industry—and we had to make it better. So in every way that was the big moment, an assignment that was far different from the things I had done in the past, where we started with low expectations that weren't hard to exceed. At *The New Yorker*, we had a property with very high expectations, and it was unknown initially how we would succeed. But with a great team in place and the brilliant editorial leadership of David Remnick, the magazine's business staged a dramatic turnaround.

There is a lot of credit to go around in running a big media battleship, and often it's a very hard job. But with launches and big turnarounds, you're kind of on the edge of your seat; you don't know for sure how it's going to end. You hope it's going to work out the way you envision, but it's a challenge for a magazine like that to thread its way through such a competitive landscape. I like that process a lot, but it can be very nerve-racking.

I think success means that at the end of the day, the week, the month, you can look at what's been accomplished and know you played a key part in making it all come true. It's knowing that it wasn't a marketplace condition that listed your rising vote, it wasn't a lucky break; it was the ability to look at a complex business situation, come up with creative ideas, execute well, and then see the results. I'm very much cause-and-effect-oriented.

In some ways, *Condé Nast Portfolio* is a culmination of a lot of things I've learned over the years. The whole media industry is in turmoil. Ad pages aren't as easy to come by. It's a tough marketplace. There are two ways to look at this: You can be anxious and fret about it, or you can recognize that your competition's business models are highly stressed, making it the perfect time to jump in and challenge them.

The skeptics of the world will always question the timing of anything new. But history shows that a time of chaos is often the very best time to do something bold. I think our timing is perfect, but it takes a lot of guts, because holes in the market aren't always apparent to everyone at first glance. The people who are most successful—especially the entrepreneurs—always wander in when people least expect them.

I've often taken jobs that other people haven't wanted. I've done so with confidence and with a clear head. Some assignments I've volunteered for; some were given to me. Given a choice between working on something that's broken, complex, and higher-risk versus something that's safe and successful, I've always chosen the former. A true entrepreneur often takes a contrarian point of view and works to find the path to success. I'm like a kid in a candy store during bumpy times—I love the chaos. I'm thinking, "Holy cow—someone's going to solve this. And I'd like to be with the people who do."

CHAPTER 45

• • •

Bob Costas

BROADCASTER, NBC SPORTS AND OLYMPICS AND MLB NETWORK

Bob Costas is sports television's most honored and versatile studio host. The nineteen-time Emmy Award winner's current broadcasting duties for NBC include hosting the *Football Night in America* studio show, prime-time coverage of the Olympic Games, and coverage of the U.S. Open, the Ryder Cup, the Kentucky Derby, and the Preakness Stakes. He joined MLB Network in 2009 as the host of special original programming and as the lead play-by-play commentator for a select number of the baseball network's live regular-season games.

Costas, who has the longest tenure of any of the network's sports announcers, joined NBC in 1980. Since then, he has hosted eight Olympics and been prominently involved in virtually every major sporting event, including numerous World Series, Super Bowl, and NBA Finals broadcasts.

Previously, Costas hosted a variety of sports programming on HBO from 2001 to 2008, including *On the Record with Bob Costas*, *Inside the NFL*, and Costas Now. He created *Costas Coast to Coast*, a popular nationally syndicated Sunday night sports radio talk and interview show that ran from 1986 to 1996. From 1988 through 1994, he hosted his own late-night interview television show, *Later with Bob Costas,* on NBC. In 2006, he returned to radio, launching *Costas on the Radio,* a nationally syndicated two-hour show featuring guests and Costas's own commentaries.

Costas began his broadcasting career in 1974 at WSYR–TV and Radio in Syracuse, New York, while attending Syracuse University. He later joined KMOX Radio in St. Louis, working as the play-by-play voice of the American Basketball Association's Spirits of St. Louis. He also called play-by-play for one season of Chicago Bulls road-game telecasts. He then went on to handle regional NFL and NBA assignments for CBS Sports while acting as the radio voice of University of Missouri basketball from 1976 to 1981.

Costas has been honored as "Sportscaster of the Year" by the National Sportscasters and Sportswriters Association a record eight times.

Bob Costas knew what he wanted to be from an early age and single-mindedly set about achieving his dream. Although his calling was clear from the outset, he rose to the top of sports broadcasting on his own terms—authentically, without pretense or imitation. Costas attributes much of his career to a couple of good breaks, but his level of achievement has nothing to do with luck. The key to his success has always been his love of the game and his innate ability to share that passion with his audience.

"MY DEFINITION OF SUCCESS HASN'T CHANGED VERY MUCH SINCE THOSE EARLY DAYS: FIND SOMETHING THAT YOU'RE PASSIONATE ABOUT, THAT FULLY ENGAGES AND INTERESTS YOU, AND THEN DO IT AS WELL AS YOU CAN."

From almost my earliest recollection, I wanted to be a sports broadcaster. I didn't love sports just from the competitive standpoint. I also

loved the storytelling and the romance of it—at least as it was trans-
mitted to a kid growing up around New York in the 1950s and early
1960s. I liked the sound of it, and no game to me was complete without the voice of the sportscaster, be it on television or radio. They
were the sound track of a great game.

Even when I was playing in Little League, or shooting baskets in
the backyard, or just throwing a rubber ball off a wall and creating
an imaginary game in my mind, I would hear the voices of the great
sports announcers in my head: Mel Allen, Red Barber, Vin Scully,
Lindsey Nelson, Marty Glickman, later Jim McKay and Jack Whita-
ker. The game to me was as much about the way it was presented and
told as it was about the competition itself.

Listening to them, I was unconsciously preparing for what I
wanted to do, absorbing a lot of what I heard—the history of sports,
the terminology, that kind of stuff, was all seeping in. And I was in-
ternalizing some of the styles and rhythms of these announcers. But
it wasn't until my sophomore or junior year in high school that any
kind of realistic path to a broadcasting career became clear to me.
Most universities in the early 1970s didn't have full-fledged communications or broadcasting majors. They had journalism majors, but
that was for print journalism. Mine was probably the first generation
of college students who had truly grown up with television and had
never known a world without it. According to my guidance counsel-
ors, among the relative handful of schools that had credible journalism programs, Syracuse University was tops for someone who was
interested in a broadcasting career. So that became my focus—to go
to one of those colleges, take the courses, but also get hands-on experience on the campus radio and television stations so I could see if
I had any aptitude for it.

Even today, for all my preparation and all my focus, I don't think
it would have made much difference if I didn't have some ability at
broadcasting. When I was growing up, I didn't know for sure that I
would have any ability at it. I had spoken into a primitive tape recorder
when I was fourteen or fifteen years old, heard my voice back for the
first time, and I was horrified. So when I got to Syracuse, I was hoping

that my ability would match my ambitions, but I certainly wasn't sure that that would happen.

Bob Hyland at KMOX in St. Louis hired me right out of Syracuse. I was twenty-two, but I looked like I was eleven. A lot of people around the station were very skeptical. They wondered, "Why would you hire this kid? He's still wet behind the ears." But Mr. Hyland saw something in me personally, and potentially professionally, and put me right into this first-rate operation, surrounded by people with tremendous ability and experience. Being in that environment helped to accelerate my development.

My definition of success hasn't changed very much since those early days: Find something that you're passionate about, that fully engages and interests you, and then do it as well as you can. Of course, luck has played a big part in my success. I have been phenomenally lucky. I was on CBS when I was twenty-four, NBC when I was twenty-seven. Over the years, I've had a number of very prominent assignments in broadcasting, but I sought almost none of them. My objective always was to be as good a broadcaster as I could be and to do the kind of work that was best suited to my interests and abilities. I never defined success as the biggest job, the biggest paycheck, the greatest degree of exposure. Now, some of that has come along with the things I've chosen to do, but I've never taken that kind of next-rung-on-the-ladder approach.

I'd consider myself a competitive person, but mostly I compete with my own notion of the best work I can do. Is this as good as I'm able to make it? Does this measure up? If it does, then I'm perfectly satisfied. It's never direct competition with anyone else. It's not like we're all running to the same finish line on the same track on the same day, or we're all playing the same golf course on the same day.

Everyone, even if they disguise it pretty well, has some fear of failure or rejection. But I've always been willing to attempt things where success isn't assured. I've always been willing to take a risk. For example, when Bryant Gumbel went to the *Today* show and they asked me to become the host of first the NFL and then all the major sports programming on NBC—eventually including the Olympics—no one at NBC knew that I'd never hosted anything on television in my life. I had never read a teleprompter. In fact, for the first four years of *NFL*

Live, I just ad-libbed everything because I wasn't used to using one. I was truly unfamiliar with the basics of a studio; I had never really done local sports on TV. All my work was radio or television play-by-play. I was a little nervous about my ability to handle it, but I thought, "What the hell? Let me just try it." It worked out fine. Then, when Dick Ebersol and Brandon Tartikoff asked me to do *Later*, I'd never done anything outside of sports besides filling in on the *Today* show for a week.

So I imagine a lot of people were skeptical about my ability to handle it. But I thought, "Bryant Gumbel crossed over from sports to news, and this isn't exactly news. It's kind of a hybrid. Let me give it a try." It took me a little while to get the hang of it, but not too long. Now I look back on that as one of the best things I ever did.

You can also paralyze yourself by wondering, "If I state my opinion or toss off a wisecrack, will someone be offended? Will someone take it the wrong way?" Believe me, somebody, somewhere, will take almost *anything* the wrong way. You can't worry about it. If you're not willing to take the occasional risk, you become generic. You sanitize all the individuality out of it.

Fairly early in my NBC career, someone wrote of me, "He's reverent and irreverent at the same time," which I thought was true. I hope that at my best I can convey a sense of fun and occasional sarcasm, but at the same time offer an appreciation for events and their history. I think the audience could sense I was genuinely happy to be at Yankee Stadium or Wrigley Field on a Saturday afternoon. But I also hope they appreciate that I recognize the elements of hypocrisy and corruption in sports and can bring some journalism to it. At the same time, if something truly great happened, I wasn't so jaded as to not enjoy it and highlight the drama of it.

If I had to pass along one piece of advice, it would be about perspective—about looking at the big picture. Taking the long view always helps. No matter how well you do what you do, someone's not going to like it. They're entitled to their opinion, of course, but you have to have enough belief in yourself and in your own standards to judge yourself. You shouldn't be swayed by easy praise or easy criticism. If I do something I think is just so-so and I could have done better, and the first five people I meet when I walk out of the studio tell me they think it's great, that's not likely to change my mind. If I do something I know is very, very good, and somebody in East Sheboygan, or *The New York Times*, for that matter, says it stinks—fine. That's not going to change my sense of it, either. By now, I have a good idea of how I should do my job.

CONCLUSION

• • •

Throughout the process of conducting the interviews for this book, we found again and again that success is a very personal notion, something nearly everyone defines differently. We interviewed forty-five people and found more than fifty unique descriptions. No one definition is broad enough to accommodate all the creative, striving people whose stories you've just read.

The people we interviewed reminded us repeatedly that the most important part of success is the process of achievement itself. The rewards of life can be tenuous, fleeting, amorphous, and difficult to quantify. They may come at work, or on the road, or at home. They may come from your colleagues, or your family, and often from both. If there's one thing we can be certain of, it's that success comes in many forms. It's not necessarily about the corner office, though it can be, or about besting your competitors, though that might be part of it. It's not really about how much money you amass, though having enough to live comfortably is certainly desirable. It's not even about how much you get. It's about the journey, the life you live along the way.

The high achievers we encountered were not only different in temperament and personality, they also came from every ethnic background. Today, this shouldn't come as much of a surprise—though if we'd been researching this book a mere generation ago, we might not have had so many contributions from Latin Americans, African

Americans, and women. We now take it for granted that women and men of diverse backgrounds are leading our society, from the boardrooms of America to the ballots of the 2008 election. The glass ceiling has been cracking for some time; by now it is all but shattered.

As the interviews collected here suggest, we found that those leaders who best understood their archetypes were most effective in their chosen fields. By the same token, there's evidence that trying to fight one's own archetype can end up being a futile endeavor. Since our expertise stems largely from representing high-profile candidates in political events, we can offer a revealing example where a midstream change has done more harm than good.

President George W. Bush is a study in how an independence seeker can wander too far. While Bush surrounds himself with legions of experts in law, public policy, foreign relations, business and finance, he has exhibited a profound committment to "go my own way" in the five-year siege of Iraq. His short-term goal was to take out Saddam Hussein, and after that was accomplished he appears to have lost interest and convinced himself that the idea was a success—as witnessed by his speech on an aircraft carrier under a banner reading MISSION ACCOMPLISHED. Once an independence seeker accomplishes his goal, he's likely to grow restless to move on to the next challenge. Whatever the conditions were on the ground, President Bush seems not to have had a clear goal after Saddam was captured and his statues were toppled. His hard-nosed approach to the challenges in Iraq—and to his critics—backed him into a corner.

It requires no partisan perspective to recognize that Bush failed to come to grips with the power and meaning of his own archetype; Bush's downfall came when he followed his too blindly and inflexibly, without understanding his true goals.

Now, Bush is being replaced in the Oval Office by a quintessential natural born leader, Barack Obama. Obama displays all of the traits of the natural born leader: from an early age, he displayed the self-confidence to achieve at the very highest levels, regardless of the obstacles in his way. His success was built on specific, well-defined achievements: admission to Columbia, election as president of Harvard

Law Review, election to the United States Senate. His exceptional rhetorical skills represent his desire to lead through inspiration, whether as a community organizer or as president of the United States. Ultimately, what made his presidential campaign so successful was the extent to which Obama stuck to his archetype: every time he told his supporters, "This campaign is not about me, it's about you," he was repeating the mantra of a true natural born leader.

What's the lesson here?

Knowing your archetype and leveraging its strengths is the key to success. While the success of Barack Obama's presidency may be defined by his policy achievements, it will be determined by his ability to stick to his archetype. And he need look no further than his predecessor to appreciate the risk of losing sight of his weaknesses.

With luck, you've been able to recognize your archetype through the categories and profiles in these pages. If you're having trouble, ask others who are close to you for their input. Some people are uncomfortable being categorized, but it's our experience that almost everyone fits into one of these four spheres. Once you identify where you fit in, working within that framework can offer important insights into your best path to success.

UNDERSTANDING AND USING YOUR
ARCHETYPE: A FIVE-STEP PROCESS

The interviews and ideas in this book are intended as guidelines to help you identify your own strengths and weaknesses and apply them to your assessment of your career and lifestyle. Through understanding how our subjects made things work for themselves, you can begin to look at your own underlying patterns and at how you can work toward the kinds of success that will genuinely fulfill you.

To help you apply the findings of this book to your own goals, follow this five-step process:

1. **DETERMINE YOUR ARCHETYPE.**
2. **DEVELOP YOUR PERSONAL DEFINITION OF SUCCESS.**
3. **IDENTIFY WAYS/SITUATIONS TO LEVERAGE YOUR DEFINITION OF SUCCESS.**
4. **CONTINUOUSLY REFLECT ON YOUR SUCCESS AND BE PREPARED TO ALTER IT OVER TIME.**
5. **ABOVE ALL, USE THE FIRST FOUR STEPS TO HELP ACHIEVE SUCCESS** *ON YOUR OWN TERMS.*

1. DETERMINE YOUR ARCHETYPE.

This is the most critical step: self-analysis. One good way to start is to review the stories of the people in this book. Check off the names of those people you identify with most closely. Are they leading the kind of life you'd like to lead? Take out a yellow legal pad and draw a line down the center. On the left-hand side, list the traits you value; on the right, list the ones that have little meaning in your life.

The archetype has to fit your value system. What motivates you? What have you done that has worked best for you? What *hasn't* worked? What do you feel guilty about not being? What do you enjoy most about your life and career? What gives you the most satisfaction, now and in looking back?

- *Explore your archetype.* You have to see yourself in the archetype for it to be meaningful. When you find your archetype, how does it help you understand yourself in new ways? What things are you doing now that fit with your archetype, and what aspects of your life suggest that you're trying to fit someone else's idea of success? As so many of our subjects demonstrate, passion and success tend to go together.

2. DEVELOP YOUR PERSONAL DEFINITION OF SUCCESS.

Make a list of the things you'd like to accomplish in your life. They can be meaningful or frivolous, selfish or philanthropic, career goals or exotic places you'd like to visit. Here's where you should let your mind wander a little. Stretch your parameters a bit. Remember, this is your life—don't make your list based on society's perception of success. Instead, listen to the voice inside you. Listing a wide variety of activities will help you focus on how to integrate them into a whole. This is important preliminary work: While you're putting your hopes and dreams into a manageable array, you'll start to see what's practical and what's not, what's achievable, what's a realistic stretch, and what doesn't work at all. Remember, this is about you, not the expectations of others—including those closest to you, like family members and friends.

- *Consider what you want to do with your life*—your goals, your values, your dreams.
- *Understand your passions and talents.* Have a clear vision to focus on. (Remember that it has to be real and attainable—and feel good when you do it.)
- *Prioritize your own core values*—not what someone else thinks they should be.
- *Focus on your own interests, values, strengths.*
- *Have fun.* It's better to be rewarded for something you like than to become successful at something you hate.

For Mario Andretti, the great race car driver, success was mostly about the exhilaration that came from winning races. "I was motivated by the joy of success," he said. "That was the best medicine for me, the best come-on. It was so fulfilling that it was easy for me to stay motivated to try to achieve it again." Supermodel Heidi Klum, on the other hand, knew she was successful when she attained a certain quality of life: "For me, success means being really happy. Having a great family, to me, is the most I can ever wish for. Success is being at peace with yourself, liking what you do, and having a family. Having money and a successful career is no success if you don't have love around you."

3. IDENTIFY WAYS/SITUATIONS TO LEVERAGE
YOUR DEFINITION OF SUCCESS

Once you have some idea of what your personal value proposition is as it relates to your definition of success, you can focus on creating situations that will help you get there. They might involve networking, character development, furthering your education, considering new paths. They should certainly involve putting yourself in situations that favor your best assets and give you advantages over your peers.

- *Use your definition of success as a lens for thinking about your goals and how you want to reach them.* Know where you are going and why.
- *Stay focused on the big picture.* Success isn't built in one meeting or one day. It's built in blocks you assemble over a lifetime, each one representing its own success.
- *Be good at what you do, and do what you're good at.*
- *Differentiate yourself—be distinctive.*
- *Compete.*
- *Be driven—nearly obsessive—in focusing on your goals.*
- *Be ready to take risks.*
- *Strive to improve yourself.* Set goals that you find challenging.
- *Don't make money a goal.* Successful people are passionate about what they do, and the money follows.
- *Find role models and learn from what they do well.*

Look at Bernie Brillstein's earlier career. The Hollywood agent and producer started in the mailroom at William Morris because it was a tradition in the entertainment business. Then he went to California because "that's where the television business was." He decided to go "where I could succeed." Joe Rose, former chairman of the New York City Planning Commission, knew money wasn't something he would pursue for its own sake, but he saw other paybacks. He told us, "For people who spend their lives accomplishing things in the not-for-profit or governmental sectors, money is not the motivating factor."

The words *fun* and *passion* can have more profound effects on a life than we can imagine. Jake Burton, the man who helped make snowboarding a worldwide phenomenon, said he liked to have fun and play sports as a youth. "I developed a passion for snowboarding, and I was convinced it could become a sport," he said.

Most really successful people don't have an aversion to risk. Gary Bettman, the commissioner of the National Hockey League, bet his career—and also the future of a major professional sport—when he canceled an entire season during a labor dispute. It took sheer guts to do it. He endured a mountain of criticism. But the gamble paid off. He survived, and the NHL thrived.

4. CONTINUOUSLY REFLECT ON YOUR SUCCESS AND BE PREPARED TO ALTER IT OVER TIME.

Remember the cliché "Life is what happens when you're busy making plans." It's the ultimate excuse for allowing serendipity to overcome logic and strategy. Sure, it's important to allow things to flow and happen in a natural way, but you must continually take that formal look in the mirror to ensure that you're on track to achieve success on your own terms. Give yourself a periodic checkup—especially after experiencing life-changing events you have little or no control over (death in the family, divorce, job furloughs, and so on).

- *Life changes.* Your definition of success evolves. Don't be afraid of that—accept it and use it.
- *If you achieve your definition of success, try recasting it.* Find something that will engage you in your new situation.
- *Be prepared for setbacks.* Everyone has them, but successful people keep going.

Could anyone experience a greater epiphany than Anna Cheng Catalano, the former oil company executive? In midcareer, she decided to make a major lifestyle change and abandon her career. Here's how she put it: "It was the first time in my career that I really felt I didn't have to keep climbing to prove anything to anyone. You spend a good part of your life trying to prove you're good, and then you reach a point in your life where you think, 'I'm done proving myself. Now I actually need to figure out if there's something else I'm supposed to do.'"

The inevitable disappointments and setbacks that come along the way are an important element in the formula to success. Here's how publisher Steve Forbes, no stranger to failure, looks at it: "In my family's line of work, you expect setbacks. . . . These things happen. But you have to keep probing and pushing, or you'll fail. It's like riding a bicycle: If you don't keep moving, you'll fall over."

Jimmy Choo's Tamara Mellon concurs: "You just have to keep going. You have to do what you do well. You have to ignore setbacks. If I had to sum up the key to my success in just one word, it would be *determination*."

5. USE THE FIRST FOUR STEPS TO HELP ACHIEVE SUCCESS ON YOUR TERMS.

So how do you ultimately measure your happiness quotient? One question you should always be asking yourself is: "How do I want to be remembered?" Many people don't give much thought to their legacy, but even those who don't may find this a good tool for assessing a life well lived. Dick Parsons, who runs Time Warner, put it rather simply when he said he wanted to be remembered as a "good man." All his extraordinary accomplishments aside, that was enough for him—and that is the whole point.

A few suggestions in closing:

- **Appreciate what you've accomplished.** Use past successes to encourage you to keep moving forward. (But don't dwell on them.)
- **Know when you're "there."**
- **Don't wait too long to enjoy your success.** There's a reason "Stop and smell the roses" is such a time-honored cliché.

In the end, you want to reach the end of your journey without a lot of regrets. Here's what former SEC chairman William Donaldson told us: "I've done what I wanted to do. I feel pretty lucky that I'm pretty healthy. I can't conceive I'm the age I am. I don't feel the way you're supposed to feel. Everybody is living longer. The idea of sailing off into the sunset and improving my golf game was not something. . . Well, I'd like to improve my golf game."

As we finished this book, we couldn't resist talking about the patterns of success we discovered with our friends, family, colleagues, and even the participants in the book. The discussion always went the same way: After we reviewed the archetypes and their qualities, invariably the response came: "So, which archetype do you think I am?" Of course, being pollsters, we asked them, "Where do you think you belong?" And so the thought process began.

We were fascinated by the lengthy silences. Many people tried to figure out which archetype they "should" be or "wanted" to be rather than the one they knew they were. The debate that followed always taught us—and, we hoped, them—more about their goals and aspirations, their hearts and minds.

But these archetypes are no mere parlor game. They're a window into your career and family, and a tool to help you enhance the value of your life. And there is no hierarchy to the archetypes—no reason that you "should" be one or another. No one archetype is better than, or preferable to, the others. The only archetype you should follow is the one in which you recognize yourself.

You are who you are. Don't deny it; embrace it. Be yourself. There are many roads to success. All you have to do is choose the one that's right for you.

ACKNOWLEDGMENTS

• • •

A book like this is truly a labor of love. Between the two of us, we have spent more than fifty years conducting thousands of polls and market research studies on behalf of political and corporate clients in more than eighty countries. So after all those projects—and the millions of people that we have interviewed over the years—why do another study? Why do more interviews? And why compile them into a book? Because as we've worked on so many projects for our clients over the years, we have observed a pattern. A pattern of success—one that characterizes not just the companies, the products, or the political campaigns we were analyzing—but the clients themselves.

We thank all those we interviewed for taking the time out of their busy schedule to share their stories with us and our readers.

There were many people who shaped this book that we would like to acknowledge:

Britt Kahn was part of the book from day one. A true independence seeker, Britt combines brilliance with charm, tenacity and attention to detail. She was instrumental in every phase and without her this book would have never come to life.

Doug Garr's profound insights and masterfully edited chapters allowed the true essence of each of our participants to come to life. Doug's deep understanding of people, their motivations, and their use of words allowed him to capture their voice as if each chapter were a conversation with a friend.

The professionalism of the team at HarperCollins—Cal Morgan and Brittany Hamblin. Your vision and masterful editing brought out the best of us.

Judith Regan was the initial inspiration for the book and she green-lighted it. Judith understood the potential power of the insights and challenged us to uncover them.

Our friends an colleagues who were always available to read, listen, and edit. Peter, David, and Tony, thank you for being there and sharing your thoughts and feedback with us.

And our partner of more than a quarter of a century, Mark Penn. We will always be together as Penn, Schoen & Berland.

INDEX

• • •